BISEXUAL HORIZONS
Politics, Histories, Lives

BISEXUAL HORIZONS

Politics, Histories, Lives

Edited by

Sharon Rose, Cris Stevens *et al*

Lawrence & Wishart
LONDON

Lawrence & Wishart Limited
144a Old South Lambeth Road
London SW8 1XX

First published 1996

British Library Cataloguing in Publication Data.
A catalogue record for this book is available
from the British Library.

ISBN 0 85315 8312

Photoset in North Wales by
Derek Doyle & Associates, Mold, Clwyd.
Printed and bound in Great Britain by
Biddles Ltd, Guildford, Surrey.

Contents

CONTENTS

CONTENTS

CONTENTS

Foreword

Joseph Bristow

Bisexual Horizons is the most comprehensive collection of materials to date on bisexual living and loving. Exceptional in its range, the book brings together many different voices to show the richness and complexity of contemporary bisexual identities. Covering topics as diverse as safer sex and political activism, the volume opens up a wide variety of perspectives on a firmly established and flourishing bisexual movement. The fifty or so contributions will be of interest to anyone wishing to engage with urgent areas of debate in current sexual politics. Rarely do collections of this kind succeed like this one in revealing why it remains impossible to separate issues of sexuality from class, (dis)ability, ethnicity, gender, and generation. By broadening understandings of where bisexuality lies in relation to feminism, to the lesbian and gay movement, and to heterosexual institutions such as marriage, *Bisexual Horizons* will have a number of uses. This volume will be discussed widely by bisexual women and bisexual men already active in the movement. The book will cause many lesbians and gay men to consider why their organisations have sometimes treated bisexuals with distrust and contempt, and why such attitudes are having to change. Striking a balance between academic and less formal writing, it will serve as a textbook for students taking courses in the humanities and social sciences. Providing an up-to-date list of helpful resources, the collection contains an immense amount of invaluable information for any reader who wants to discover more about bisexuality.

The 1990s have turned out to be a decade in which progressive ideas about sexuality and sexual identity have undergone a welcome upheaval, particularly among activists involved in a variety of political campaigns against discrimination. In this ferment of debate, bisexuality has become a central issue. Bisexuality has shown exactly why for many people it remains difficult to belong to one side of the bleak divide between heterosexuality and homosexuality. In some respects, queer politics shares a similar impulse to bisexual activism. Queer politics arose out of an urgent need to transform an introspective lesbian and gay movement that often set rigid boundaries around itself. One of the tremendous achievements of the past decade has been the growing acceptance that sexual identities are not fixed forever and cannot be readily contained by clear-cut categories. They are subject to change and to transformation. They are full of possibility, if not without ambiguity and some conflict.

Bisexual Horizons forms part of an increasingly broadening awareness that there must be more open discussion of sexuality in contemporary culture – from sex education in the classroom to intimate conversations in the bedroom. It is in this spirit that the Off Pink Collective have edited this collection. The writings contained in this volume celebrate the potential to explore many aspects of sexual life, enabling us to expand the terms through which we can articulate our desires.

Acknowledgements

No undertaking of this kind could be achieved without the input and assistance of many people. We have been meeting and talking and eating in each other's houses for the last four years, working on this book in our spare time, whilst keeping the rest of our lives going, so we owe a great debt of gratitude to many people. Our colleagues in the bisexual movement have been generous with their support, encouragement and ideas; especial thanks to all the people whose articles we were not able to include. In particular, we would like to thank Sue George, Gyan Mathur, David Burkle, Nina Silver, Wayne Bryant, Nicola Field, Hugh, Russell Gardener, Roberta Wedge, Anne Nyssen, Susan Deacy, and Fritz Klein. Our biggest personal thank you must go to Joseph Bristow, without whose support and perseverance this book may never have been published at all. For the smoother running of meetings, we would like to thank Diana and David for doing more than their share of childcare; the residents of The Enclave for letting us trample through their house so often; and Colin Cracknell, for providing the right word in moments of crisis. We also wish to thank Sally Davison and other staff at Lawrence and Wishart for their flexibility and enthusiasm.

I Sing the Body Electric

I have perceiv'd that to be with those I like is enough,
To stop in company with the rest at evening is enough,
To be surrounded by beautiful, curious, breathing, laughing flesh
    is enough,
To pass among them or touch any one, or rest my arm ever so
    lightly round his or her neck for a moment, what is this
    then?
I do not ask any more delight, I swim in it as in the sea.

There is something in staying close to men and women and
    looking on them, and in the contact and odor of them, that
    pleases the soul well,
All things please the soul, but these please the soul well.

                                        Walt Whitman

Introduction

This is the second book commissioned and edited by the Off Pink Collective, a group of bisexual activists, some of whom first got together to produce *Bisexual Lives* (self-published in 1988). Both that book and this one are products of their time. *Bisexual Lives* appeared when the active bisexual movement in Britain was still young, and no serious book on bisexuality had been published here for ten years. Since 1988, the bisexual movement has grown enormously, both in Britain and around the world, if not to complete maturity, then at least to late adolescence – with all the advantages of energy and enthusiasm, as well as some of the disadvantages of not having quite established its precise identity yet. But maybe that, too, is an advantage – we have seen too many examples of the kinds of problem that rigidity in political and personal definitions can bring – a theme taken up by almost all the contributors to this volume. One of our uncertainties is whether we have now developed sufficiently to be able to talk of this coming together of bisexuals as a movement – a theme that is explored more thoroughly in the introduction to Section IV.

Despite enormous differences, most bisexuals seem to share a rejection of society's many attempts to force everybody into conforming to standards which are not only rigid, but static. In opposition to this, Jo Eadie's article in this book argues that the idea of a monolithic persistent identity is an illusion, and proposes an alternative model of tactical identification. This is a dynamic model which implies a different relationship to time: 'Identity is an identification which we go on making.' He envisages the deconstruction of all oppositions, including homosexual/heterosexual, bisexual/monosexual: and perhaps most importantly, he cautions the bisexual movement itself not to get caught up in its own orthodoxies and develop its own monolithic culture.

For, as June Jordan so elegantly points out in the article which opens this collection, and which provides the keynote for the whole volume, one cannot fight a single oppression in isolation. She advocates creating

1

links between struggles, since, at an individual level, 'freedom is indivisible', and to neglect one area in favour of others cannot lead to effective liberation. Both June Jordan and Yasmin Prabhudas (also in this collection) make an analogy between bisexuality and 'mixed-race' identity, and of the possibilities these identifications create to transcend the present partitioning of political issues. 'As a social construct, these polarities are increasingly recognised as obsolete – people's ethnic origin or sexual orientation is no longer a clear-cut matter, but rather a merger of identities, which everyone could fully explore,' says Prabhudas, who also argues for a single movement 'embracing a philosophy of unity rather than one of division, making sexuality everyone's issue, making race everyone's issue'.

In the real world, individuals do not carry a single identity, but identify in a number of ways simultaneously, eg, as bisexual, black, working-class, etc. Such a multiplicity of identities requires multifocused political struggles. As we show, bisexually-identified people are often also politically involved around their other identifications, creating links between the bisexual movement and feminism, anti-racism and class-based politics, in addition to the lesbian and gay movements.

In general, politically active bisexuals have rejected the most common negative stereotypes levelled against us – that we are neither one thing nor another, neither heterosexual nor homosexual, unable to make up our minds, not fitting in either camp. Bisexuals in this book tend towards seeing these as great strengths, because we draw things together and challenge existing dualities, going for a both/and solution, instead of either/or options. This affects what happens when we are active in other political movements – we challenge the framework within which people think. Many of us refuse to be pigeon-holed neatly, or at all. There are feminists challenging the notion that all men are the enemy, by refusing gender stereotypes; and black people and people with disabilities demanding that everybody learn from the mistakes of feminism and the lesbian and gay movements, and work for freedom from oppression for everyone, not just white middle-class, able-bodied people.

It will also be obvious in reading this book that not all bisexuals, even those who are ready to self-awarely adopt that label, perceive themselves as political people or as affiliated to an identifiable bisexual movement. The current book differs from *Bisexual Lives* in that it has moved on from being exclusively about personal histories, to include a broad range of more analytical pieces and an international perspective, including a number of contributions which reflect an increasing recognition of cultural diversity among bisexuals. We include contributions from Australia, Aotearoa/New Zealand, Belgium, Germany, Ireland, The Netherlands, Tunisia, and the USA, as well as Britain. None of this could have been achieved without the development of some coherent political thinking among those who do consider themselves part of the bisexual movement or community. At the same time, we do not wish to lose sight of the value of recording and learning from diverse individual experience.

It is impossible to start discussing personal experience without getting involved in some of the debates about labelling and identity. These preoccupy all sexual politics theorists, but have a particular resonance when discussing bisexuality. For 'bisexual' is, above all, a label you choose for yourself, covering, as it does, such a range of human behaviour, and indeed, being chosen by many people whose actual behaviour is indistinguishable from that of many others who reject this very definition. One of the main conclusions in an important recent study by Paula Rust,[1] in which she compares lesbian-identified and bisexually-identified women, is the inaccuracy of conventional ideas about lesbian or bisexual identity compared with the actual behaviour of women who identify in these ways. A considerable overlap in behaviour was found, with the main difference between many individuals being simply their stated self-identity. Moreover, as is shown, for example, in the interview with Muhammed in this book, in many other cultures, extensive bisexual behaviour can occur without individuals identifying as 'bisexual' at all.

What, then, if anything, do people who choose to define themselves as bisexual have in common? It emerges clearly from the life stories recorded here that, whatever our differences, we all share the experience of a personal struggle with our sexuality and a search to construct an identity we feel happy with. Very often, these struggles have brought us into conflict with those close to us, and though many of us are contented, very few of us are relying on the proverbial happy ending! Another characteristic we all seem to share is a deep mistrust of any received wisdom, as, having been forced to trust our own thinking, we have found we like doing so. Thus, we emphasise the importance of self-identification and of resisting established labels, which are seen in many cases as cultural constructs. Some bisexuals suggest that the label of 'bisexuality' itself is a cultural construct, and they adopt it temporarily, as a means to the end of dispensing with labels altogether. Others in the bisexual movement disagree with this position, and see retaining the bisexual label as an important part of our political struggle to be taken seriously by the rest of the sexual politics movement.

It is a clear example of the increasing sophistication of our movement that we feel it is important to debate such issues, and that our researchers have been doing the work to enable us to do so. Moving from the simple linear scale of sexual identity presented by Kinsey's early work[2] to the multiple dimensions of emotional and sexual preferences recorded in Fritz Klein's Sexual Orientation Grid,[3] we can note the development of a more subtle appreciation of how people's sexual identities are constituted. For example, the contribution in this book by Michael S. Montgomery illustrates the ongoing process of self-identification which characterises his life, and that of many other bisexuals, which do not conform to the ideology that everyone should stick to a life-long quasi-biological essential identity. Unfortunately, publications which address the theoretical underpinning of bisexuals' intuitive understanding are still very thin on the ground – the books by Fritz Klein,[4] Charlotte Wolff,[5] Sue George[6] and Martin S. Weinberg et al[7] are the only substantial contributions to date. Another two important analytical volumes will be published in autumn 1995[8] – further evidence of the current vigour of the bisexual movement.

As Amanda Udis-Kessler points out in her article in this book, present attitudes to sexuality in the West are highly culturally specific. A key turning point in attitudes was the late nineteenth century, when same-sex acts began to be seen as the expression of a person's identity. An activity or behaviour was thus transformed into an identity, and this identity was understood as being part of a person's 'inner core' – an *essential* part of their being. These were the foundation stones of an essentialist approach to sexual identity – one which gay people themselves have sometimes adopted. Both Jeffrey Weeks[9] and Michel Foucault have analysed these changes in attitudes, Foucault expressed it sweepingly; 'The sodomite was an aberration, the homosexual became a species.'[10] But while Foucault and others have made very helpful contributions to our thinking, they are often oblivious to the notion of bisexuality. Their analysis of sexuality therefore unthinkingly adheres to a model based on a binary opposition between homo- and heterosexuality. Sue George's book,[11] has succeeded in moving the debate forward by irrevocably validating the existence of bisexual women, but although it is a ground-breaking work, it needs companion volumes by other bisexuals (not least, somebody to do the same job for bisexual men) to develop our analysis beyond what we already know.

Our intention in this book is to show, through a range of personal and analytical pieces, how the rise of bisexuality as an identity has affected many individuals, some of whom identify with the bisexual movement and some of whom do not. When we started work on collecting material, we had a notion of inclusivity which was very dear to us, as we know how hurtful it is to be excluded. And we certainly have tried to represent as wide a variety of bisexual thinking as possible in the finished volume. But as the articles came flooding in, it was clear that we could not include everything we were sent, and an important consideration was to provide an approachable book for a wide variety of readers. Our companions in the bisexual movement, who have waited patiently for some years as we have toiled, will doubtless find some topics missing that they care about deeply – inevitable in such a diverse collection of people – while others may feel we have been indulgent. But despite the need to edit and select, this collection represents the experiences and current state of thinking of a wide range of bisexual people.

In one respect, in particular, we wish that the cumulative effect of the contributions had been different – in the way that the relationship between the lesbian and gay movements and bisexuals comes across. Reading this book, one gets the impression of a sense of alienation from the lesbian and gay movements, but this is not the way bisexuals, and probably most individual lesbians and gays, want it to be. It is an honest reflection of the current situation, and we hope that one of the beneficial results of this book may be to help overcome the problems of recent years.

Difficulties have partly arisen because most bisexuals see lesbians and gays as their natural allies, and so we are even more disappointed if we are rejected by them. All people who refuse or are unable to conform to restricting societal norms are oppressed and threatened by those in power, so we sometimes tend to attack each other, as it can be so difficult to fight back effectively against all the parts of society which are oppressing us. Also, as Nina Silver has pointed out, there may be other psychological factors playing a part in this dynamic, such as lesbians sometimes perceiving bisexual women as a threat to their personal security.[12] In addition, the frequent exclusion of bisexuals from lesbian and gay politics and culture is often a result of the essentialist approach to sexuality mentioned earlier, as Amanda Udis-Kessler discusses in her article in this book. Some commentators, including Sue George and Jeffrey Weeks, argue that this exclusive approach to gender and sexuality has developed over the last twenty years or so. And to a significant degree, the current bisexual movement has grown out of the unwillingness of the modern lesbian and gay movements to consider the issue of bisexuality.

This view of history maintains that lesbian and gay liberation evolved from being an inclusive movement for sexual liberation in the late 60s and 70s into the exclusive lesbian and gay movement that became familiar from the mid 70s. The spirit of the early gay liberation movement grew out of the counterculture, and thus sought to question and challenge as many social categories as possible. The meaning of the term 'gay' at this point was quite wide. Wayne Bryant,[13] a leading figure in the US bisexual movement, argues that initially there were gay people, those who were sexually attracted to their own gender. But then a progressive narrowing of the term 'gay' took place over the years, first with a split between gay men and lesbian feminists, and then more recently, over the last ten to fifteen years, with homosexual identity taking on an 'ethnic' meaning. Whereas before it was enough to love members of your own sex to be considered gay, now it is necessary never to have loved or experienced attraction to members of the opposite sex, or to repudiate such feelings if you ever had them.

Over the last ten or so years, several distinct groups of people have wanted to recapture the early gay liberation spirit of challenging rigidities of sexual definition – and at times, the challenge has been as much to the lesbian and gay movement itself as to the wider society. This emergence of diversity is known as queer politics, although as befits such a diverse and amorphous cluster, nobody can agree precisely what it is. The term 'Queer' seems to have been taken on initially by mainly young, disenfranchised people, many of them poor, female and/or black, who felt excluded and disgusted by the middle-of-the-road, predominantly white and male, gay movement in the US. They were angry that years of respectable, assimilationist politics had done nothing to end the kind of discrimination that left so many of their friends dying of AIDS, and angry at the US government's failure to spend the millions of dollars of funding available to them for research, for treatment, or even for education to prevent the spread of HIV. They took the opportunity to create an activist coalition, to fight around AIDS issues, and against institutionalised homophobia and other kinds of discrimination. The guiding principle of the early days was, 'If you're here, you're queer'. Minority heterosexuals and intravenous drug users were also a part of the queer movement then, since they, too, were facing ill-treatment and death through neglect.

The notion of Queer was rapidly taken up by sexual theorists and academics, some of whom did not connect it with any sort of activism. Agreement about definitions of Queer and, even more so, agreement about whether it is a good thing or not, has been hard to find, but its characteristics include reclaiming for sexual politics a sense of outlawry and resistance, and a lifestyle and sexuality outside the bounds of the conventional nuclear family. For some people, Queer has been a way of thinking about sexuality which is more radical and fruitful than keeping gayness in a rigid box, which often leads to a politics focused on trying to make the status quo more gay-friendly. Some theorists have found that the fluidity of queer politics links in to theories of post-modernism and the fragmentation of identity, although some of the writing in this area owes more to fashionable academic trends than to real substance.

As with any new intellectual or political development, while many lesbians and gay men are excited by the potential for diversity offered by queer politics, many others are very threatened by such developments. For example, there are lesbians, gays and bisexuals who find it disturbing that some lesbians and gay men can have sex with each other, without it seeming to disturb their fundamental sexual/political identities. While some people think that organisations such as Outrage and the recently formed Lesbian Avengers represent the activist arm of queer politics in Britain and are generally a good thing, others are concerned that their focus on straight society as the enemy simply makes people feel guilty and divided, and does not make it clear that everybody will benefit from the ending of sexual oppression.

It is clear that the concept of Queer, at its best, opens up a lot of potential space for bisexuals, and it is up to us to get involved, and make ourselves a central part of an inclusive sexual politics movement. Our communities have already been turned in this direction by the tragic impetus of HIV/AIDS, which has affected so many of us. Disgust at media and government reaction to AIDS has led many people to work together who might not previously have done so, although it has not entirely alleviated the suspicion of bisexuals among some lesbians and gays. We hope that the articles about HIV/AIDS that are included in this book will help to dispel some of the more prevalent myths and anxieties.

Since we have been working on this book, coverage of bisexual issues in the mainstream and lesbian and gay media has increased substantially, but life for individual bisexuals has not been dramatically transformed. It is upsetting to note, for example, how many of this book's contributors have felt compelled to use pseudonyms to protect themselves. We hope that our work will be a timely contribution to developing further understanding, both of bisexuals as individuals and of the political contribution of the bisexual movement, so that, in future, such reticence will be unnecessary.

Cris Stevens, Sharon Rose, Zaidie Parr, Francoise Gollain, Alison Behr, Kevin Lano, Vicky Wilson, Guy Chapman, David Sands.
May 1995.

Notes

[1] Paula Rust, 'The politics of sexual identity: sexual attraction and behaviour among lesbians and bisexual women', in *Social Problems*, vol.39, pp366-386, 1993.

[2] Alfred Kinsey, W.B. Pomeroy, C.E. Martin, and P.E. Gebhard, *Sexual Behaviour in the Human Male*, W.B. Saunders, Philadelphia 1948; and Alfred Kinsey, W.B. Pomeroy, C.E. Martin, and P.E. Gebhard, *Sexual Behaviour in the Human Female*, W.B. Saunders, Philadelphia 1953.

[3] Fritz Klein, Barry Sepekoff and Timothy J. Wolf, 'Sexual orientation: a multi-variable dynamic process', first published in the *Journal of Homosexuality*, special issue on bisexuality, vol.11, 1/2, 1985, and widely reprinted.
The Klein Sexual Orientation Grid is an elaboration of the scale developed by Kinsey, which places people's sexuality along a heterosexual to homosexual continuum from 0 to 6. The Klein grid recognises that people's sexuality may change over time, and that their behaviour and what they would like to do is often significantly different. People filling in the grid are asked to identify, on a scale of 1 to 7, their level of heterosexuality to lesbianism/gayness, in the past, in the present, and as an ideal, in seven areas of life; sexual attraction, sexual behaviour, sexual fantasies, emotional preference, social preference, self-identification, and lifestyle. A clear illustration of the use of the Klein grid can be found in Sue George's book, *Women and Bisexuality*, Scarlet Press, 1993 (pp170 to 181), where she analyses the results of the grids filled in by 97 of her respondents.

[4] Fritz Klein, *The Bisexual Option*, 2nd edition, Haworth Press, 1993; Fritz Klein and Timothy Wolf (eds), *Two Lives To Lead: Bisexuality in Men and Women*, Harrington Park Press, 1985.

[5] Charlotte Wolff, *Bisexuality – a Study*, Quartet, 1977.

[6] Sue George, *Women and Bisexuality*, Scarlet Press, 1993.

[7] Martin S. Weinberg, Colin J. Williams, and Douglas W. Pryor, *Dual Attraction: Understanding Bisexuality*, Oxford University Press, 1994.

[8] Naomi Tucker (ed), *Bisexual Politics: Theories, Queries and Visions*, Binghamton, NY, Howarth Press, 1995; and Paula C. Rust, *Sex, Loyalty, and Revolution: Bisexuality and the Challenge to Lesbian Politics*, New York University Press, 1995.

[9] Jeffrey Weeks, *Coming Out*, Quartet, 1977.

[10] Michel Foucault, *The History of Sexuality*, Allen Lane, 1979, p43.
[11] Sue George, *op.cit.*
[12] Nina Silver, 'Can we be friends if I'm bisexual?: the dialectics of loving', unpublished paper, 1990.
[13] Wayne Bryant, 'Who is the Gay Community?', unpublished paper, 1992.

Section I:
Theory and
Representation

A New Politics of Sexuality

June Jordan

I believe the Politics of Sexuality is the most ancient and probably the most profound arena for human conflict. Increasingly, it seems clear to me that deeper and more pervasive than any other oppression, than any other bitterly contested human domain, is the oppression of sexuality, the exploitation of the human domain of sexuality for power.

When I say sexuality, I mean gender: I mean male subjugation of human beings because they are female. When I say sexuality I mean heterosexual institutionalisation of rights and privileges denied to homosexual men and women. When I say sexuality I mean gay or lesbian contempt for bisexual modes of human relationship.

The Politics of Sexuality therefore subsumes all of the different ways in which some of us seek to dictate to others of us what we should do, what we should desire, what we should dream about, and how we should behave ourselves, generally, on the planet. From China to Iran, from Nigeria to Czechoslovakia, from Chile to California, the politics of sexuality – enforced by traditions of state-sanctioned violence plus religion and the law – reduces to male domination of women, heterosexist tyranny, and, among those of us who are in any case deemed despicable or deviant by the powerful, we find intolerance for

11

those who choose a different, a more complicated – for example, an interracial or bisexual – mode of rebellion and freedom.

We must move out from the shadows of our collective subjugation – as people of color/as women/as gay/as lesbian/as bisexual human beings.

I can voice my ideas without hesitation or fear because I am speaking, finally, about myself. I am black and I am female and I am a mother and I am bisexual and I am a nationalist and I am an anti-nationalist. And I mean to be fully and freely all that I am!

Conversely, I do not accept that any white or black or Chinese man – I do not accept that, for instance, Dr Spock – should presume to tell me, or any other woman, how to mother a child. He has no right. He is not a mother. My child is not his child. And, likewise, I do not accept that anyone – any woman or any man who is not inextricably part of the subject he or she dares to address – should attempt to tell any of us, the objects of her or his presumptuous discourse, what we should do or what we should not do.

Recently, I have come upon gratuitous and appalling pseudoliberal pronouncements on sexuality. Too often, these utterances fall out of the mouths of men and women who first disclaim any sentiment remotely related to homophobia, but who then proceed to issue outrageous opinions like the following:

That it is blasphemous to compare the oppression of gay, lesbian, or bisexual people to the oppression, say, of black people, or of the Palestinians.

That the bottom line about gay or lesbian or bisexual identity is that you can conceal it whenever necessary and, so, therefore, why don't you do just that? Why don't you keep your deviant sexuality in the closet and let the rest of us – we who suffer oppression for reasons of our ineradicable and always visible components of our personhood such as race or gender – get on with our more necessary, our more beleaguered struggle to survive?

Well, number one: I believe I have worked as hard as I could, and then harder than that, on behalf of equality and justice – for African-Americans, for the Palestinian people, and for people of color everywhere.

And no, I do not believe it is blasphemous to compare oppressions of sexuality to oppressions of race and ethnicity: Freedom is indivisible or it is nothing at all besides sloganeering and temporary, short-sighted, and short-lived advancement for a few. Freedom is indivisible, and either we are working for freedom or you are working for the sake of your self-interests and I am working for mine.

If you can finally go to the bathroom, wherever you find one, if you can finally order a cup of coffee and drink it wherever coffee is available, but you cannot follow your heart – you cannot respect the response of your own honest body in the world – then how much of what kind of freedom does any one of us possess?

Or, conversely, if your heart and your honest body can be controlled by the state, or controlled by community taboo, are you not then, and in that case, no more than a slave ruled by outside force?

What tyranny could exceed a tyranny that dictates to the human heart, and that attempts to dictate the public career of an honest human body?

Freedom is indivisible; the Politics of Sexuality is not some optional 'special-interest' concern for serious, progressive folk.

And, on another level, let me assure you: if every single gay or lesbian or bisexual man or woman active on the Left of American politics decided to stay home, there would be *no* Left left.

One of the things I want to propose is that we act on that reality: that we insistently demand reciprocal respect and concern from those who cheerfully depend upon our brains and our energies for their, and our, effective impact on the political landscape.

Last spring, at Berkeley, some students asked me to speak at a rally against racism. And I did. There were 400 or 500 people massed on Sproul Plaza, standing together against that evil. And, on the next day, on that same Plaza, there was a rally for bisexual and gay and lesbian rights, and students asked me to speak at that rally. And I did. There were fewer than seventy-five people stranded, pitiful, on that public space. And I said then what I say today: That was disgraceful! There should have been just one rally. One rally: Freedom is indivisible.

As for the second, nefarious pronouncement on sexuality that now enjoys mass-media currency: the idiot notion of keeping yourself in the closet – that is very much the same thing as the suggestion that black folks and Asian-Americans and Mexican-Americans should assimilate and become as 'white' as possible – in our walk/talk/music/food/values – or else. Or else? Or else we should, deservedly, perish.

Sure enough, we have plenty of exposure to white everything so why would we opt to remain our African/Asian/Mexican selves? The answer is that suicide is absolute, and if you think you will survive by hiding who you really are, you are sadly misled: There is no such thing as partial or intermittent suicide. You can only survive if you – who you really are – do survive.

Section I: Theory and Representation

Likewise, we who are not men and we who are not heterosexist – we, sure enough, have plenty of exposure to male-dominated/ heterosexist this and that.

But a struggle to survive cannot lead to suicide: Suicide is the opposite of survival. And so we must not conceal/assimilate/integrate into the would-be dominant culture and political system that despises us. Our survival requires that we alter our environment so that we can live and so that we can hold each other's hands and so that we can kiss each other on the streets, and in the daylight of our existence, without terror and without violent and sometimes fatal reactions from the busybodies of America.

Finally, I need to speak on bisexuality. I do believe that the analogy is interracial or multiracial identity. I do believe that the analogy for bisexuality is a multi-cultural, multi-ethnic, multi-racial world view. Bisexuality follows from such a perspective and leads to it, as well.

Just as there are many men and women in the United States whose parents have given them more than one racial, more than one ethnic identity and cultural heritage to honor; and just as these men and women must deny no given part of themselves except at the risk of self-deception and the insanities that must issue from that; and just as these men and women embody the principle of equality among races and ethnic communities; and just as these men and women falter and anguish and choose and then falter again and then anguish and then choose yet again how they will honor the irreducible complexity of their God-given human being – even so, there are many men and women, especially young men and women, who seek to embrace the complexity of their total, always-changing social and political circumstance.

They seek to embrace our increasing global complexity on the basis of the heart and on the basis of an honest human body. Not according to ideology. Not according to group pressure. Not according to anybody's concept of 'correct'.

This is a New Politics of Sexuality. And even as I despair of identity politics – because identity is given and principles of justice/equality/ freedom cut across given gender and given racial definitions of being, and because I will call you my brother, I will call you my sister, on the basis of what you *do* for justice, what you *do* for equality, what you *do* for freedom and *not* on the basis of who you are, even so I look with admiration and respect upon the new, bisexual politics of sexuality.

This emerging movement politicises the so-called middle ground: Bisexuality invalidates either/or formulation, either/or analysis.

14

A NEW POLITICS OF SEXUALITY

Bisexuality means I am free and I am as likely to want and to love a woman as I am likely to want and to love a man, and what about that? Isn't that what freedom implies?

If you are free, you are not predictable and you are not controllable. To my mind, that is the keenly positive, politicising significance of bisexual affirmation:

To insist upon complexity, to insist upon the validity of all of the components of social/sexual complexity, to insist upon the equal validity of all the components of social/sexual complexity.

This seems to me a unifying, 1990s mandate for revolutionary Americans planning to make it into the Twenty-first Century on the basis of the heart, on the basis of an honest human body, consecrated to every struggle for justice, every struggle for equality, every struggle for freedom.

This essay was first published in *Lyrical Campaigns*, essays by June Jordan, Virago Press 1992.

Being Who we Are (and Anyone Else we Might Want to be)

Jo Eadie

In order to defend ourselves against oppression, we often take up and champion the accusations that our oppressors make against us. For instance, as bisexuals we are regularly told that we have 'the best of both worlds' and because of this privilege our rights are not an important area of struggle. But equally, in affirming what is good and powerful about ourselves we often seem to come back to that very point: that we are more flexible, more open, we don't reject any option – that we do indeed have the best of both worlds.

What I see emerging from this are the first signs of a bisexual orthodoxy, in which to be committed to only one choice is labelled 'limiting' or 'constricting'. This came home to me very strongly when reading the new American collection *Bi Any Other Name* where many of the contributors were using the word 'monosexual' as a dismissive term for people loving only one sex. It is both ironic and scary that we, who spend our lives victimised by the either/or ideology, should be setting up a new binary opposition: either you're bisexual or you're monosexual (and one is better than the other ...).

At the eighth national bisexual conference we hit a similar problem with monogamy. There we all were, trying to define the difference between being monogamous and having multiple relationships, and trying not to assert the superiority of one choice over the other. But we realised that what we were doing was setting up monogamous/non-monogamous as if it were a stable, persistent, universal binary, with everyone belonging on one or other side. But, for instance, which are you if you've just switched from one to the other? or if you only have one partner now but might want more? or if you're having a temporary monogamous phase in an otherwise open relationship? and what about if you're in a triad and never have sex outside those relationships – what do you call that? and what about celibacy? So we made moves to deconstruct that opposition, just as we have deconstructed the heterosexual/homosexual one. These choices change over time, and co-exist, and fluctuate. Some of us have been both bisexual and monosexual at different times in our lives, some of us move up and down a scale between the two, some of us are strongly bisexual but only as of yesterday.

Many of these problems gather around the need to protect a threatened identity or lifestyle. This is often done by creating a strong idea of 'who I am' or 'who we are' and projecting everything which does not fit it on to some rejected 'Other'. It is clear enough that much lesbian and gay biphobia is a panicky enactment of their rejection of their own heterosexual desires. Since to be lesbian or gay is to be threatened and oppressed, it becomes very important to prop up your identity in the face of its denial by mainstream culture. The easiest way to do that is to deny all those parts of yourself which undermine such an identity. To show how strongly you are gay, you assert that there is nothing about you which is heterosexual (a recent *Outrage* ad runs: 'Rejoice at being saved from HETERO HELL'). It therefore becomes very threatening to find, say, bisexual men saying 'yes, I'm gay *and* I love women'.

Bi people can be found doing exactly same thing, affirming our bisexuality by saying: 'it's so much better than being monosexual, and none of us are at all monosexual, so we really do exist as a sexuality in our own right'. The fear is that if so many of us who are bisexual are also, and have also been, and will also be its (supposed) opposite, then bisexuality cannot exist 'in its own right'.

To see that bisexuality exists as a real, distinct sexuality is essential for our survival and well-being – but it can also lead into a bisexual orthodoxy about what it means to be a 'real bisexual' which is alienating and destructive. For instance, at the eighth national conference there was a lot of celebration that 'we' had finally got over the fear of not being gay or, especially, lesbian enough, and that 'we' now knew that being bisexual was an identity to be proud of, not a pale imitation of its more committed and coherent and oppressed brothers and sisters (as they so often tell us). But for many of us just coming out, those problems of identification were still at the top of the agenda, and to hear that 'we' had finally got over them, and were stronger because of it, and that to bring them up again would threaten our stability, simply felt rejecting. And recently I caught myself promoting my own orthodoxy by saying of bi singer Tom Robinson's involvement in *Outrage* 'he should be with us, not with them'. This raises the fundamental question in any communal discourse: which 'we' is this being talked about, and doing the talking?

The tensions between communal identity and individual difference always need to be addressed. Everyone who uses the word 'we' smooths over real differences. The West has an inadequate model of a unitary, strong, single, phallic identity, which is applied to being gay, black, a woman, and now bisexual. I don't believe that this model of identity adequately reflects the desires of anybody: any monolithic identity excludes parts of ourselves. And those excluded parts end up being projected on to, and rejected in, some other: S/M, monogamy, paganism, marriage, lesbian/gay identification, apoliticism, monosexuality – what are the repressed desires that we are rejecting in others? Is it really them that we are angry at for being like that – or is it ourselves? Indeed, this entire text, in rejecting unitary identity and binary oppositions is rejecting (by accusing others of it) my own desire for precisely that stability.

To take up any position is to take it up with respect to others. To be a gay-identified bisexual man is my way of dealing with heterosexism's wholesale rejection of homosexual desire, and the rejection of the gay community by some of my bi friends, and the rejection of my place in 'their'/our struggle by sections of the lesbian and gay movement. In this sense it is not a solid or stable identity – but a *tactical identity*. I take it up as a response to attempts to deny or disparage certain things about myself.

I believe that all identities, attributes, personality traits, beliefs and desires are negotiated differently in different conditions. In particular situations some parts of 'me' are simply not relevant – but I cling to them because 'that is who I am'. I found it very hard recently to acknowledge that I wanted a monogamous relationship, because I was so committed to myself as 'a person who has multiple relationships': and that commitment was itself a tactical way of resisting the power exercised against that choice by mainstream culture. We need to make such assertions in the face of oppressive power – but at what price? Might it not be more productive to recognise that many of these preferences are specific to certain contexts: when I say that I have multiple relationships, what I mean is that at some points in my life, with certain people, under certain conditions, I have several lovers. Does that make me 'somebody who has multiple relationships'? I think that it reflects one part of me, which is relevant only sometimes. The problem comes when some aspects of me are threatened and denied – or aroused and stimulated – so often that I find myself wanting to assert (and enjoy!) them almost all of the time. This is particularly true of bisexuality, both as an oppressed desire which I need to assert, and an erotic preference which I want to enjoy. So they solidify into identities: yes, I'm always bisexual, all the time, it's always relevant, that's always who 'I' am.

But even as we construct them out of specific moments of desire and insight, these identities disperse with the pressure of multiple contexts, they become irrelevant: we want something else. I drift. If we can be open to it, new moments enable new, temporary, identifications.

Where does this leave the need for a sense of belonging? We often use a very limited meaning of 'belonging' to refer to the imaginary single place where we will feel at home. I believe that we belong wherever we are engaged in actions, or ways of being, flowing from our desires: action as politics, as sex, as art, as friendship, as a walk around a neighbourhood. In his book *Communities of Resistance*, A. Sivanandan provocatively argues that 'we don't need a cultural identity for its own sake, but to make use of the positive aspects of our culture[s] to forge ... alliances and fight ... battles'. Where our sense of belonging is most powerful is when it comes out of a togetherness in action. To 'be bi' is not for me simply to announce my sexuality, but rather to live out my sexuality by making, with my brothers and sisters, a world in which bisexuality has the important place it deserves. Adapting Marx, Sivanandan says of identity: 'the whole purpose of knowing who we are is not to interpret the world, but to change it'. In this way we can look beyond a monolithic, eternal *identity*, and see instead a range of tactical *identifications*. In this sense an identity is an identification which we go on making; and an identification is an identity that we hold only in particular circumstances.

Identification with a group or a culture enables us to belong by working, loving, celebrating and thinking together. That is what strengthens our own power, and our own feeling of belonging in the world: and of belonging in many places in the world. Those identifications do not fix our actions, or our selves. They enable us to do *more*, rather than confining us to doing *less*. I am not suggesting here a pre-political 'I'm just me' or 'I don't like labels' position: I think that the need for stable identities, and politically committed identities, is something that we must work with in the process of building something less confining. We can work towards a new understanding of identity and identification, so that when a woman says 'I'm a lesbian' it doesn't come attached, for her or anyone else, with all the baggage of 'so then you must also be ...' (and that includes 'so you don't sleep with men'). My vision is of the freedom to keep identities at that point before they become solid, when they are enabling and empowering. At that point they are made up of a brief coalition of desires, while other identities are available for other such 'coalitions': and none of them are final, or permanent, or exclusive.

My hope is that as a movement, precisely because we have experienced so strongly the tyranny of the either/or ideology, bisexual men and women can steer clear of these traps, and not set up a new orthodoxy, or a set of entry requirements, or a bisexual thought police. We need to ask how we can take up our pride and power as an oppressed group, and at the same time not oppress ourselves by taking up communal identities which can come into being only by the exclusion of everything that does not fit into some rigid definition of 'being bisexual'. And this takes me to the impossible proposition that the most powerful bisexual movement is one in which, to reverse our old slogan: nobody's bisexual really.

An Old Bottle for Old Wine: Selecting the Right Label

Michael S. Montgomery

When I was twelve I secretly studied my father's copy of the Kinsey Report, where in the section on 'Bisexuality' I carefully examined a diagram of the famous 'Heterosexual-homosexual rating scale' that places individuals' 'psychologic reactions and overt experiences' of sexuality on a seven-point continuum from exclusive heterosexuality to exclusive homosexuality. There too I raptly read that 'nearly half (46%) of the [male] population engages in both heterosexual and homosexual activities, or reacts to persons of both sexes, in the course of their adult lives.'[1] Two years later (in 1963) I furtively bought the only paperback on sexual orientation for sale in Tucson, Arizona, Edmund Bergler's infamous *Homosexuality: Disease or Way of Life?*, which informed me in a chapter entitled 'Does Bisexuality Exist?' that 'bisexuality – a state that has no existence beyond the word itself – is an out-and-out fraud, involuntarily maintained by some naive homosexuals, and voluntarily perpetrated by some who are not so naive.' Some 'homosexuals', the psychiatrist continued, 'are occasionally capable of *lustless mechanical sex* [his italics] with a woman ... They tend to marry as a means of proving to themselves and especially to the environment that they are completely normal.'[2] Another two years on I tried to talk about my latest girlfriend with my buddy Rob (whom I'd come on to sexually several times, with limited success), only to have him respond, 'If you like girls now, Mike, you must be a lesbian.' I understood immediately what he was implying about my gender identity – and his wit earned an appreciative if uncomfortable laugh – but the experience suddenly deepened by several fathoms my sense that the question of my 'real' sexual orientation wasn't going to be an easy matter for me to sort out.

Over the next three years, in a concentrated effort to deduce from definitions and situational responses 'what I was', I experimented rigorously, engaging in sexual relations with about an equal number of females and males. (Was that last night *lustless mechanical sex*, or what?) I considered, but rejected, the 'bisexual' label. Only one person I knew identified herself that way, and there was no bisexual community. Nor could I conceptualise being or feeling bi: any mental picture of myself in bed with a man and a woman at the same time made me limp with imaginative overload; when I was being sexual with a female I felt straight, and when having sex with a male I identified as gay. Also, I believed that to feel homosexual feelings at all was complication enough and theorised that the adoption of a 'bisexual life-style' (whatever that might mean) would be unworkable in practice. A two-month experiment with Sue and Bill during the summer before I left for college in Manhattan delighted me in many ways but did not dispel my notion that in the long run everybody involved would become increasingly jealous or confused or both.

The watershed came when I was nineteen and Sue decided to break up with me after I confided to her my seduction of a male friend of my freshman roommate's. A couple of months later I joined America's first recognised campus homophile group and experienced 'accepting myself as a gay man' as a definitive rite of passage. In that largely essentialist environment,[3] I was persuaded that Bergler, so egregiously wrong about homosexuality as a disease, was nevertheless right, at least in my case, about the fraudulence of bisexuality: henceforth, I vowed, I would no longer pretend to heterosexuality. So for the next decade sex with men sufficed.

Or would have sufficed had I not been recurrently reminded that I still enjoyed sex with women. I was, in those times, a fairly easy lay, and I seldom refused any attractive man or woman who came on to me – although afterwards I sometimes asked myself why I – a gay man – had gone along with the women. It was somewhat to my surprise, therefore, when it became evident that one of these women was going to be my life-partner. I tried to warn her off on our first date, but fortunately I was unsuccessful. The marriage has succeeded for fifteen years because of several truths that we established between us on that date: that I had a perennial, perdurable sexual attraction to men, that sexual constancy could be distinguished from sexual fidelity, and that for two old hippies like us sexual exclusiveness could not be a desideratum. In fact, however, from 1979 to 1986, with new fathering pleasures and responsibilities and a new career to occupy me, and with mysterious new diseases devastating the community of gay men, I had sex with no one else. During this period I would have labeled myself as

22

a happily, heterosexually married gay man who chose not to sleep with men.

Six years ago I decided I wanted a major man in my life again, and for the past five years I have had a male lover (also contentedly married to a woman), whom I see once a week or so. This friend identifies himself as 'ambisexual', but under the joyful, comfortable influence of my relationships with him and with her, I have taken up and dusted off the old 'bisexual' label that I first encountered in Kinsey over thirty years ago and had neglected or rejected since.

I find that several of Kinsey's demurs regarding the term still make sense to me: that if the word is taken to imply that bisexual persons are anatomically, physiologically, or psychologically partly male and partly female, or both at once, then its use is indeed 'rather unfortunate'; and that 'the term as it has been used has never been strictly delimited, and consequently it is impossible to know whether it refers to all individuals who rate anything from 1 [predominantly heterosexual, only incidentally homosexual] to 5 [the reverse], or whether it is being limited to some smaller number of categories, perhaps centering around 3.'[4] If one takes the 1-5 range as definitive, then the label is wildly imprecise and uninformative (however politically expedient); if on the other hand the range were arbitrarily narrowed to, say, 2.5 to 3.5, then my lover would judge the lower limit too high for him to qualify, and I the upper limit too low.

Still, I find that the label works for me today when, as sometimes happens, I need one. Thinking inductively, synthetically – taking into account my thousands of varied dreams, fantasies, erections, and orgasms, and the genders of my various friends, tricks, and lovers over the years, and the several identities and life-styles I have sequentially or simultaneously adopted – I find that only 'bisexual' (or, affectionately, 'bi') describes accurately and succinctly both my past history and my present way of life. Its very breadth and imprecision, it seems to me now, are great strengths: it is the only descriptor flexible enough to cover the case of one whose numbers on the Klein Sexual Orientation Grid span nearly the entire range.[5] It obviates awkward constructions like 'I'm married, but' and 'I'm mainly gay, but'; when I say, 'I'm bisexual', the 'but' disappears and can be replaced by 'and' if my interlocutor wishes to continue the conversation. It is the word I now find slipping most easily from my lips at work, as I slowly come out there in the service of the campus lesbigay community, and it was the word most natural to use when I first discussed my sexuality with my then nine-year-old son.

Since I began writing for the gay and lesbian press in 1986, and more recently as I have become active locally, part of my own agenda has been to promote awareness and acceptance of a variety of alternative life-styles and sexual self-images. Both the feminist and gay liberation movements benefit, it seems to me, from anything that widens support by discouraging antipodal thinking about men *v* women, gays *v* straights, or lesbians *v* gay men. For this purpose the notion of a 'bisexual identity' is elegantly constructed. I have watched self-righteous fanatics – essentialist fundies and exclusionists and separatists and anti-assimilationists – squirm or change color when the *b*-word is uttered; and I have smiled to see it. 'Bisexual' (like 'multiculturalist') is a rare label that subsumes the goal of social inclusiveness. The term may be a transitional one, for the language or for me, but using it feels comfortable to me today, and I expect to continue using it for a while.

Notes

[1] Alfred C. Kinsey *et al*, *Sexual Behavior in the Human Male*, W.B. Saunders, Philadelphia 1948, pp638, 656.
[2] Edmund Bergler, *Homosexuality: Disease or Way of Life?*, Hill and Wang, New York, 1956, p89.
[3] But not exclusively: Stephen Donaldson, founder of the Student Homophile League-Columbia University, identified himself as bi then and now (personal communications, March 1968 and November 1991).
[4] Kinsey, pp656-58.
[5] Fritz Klein *et al*, 'Sexual Orientation: A Multi-Variable Dynamic Process', *Journal of Homosexuality* 11, 1985 pp35-49; since reprinted in several bi anthologies. The KSOG was developed 'in an attempt to better demarcate and understand the complexities of human sexual attitudes, emotions, and behavior'. See footnote 3 of the introduction for further information.

Towards a Free and Loose Bisexual Future

Heather Came

This article is a personal and political one, starting from a bisexual feminist perspective that recognises that both the heterosexual and homosexual (as in lesbian and gay) worlds consciously and subconsciously marginalise the experience of bisexuals.

Because labelling is so contentious in sexuality politics, I think it is necessary to explain my understanding of bisexuality. For me, a bisexual is simply someone who chooses to identify as such. We are 'people who have the capacity to love men and women in whatever form that love takes and in varying degrees, whether the attachment be emotional, physical or a combination of the two'. I came out as a bisexual woman when I realised that I loved both a man and a woman simultaneously. I think it was due to my circumstances at the time (but by choice since then), that bisexuality has come to mean non-monogamous relationships for me, implying a free and loose lifestyle. Through open relationships with my significant others, we develop our sexuality more fully. I have tried to maintain monogamous relationships, but they do not work for me.

As a bisexual feminist, my identity has always been a political public choice as well as a personal one. Even though I am not currently 'involved as such' with a woman I continue to identify as a bisexual, because for me bisexuality, and more particularly bisexual feminism, is much more than who I might sleep with. Rather, it is fundamental to the way I live my life, with visibility always being important.

Even though I believe everybody has the potential to identify and live as a bisexual, it is not possible for many to do so because of the continued hostility of both the heterosexual and homosexual worlds to bisexuals. Because of this hostility, much of the potential depth of our community lies closeted, and our stories remain largely untold. The history of bisexuality is therefore often a tragic one, clouded in myths and misunderstandings. We bisexuals are in a unique political position and can recognise both heterosexism and homosexism as forces acting in our society. We can use this understanding to work towards greater dialogue between people.

When I moved to Auckland at the age of eighteen, I enjoyed for the first time meeting people who identified as gay. As I watched them shunned by educated liberal heterosexuals, I felt very challenged. When I finally realised I was bisexual, I began to understand the power of compulsory heterosexuality. I gained insight into heterosexual nuclear families, heterosexual romance on television and in novels. Everywhere I saw heterosexual institutions validating the experience of heterosexuals, while there was very little affirmation of my own women-loving nature.

The effect of portraying heterosexuality as the only natural sexuality, and of stigmatising sexual variance, is quite devastating to many in the homosexual community. Heterosexism is a direct cause of our often closeted lives and the traumas this entails. Being stigmatised by the straight community often confuses us and makes us feel guilty about our sexuality. Such heterosexism often comes from our family and friends. And it continues to thrive because alternative information is very limited, and the self-consciously identified bisexual community is small. The contradictions between heterosexual myths and our realities is a burden we have therefore had to attempt to iron out in isolation. Heterosexism takes a heavy toll on the queer community, as reflected in our high rates of mental illness, suicide and various forms of addiction.

However, heterosexism has not had only negative effects on sexual variants. It has motivated our community to organise, to provide ourselves with support groups and counselling services, to uncover our own herstory – to make sexual variance an easiers option in the future, so that our community may grow. The whole gay liberation movement was born from a rejection of the stigma placed upon us by heterosexuals. Likewise, visibility has been invaluable in counteracting myths and stereotypes about us.

For me, discovering heterosexism has been a radicalising experience, switching my feminist concerns from the sexist to the heterosexist and giving me a definite focus for my political beliefs as well as a new understanding of sexuality. I was lucky to avoid taking on the stigma of sexual variance, and those of my friends who did not support my bisexuality rapidly lost my friendship.

My response to heterosexism has been to make myself as visible as possible. As a form of individual political action, I talk about sexuality with anybody who is prepared to listen, sometimes even when they are reluctant. By encouraging people to talk about sexuality, I can squash many myths and sometimes challenge the heterosexist thinking at the core of their lives. Within the university, in much the same way as I protest sexist language, I also protest heterosexist assumptions. At times I feel like a guinea pig on show, the token bisexual, but by being visible I create choices for others and a more supportive place for myself. Heterosexism is a central reality of my life.

Homosexism, on the other hand, is about compulsory homosexuality within the sexually variant community, and political correctness and hierarchies of feminism, with lesbian feminism being held up as the pinnacle, the 'true' feminism. Although homosexism is not as rampant as heterosexism, it is a powerful force within the politically active sector of the sexually variant community, where it effectively gets in the way of the natural alliance between all women-loving women.

The strength of homosexism can be seen in bisexuals' lack of visibility in the gay community, as well as in the strong pressure to conform to the community's unspoken code of ethics. These ethics regard relationships with the opposite sex as unacceptable. Our woman-loving credentials are judged by how much we look like dykes, how much prejudice we have faced, how long we've been out.

Homosexism has been far more devastating for me than heterosexism, because I expected much more from other women-loving women. I find my welcome in the straight world, no matter how outspoken I am, is nearly always friendlier than in the 'gay' community. In the straight world I can be freer, and the judgements seem to mean less and are less severe.

Homosexism deprives bisexuals of a safe place. For many of us this means resorting once again to the secrecy and trauma of closets in order to get the unquestioned affirmation of our women-loving selves. For me, moving to Christchurch, where I knew no women-loving-women, let alone bisexuals of any shape, size or form, the idea of finding an all-women sexually variant group was a very scary and necessary ambition. When I heard of the *Lesbian Collective* in one of my classes, I jumped at the possibility, determined to learn more about my woman-loving nature. These older lesbians, who all seemed to know each other, didn't ask whether I was bisexual. I somehow knew that if I was to stay in the group I couldn't tell them.

I despised every minute of the deceit, but I learned more than I had expected about women-loving women, and I maintained my visible bisexual status in the rest of my life. Until my involvement with the mainstream 'gay' community, my bisexuality had never been an issue. I had not known about homosexism. Yet a couple of months later my sexual identity had changed largely as a result of it. I enjoyed my new lesbian status for nearly a month before a friend challenged the validity of my new 'pure' lesbian status. Since then I have vigorously reclaimed my bisexual label and removed all suggestions of closets from my life. I feel very much stronger for it.

However, attempting to be visible in the sexually variant community presents an enormous challenge to bisexuals; every inch we gain has to be fought against the myths and pressure of homosexism. Even ground we have already won has had to be fought for to be maintained. We now have a women's group in Wellington, and an article about bisexuals appeared in a recent *Broadsheet* – the bisexual liberation movement has made a humble beginning in Aotearoa.

Homosexism is maintained primarily as a reaction against heterosexism, meeting the need for safe, secure places for homosexuals. These places are precious in that they protect and nurture a homosexual identity away from the straight world. The inclusion of bisexuals in such spaces is seen as undervaluing the exclusive experience of homosexuals. Allowing bisexuals who still retain some links with the straight world to share these spaces is seen as jeopardising them altogether.

I also see lesbian feminists, in particular, believing it is in their interests to perpetuate homosexism in order to retain their position as the 'true' feminism. So long as heterosexism threatens the homosexual community, it seems that homosexism will continue as a response.

The difference beween a heterosexual future and a bisexual or lesbian one lies in the absence of rigid gender roles. More particularly, as a result of our involvement with other women-loving women (and our recognition of this possibility itself), we are able to appreciate alternative approaches to childcare, domestic, and emotional work in relationships, leaving ourselves time for involvement in political action.

When we bring this understanding back into our opposite sex relationships, we are less likely to become isolated from other women, to become economically dependent on male partners or to invest all our self-worth in the success of that relationship. Instead, we are likely to develop alternative support systems, have the confidence to make choices for ourselves and to sustain an attitude to life which allows us to assume many different roles, both in our emotional and political lives.

Bisexuality holds radical possibilities for change, particularly for non-monogamous bisexual situations like my own. Multiple 'open'

TOWARDS A FREE BISEXUAL FUTURE

relationships become serious possibilities for women, offering great potential for personal growth and self-awareness. Women could develop greater depth in their support networks by establishing varying levels of intimacy with people, dissolving the artificial distinction between friend and lover. Placing the highest value on people and relationships could challenge the entire capitalist value system and work ethic. Sexuality labels would wither away together with patriarchy, as individuals began to think for themselves and find their own niche within a truly free and loose world.

This article was first published in *Race Gender Class*, issue 11/12, 1991. It was written in 1989 and Heather Came would like to note that her ideas have changed since then.

Notes

[1] Barry Kohn and Alice Matusow, *Barry and Alice: Portrait of a Bisexual Marriage*, Prentice Hall Inc, Englewood Cliffs, New Jersey, 1980.

Bisexuals and People of Mixed-Race: Arbiters of Change

Yasmin Prabhudas

To be bisexual is to be both gay and straight. It means that we benefit from fulfilling relationships with people of both sexes.

To be mixed-race is to be both black and white. It means that we benefit from the richness of two different cultures.

Bisexuals and people of mixed race are often confronted by parallel difficulties – both may feel alienated from the established group categories of gay/straight, black/white and are frequently derisively dismissed as 'in-betweens'. This negative experience can, however, be turned on its head and used to positive effect.

Bisexuals and people of mixed-race have a positive role to play in bringing together the frequently very separately perceived realms of 'gay'/'straight', 'black'/'white', through our experience of each of these realms as interwoven threads of one world. As social constructs, these polarities are increasingly recognised as obsolete – people's ethnic origin or sexual orientation is no longer a clear-cut matter, but rather a merger of identities, which everyone could usefully explore.

Yet we appear to be conspiring with society's consistent efforts to set minorities against each other, to continue a policy of 'divide and rule'. Whilst it is important to set up our own separate groups, based on race, gender, sexuality, disability and other identities which are discriminated against, as these provide safe and comfortable environments, where people do not feel intimidated, this can only represent a short-term measure against oppression.

On a long-term basis, a policy of separation only reinforces a ghetto culture, enabling society as a whole to 'pass the buck' where minority issues are concerned, and helps to perpetuate already prevalent myths, cultivated through ignorance. It is time we sought to challenge this ignorance by broadening our view, and embracing a philosophy of unity, rather than one of division, making sexuality everyone's issue, making race everyone's issue.

Under the banner of queer politics, bisexuals who are also people of mixed race can help to establish a dialogue between different oppressed groups. This will enable us to focus on common issues and concerns, whilst at the same time celebrating difference. There is no doubt that single issue politics is important and has made considerable headway in the past few decades, but how much stronger our voices would be if we worked more closely with one another through setting up networking groups, organising joint actions and sharing resources, expertise and experiences. The political power which such co-operation accesses, by bringing people together from a range of minority groups to debate issues of concern to everyone, is immeasurable.

This all requires a great deal of effort and a strong commitment to co-operative working. Bisexuals and people of mixed race are well-placed to embrace this vision.

Yasmin Prabhudas now defines herself as a mixed-race lesbian. She continues to support the rights of those choosing to define themselves as bisexual.

Passing: Pain or Privilege? What the Bisexual Movement Can Learn from Jewish Experience

Naomi Tucker

I defy the categories. I am a Jewish woman with white skin, a minority with no face to prove it, tied to a culture that many say is not a real culture. I shatter the illusions of innate sexual orientation. Because mine is fluid, changing, chosen. I was raised in a family with solid working-class values that gradually worked its way into solid middle-class money, living trapped between my morals and material possessions. My maternal tongues were English and French: my childhood roots are on two coasts. Some of my friends and lovers are the same people. I'm an earth mama with hairy legs who dresses in black with flashy jewelry. A walking contradiction. I'm not a top or a bottom, a butch or a femme, straight or gay, San Franciscan or New Yorker, Religious or Atheist. I am all of these things together but no one can figure me out.

This is a journey, as a Jewish bisexual feminist woman, through a society where the norm is Christian, heterosexual, and sexist. It is about levels of invisibility – from internalised to institutionalised oppression, from passing (allowing others to assume we are part of the mainstream) to assimilation (giving up our identity in an attempt to *become* part of the mainstream). It is about how I was living life on both sides of the oppressor/oppressed fence – because of my white Jewish background and because of my bisexuality – until I realised there is no fence.

PASSING: PAIN OR PRIVILEGE?

I grew up in a household where being Jewish was a language, a gathering point of family, a history that we celebrated at certain times of year, a value system based on the need to proudly push our individual potentials to the utmost in order to survive and flourish. I remember clearly that expressing my opinions, sticking up for what I believed in, and succeeding in whatever I chose to do, were central to our ethic of how to live life. So in some ways I have my Jewishness to thank for my strength as a woman and my self-acceptance as bisexual.

Bisexuality was not a label I used until I realised that I needed a community to fit my sexual identity. As a teenager I was always in love with my girl friends, but never translated this into conscious sexual desire. I was not particularly attracted to boys either, and I sometimes thought I might never be, which made me faintly aware that I was not and might never be socially acceptable as a woman.

My first sexual experiences were with men in college. But my first loves happened almost simultaneously with a close male friend and a 'nice Jewish girl' from my college dorm. Unfortunately, the women's community where I had always felt at home could barely tolerate me relating sexually to a man, so I began to keep quiet about that relationship. Outside that community I could not always safely speak of loving a woman, and my woman-loving self was often rendered invisible by others' presumption of heterosexuality. I felt split between the two worlds of which I was a part.

When I joined the newly-formed bisexual group on campus in my fourth year, and began to claim that word as my identity, this split was at least partially healed. As I started to come out publicly, I longed even more to bridge the philosophical and political gap between my claim to my Jewishness and my increasing feminist bisexual identity. But instead, I joined the Anti-Apartheid movement, the battered women's movement, the pro-choice movement, the campaign to help women struggling with body image and food issues. My priorities were in radical left and women's politics, and these did not include the Jewish community or combatting anti-semitism (as these causes didn't seem political enough). I didn't think I was 'Jewish enough' to be part of the organised Jewish community on campus, which was fairly heterosexual anyway, much in the same way that I had never felt I was 'lesbian enough' to be part of the women's community. These experiences of passing – allowing my lesbian friends to assume I'd given up men, allowing my political friends to forget I was Jewish or assume it didn't matter – always involved the painful suppression of some aspect of my identity.

Who would have thought that some day, I would be drawing parallels between Yiddishkeit and bisexuality? Clearly, coming out as bisexual, and coming home to my Judaism, both contextualised in feminism, were keys that unlocked some of my greatest joys about who I am, as well as some of my deepest fears about my place in the world. Stereotypes equate Judaism with greed for money and power, and bisexuality with greed for sex. Both identities are seen as privileged, despite the fact that we are the objects of worldwide rage and murder. Both identities have taught me about passing (for straight, for lesbian, for Christian ...) But the move from complacency and silence to proud confrontation of people's assumptions about me had to come from examining the history of Jewish assimilation for survival in a hostile world, and then bringing it home to my own family.

Even on a progressive college campus, the very Jewishness and bisexuality that moved my thoughts and desires were familiar targets of hatred. The scope of this hatred on this planet is so vast that I cannot feel truly, completely safe anywhere. I learned that there is no safe homeland for Jewish queers.

My mother has always tried to preserve her traditional Jewish culture without losing her modern independence. Yet even this strong believer in maintaining the loving traditions of her background has not escaped the Americanisation process. From her grandmother who never learned English, to her parents who spoke a mixture of Yiddish and English, her childhood bilingualism faded to a smattering of Yiddish words by the time I was born. Her maternal tongue was lost to the shame she swallowed throughout her life, as the daughter of immigrant Jews in New York. And I think: will the next generation of Jewish children even know what Yiddish is? What will it sound like to be an Ashkenazi Jew without familiar inflections, tone of voice, accent, which have been passed down from our Yiddish-speaking grandparents?

Assimilation seems to grow thicker with each generation. When I was a child, I laughed at my mother's seemingly outrageous fear that I might not pass on my Judaism to my children. Although she always said that above all I should be happy, and that she would accept my relationships whether they were with a woman or a man, Jewish or not, she would always end with 'so long as you raise your children Jewish'. For the longest time, she was crushed by my staunch declaration that I was *not* going to have any children ... not because she wanted to be a grandmother, but because she was possessed by a deep fear that the Jewish people were dying out, and that it was our responsibility to pass on our traditions to the next generation. As I come to understand my mother's fears, I, too, start to wonder about my responsibility as a Jew in this world. I have learned that it is my responsibility *not* to deny my Judaism, much in the same way that as a bisexual woman it is my responsibility to be out and proud. My visibility makes a public statement that being Jewish, or being bisexual, is a wonderful thing, so that others, in turn, may be empowered to be proud of themselves. Each individual's visible statement of pride in their heritage or identity is a building block of community.

Jews are an example of what a government's racism can actually do to a group of people: slavery in Egypt, the Inquisition in Spain, the extermination of half of our worldwide population only a generation ago. How quickly we forget these events, or brush them off as merely a part of the past. In 1991, a candidate for governor of the State of Louisiana, David Duke, claimed the Holocaust never happened, and in the United States today Jews are buying the myth that anti-Jewish oppression ended in 1948. Such pervasive denial is a frightening example of anti-Jewish oppression at work, and it is testimony to the power of institutionalised oppression.

The bisexual community would do well to look at this history, because we risk similar extermination. The difference is, we are not born into bisexual families with strong oral histories of centuries of biphobia, the pain of passing, the life-or-death need to assimilate. That's why it is imperative that we make ourselves visible and face our real enemies: the heterosexist institutions that seek to isolate and eliminate us. Only then will we know what we're up against, and understand how to dismantle the power structure of our oppressors. Only if we are visible will other bisexually-identified people know that we exist, so that they can join the struggle for bi liberation, or at least know that there are other people like them.

My experience of anti-Jewish oppression is different from that of previous generations of Jewish women. I was raised to value being Jewish, and I am privileged in not having to fear for my life when I walk out of my front door. Yet I have inherited the historic memory of a people afraid of extinction, and that cultural connectedness shapes who I am and how I think.

My political friends who fight against racism, sexism, homophobia, think I contradict myself in not giving up my Jewishness. To them it is just another organised religion, and a sexist one at that. So how could I be Jewish and still be feminist, queer, and non-conformist? I did spend some time questioning how connected I could really be to my Judaism,

35

and therefore distanced myself from Jewish culture. Having missed many opportunities to learn about my own culture is one of the most painful parts of assimilation.

So I come back to the shame I felt in the lesbian community when I 'admitted' that I was in love with a man, to the times when I stood silently by while somebody assumed I was straight. When I 'pass' as the norm for whatever group I might be in, I give up personal integrity, honesty with myself and the world. When I am a traitor to a significant part of who I am, there is an underlying element of not feeling good about myself. This happens when I internalise the mass culture's perceptions of compulsory heterosexuality and christianity, or even the pure-woman-loving values of cultural lesbian feminism. When I take these external morals and internalise them into my own personal belief system, despite my strong intellect and understanding of how internalised oppression works, it shows just how powerful these forces are.

Our oppressors gain ultimate control when we do their work for them. When thousands of Jews in the US today feel disconnected from or ashamed of their Jewish heritage, WASP (White Anglo-Saxon Protestant) culture no longer needs to put 'Jews not welcome' on their meeting room doors, because we will not come to their meetings as open Jews. When lesbians and bisexual women spend our energy fighting each other about who loves women more, our enemies score a point for keeping us divided and therefore less able to join forces against heterosexism. When women swallow the myth that we have to be thin and submissive in order to be attractive, men no longer need to blatantly insult us in order for us to feel shame. We feel the shame anyway, and we will endlessly torture our bodies with chemicals and surgery and starvation to meet unrealistic, sexist norms of 'traditional beauty'. We will even judge other women as fat, ugly, or unfeminine – the ultimate act of doing our oppressors' work.

After generations of being oppressed, the result is Jews who hate their own Jewishness, people who are ashamed of their own sexuality, and women who think that sexism doesn't affect them. As we struggle to fight the oppression of Jews, bisexuals, lesbians, gays, women, transsexuals, people of color, people with AIDS, people with backgrounds or lifestyles or abilities different from the societal norm, we must remember the source and power dynamics of these oppressions. Yes, I believe in being out and proud and visible. But blaming each other for the 'privileges' some of us hold on to for survival will only further the oppressive systems by dividing our energies. Instead of directing our anger at straight-identified bisexuals or assimilated Jews, let us direct our anger at the systems that force people to make those choices and deny our true selves.

As a white-skinned person living in a Western country, I do have some societal privilege. When I walk down the street with a man, I do gain more societal acceptance than when I walk down the street with a woman. I recognise these privileges; they motivate me to fight even harder to end the oppression that makes them privileges in the first place. I should be held accountable for my racism, for instance, because that is my responsibility as part of an oppressor group. But I am not being oppressive to other Jews, women, or queers if my strength occasionally caves in under the weight of anti-semitism, sexism, homophobia, or biphobia.

What we *can* do as Jewish bisexuals is to examine what we have internalised, and to claim all of who we are. The next time someone talks about the 'privilege' of being Jewish or bisexual because these are identities that are not necessarily marked by the way a person looks, think about the pain of invisibility that goes along with passing. And ask yourself: is this really a privilege?

Bisexuality and Feminism: one Black Woman's Perspective

Valerie Barlow

My own definition of bisexuality is the freedom to choose my partners on the basis of our criteria rather than on the basis of a societally prescribed sexual choice. It is a rejection of the oppression of sexual stereotyping and the expectations in our relationships which lays down a challenge to both our heterosexual sisters and brothers, and our gay brothers and lesbian sisters. My definition of feminism is a commitment to addressing the issues of women's oppression and the inequality and discrimination that we face. However, within the women's movement, feminism became an examination of issues which were pertinent to white middle-class women.

So what are the possible connections between bisexuality and feminism? Both schools of thought challenge the status quo. Both are commitments to liberation from an oppressive and exploitative prescription of values, attitudes and behaviour. Both are a choice to reshape our destiny in the values of liberation, equality and freedom. The women's movement was centred around the ethos and principles of feminism. It gave women from varying schools of feminist thought a focus around which to advocate equality and often offered the opportunity for a unified voice. However, for a variety of reasons, the movement today does not have the profile that it once had. Although at present it cannot be said to speak for the body of women as it previously did, I hope that perhaps one day it will once more attain that power.

One of the factors that contributed to the movement's present position was its inability to address a wider political agenda of societal inequality. As a black woman, the women's movement did not address my triple and combined oppressions of racism, sexism and poverty and their pernicious cumulative effects. Feminism was interpreted in the language of articulate and educated white middle-class women who identified the issues from their own experience. It feels to me as though this was a missed opportunity. However, now that the lesson has been learnt we can try to ensure that this does not happen again through the adequate representation of working-class and black women, and by listening respectfully to their voices.

A black women's definition of feminism encompasses the reality of globally unequal distribution of wealth, opportunity and resources to all socio-economic groups. In our daily lives the issues are not only about sexism and racism but also include all other forms of oppression. 'Black Feminism', renamed as 'womanism' by Alice Walker, is a movement that has been possessed through our struggle. We come from a position of strength to share our common experiences with our Black sisters all over the world. Holding this wider picture places us in a unique position. This experience, and the communication of this perspective, offers us a great opportunity for leadership and offers others a great opportunity for learning.

While the voice of the women's movement continues to speak for many women in the world of academic thought, debate and institutions, the bisexual movement is in the process of moving from its stage of infancy to early maturity. As part of this growth it would do well to pay particular attention to the valid lessons learnt from the women's movement. It is important that we in the bisexual community are continually aware of other forms of oppression, their effect and operation. The eradication of racism, classism and sexism should be as important to us as the final removal of all traces of homophobia, behavioural expectations and sexual stereotyping.

Angela Davis, in *Women, Culture and Politics* (published by the Women's Press in 1984), comments: 'The roots of sexism and homophobia are found in the same economic and political institutions that form the foundation of racism'. She goes on to make the point that our political activism must clearly manifest our understanding of all these connections. Without this broad and encompassing agenda we in the bisexual movement will inevitably sow the seeds of our own marginalisation. It is also important that we reach out to other liberation movements communicating our primary concerns and listening to theirs.

We have a golden opportunity before us – to build a new land with some of the still strong foundation stones of feminism, socialism and other liberation philosophies. We can learn from the mistakes of those who have gone before us. We can stand on the shoulders of giants and see clearly over the wall as we continue to build and strengthen our bisexual community. In the words of Angela Davis 'If we wish to be radical in our quest for change – then we must get to the root of our oppression. After all, radical simply means "grasping things by the root".' A clear analysis of the roots of our oppression shows it to be a wide-ranging pattern of societal exploitation, discrimination and imposed disadvantage, with homophobia and heterosexism as part of this 'mosaic of oppression'.

As a 'Womanist', I will leave the last word to the Combahee River Collective:

> If Black Women were free it would mean that everyone else would be free, since our freedom would necessitate the destruction of all systems of oppression.

Let us not forget that we are not doing this 'for other people' but primarily for ourselves, and if this is true we can rewrite this statement to read:

> If all Bisexual women and men are free it would mean that everyone else is free, since our freedom would necessitate the destruction of all systems of oppression.

For our own survival and for the sake of the commitment to liberation to which we hold true, it is important that we take this vision on board, and that this becomes our wider picture. Sisters and brothers, let's go for it!

Bisexual Feminism: Challenging the Splits

Susan M. Sturgis

Bisexuality and feminism are so intertwined in me that it is difficult to write about one *without* writing about the other. My attraction to women – then still unacknowledged – led me to feminism, and my discovery of feminism led me to question my sexuality. In my day to day life, my bisexual resistance to enforced heterosexuality challenges the homophobia used to prop up sexism, while my feminist resistance to male domination challenges a gender order supported by enforced heterosexuality.

Of course, in the straight- and male-dominated world at large, bisexuality and feminism are not seen as intertwined, or necessarily even related. But as a bisexual feminist I am frustrated when the feminist and lesbian and gay movements fail to see their connection to the bisexual movement. It is critical for bisexual feminists to make these connections, to fill in gaps in either/or theories which fail to account for our both/and existence. The lesbian and gay movement's challenge to enforced heterosexuality, the feminist movement's resistance to male domination, are weaker for not acknowledging bisexual existence. Bisexual feminism has much to offer resistance to both enforced heterosexuality and male domination.

Bisexual-conscious feminist theory and feminist-conscious bisexual theory have the potential to challenge western ways of thinking; and these western models form the basis not only of the oppression of bisexuals, lesbians and gay men, not only of women, but of the very construction of oppression. Western philosophy conceptualises the world along deep splits. Fragmenting human from animal, man from woman, mind from body, self from other, reason from emotion, culture from nature, enquirer from object of enquiry, and black from white, metaphysical dualism imposes polarities on what is in reality interconnected and interdependent. The splits are created in a context of domination, one half of each split pair privileged – and assigned gender. Human, mind, self, reason, culture, enquirer, white become masculine. Animal, body, other, emotion, nature, object of enquiry, and black are deemed 'feminine', subordinate to their 'masculine' counterparts. A recent split, created by nineteenth century science, is heterosexual versus homosexual. Heterosexual is conceptualised as masculine, homosexual as feminine. This association of homosexuality – male homosexuality – with the feminine contributes to the cultural erasure of lesbianism.[1]

By challenging this heterosexual/homosexual split and the construction of the 'sexual other', the bisexual movement provides a theoretical framework to resist all dualisms and constructions of 'otherness' – constructions which fracture our selves and society, and enable hatred and violence of all kinds to continue. That bisexuality resists these splits is hinted at in the anxieties bisexuals create for both heterosexuals and lesbians and gays. Biphobia is often articulated around fears of contamination, vividly demonstrated in the conflation of biphobia and AIDS phobia. Heterosexuals accuse bisexual men of spreading AIDS to them, while some lesbians accuse bisexual women of carrying AIDS into the lesbian community. The assumption on the part of both heterosexuals and lesbians here is that they exist in a world apart from each other, and that when bisexuals inappropriately cross the boundary, death results.

The destruction bisexuals are accused of wreaking is sometimes metaphorical: some lesbians and gay men, embracing the straight/queer split as a source of personal and community identity, accuse bisexuals of destroying the 'purity' of their movement and community through a presence which they biphobically view as confused, confusing, and straight-tainted. Much to the anxiety of those who imagine themselves on one or the other 'side', bisexual existence brings the straight and gay worlds together, attesting to the existence of a sexual continuum, rather than two separate worlds separated by an impenetrable fence.

After the medical establishment's creation of homosexuality as a phenomenon worthy of examination, mixed-gender relationships came to be seen as a biological 'truth' and same-gender relationships as a biological error. Homosexuality and bisexuality were viewed as illnesses. Heterosexuality became medically compulsory. In a curious parallel, in the late 1960s feminist resurgence, a strand of feminism emerged which viewed women's oppression as universal and fundamental. Radical feminism's emphasis on examining how women are oppressed through sex and reproduction gave it decidedly biological overtones, at times to the point of being as biologically determinist as conservative anti-feminism. Viewing men *qua* biological men as the problem naturally led to the political practice of separatism. Some radical feminists even came to see same-gender relationships as a political necessity and mixed-gender relationships as a political error, gender treachery. Thus radical feminism answered enforced hetero-sexuality with enforced homosexuality.

Both conservative anti-feminism and radical feminism demand that certain behaviour be determined by gender. But bisexual feminism resists this dualistic, polarised conception of gender. It queers up imposed gender order, rejecting the idea that the gender you fuck is determined by the gender you are. It broadens the zone of sexual liberation.

By its inherent rejection of gender separatism, bisexual feminism also avoids the radical feminist trap of biological determinism, in which the assumption is made that women are oppressed and men oppress because of their biology. Because it acknowledges that sexism is a basic problem and that men are a part of its world, bisexual feminism demands that men be included in any feminist change project. Bisexual feminism rejects the fatalism of both conservative anti-feminists and radical feminists. It rejects the conservative view that says women's oppression is biologically inevitable, so nothing can be done about it. Equally, because it insists on including men in our lives in deeply personal ways – out of choice, not out of compulsion – it requires political engagement with men in the hope that change is possible. In so doing bisexual feminism rejects the fatalism of radical feminists that says men's oppressiveness is biologically inevitable, with gender separatism the only option for freedom.

Some nonfeminist bisexuals might query the need for a bisexual *feminist* movement. If we are to work toward tearing down the divisions, why not bisexual *humanism*?

Embracing a 'we're-really-all-the-same humanism' obscures the very real power structure of male domination. Certainly men are also hurt by sexist dualism, just as whites are hurt by racism and straights by heterosexism. But to imply that men's experience of male domination is the same as women's, or whites' experience of racism is the same as blacks', is to trivialise the very real and immediate violence experienced by those who happen to fall on the subordinate side of the split. Men – and all of us who find ourselves on the privileged side of a division – need to acknowledge our privilege in order to struggle against it. Ignoring or denying the split won't make it, or the power imbalance, go away – that requires struggle conscious of existing realities. By embracing bisexual *feminism* over 'humanism', I acknowledge and challenge the existing power differential while at the same time challenging the structure that allows the imbalance to continue.

This is not an argument for bisexual superiority, a call for straight and lesbian and gay people to throw way their identities and call themselves bisexuals. The perspectives of those falling closer to the ends of the sexual continuum have contributed much to feminist and queer thought and movement. However, the voices of those of us in the middle of the continuum, long trapped in inadequate reality constructs that condemned us to silence, need to be heard.

Nor is this an argument against separatism. It is not useful for bisexuals to dispute all lesbian- or gay-only space, or for men to dispute all women-only space. Separatism is necessary at times – I certainly think there are times when we need bisexual-only space. But there are political and cultural moments when it makes sense, and when it is imperative, for lesbians, gays, and bisexuals, women and men, to join together.

The bisexual movement is burgeoning. It addresses cultural assumptions of dualism that obscure a real underlying continuum, while feminism challenges the power differentials resulting from dualism. A theory and movement – bisexual feminism – that combines these perspectives has the potential to disrupt the very structure of oppression.

Notes

[1] In a similar way, the 'feminisation' of the black man – historically symbolised by white supremacists through castration and lynching – contributes to western culture's erasure of the black woman. See the introduction to the women's studies anthology, *All the Women Are White, All the Blacks Are Men, But Some of Us Are Brave*, Gloria T. Hull, Patricia Bell Scott and Barbara Smith (eds), The Feminist Press, New York, 1982.

Challenging the Stereotypes

Amanda Udis-Kessler

> Bisexuals are seen as 'fence-sitters, traitors, cop-outs, closet cases, people whose primary goal in life is to retain 'heterosexual privilege', power-hungry cold-hearted seducers who use and discard their same-sex lovers like so many kleenex.[1]
>
> Lisa Orlando

As bisexual movements in parts of the US, Europe and Australia have grown, those of us involved in them have discovered just how much resistance there is to the idea of bisexuality and the support of bisexuals. The anger, discomfort and patronising attitudes which a number of us have encountered are fuelled in part by an unfortunate set of stereotypes about bisexuality and bisexuals. This essay attempts to lay out these stereotypes and respond to them in some detail.

There are a number of stereotypes which we encounter with more or less frequency. Here I will focus on the ten which I have experienced as the most common:

1. 'People who consider themselves bisexual are confused/undecided/fence-sitting/going through a phase. Ultimately they'll get it together and settle down one way or the other.'
2. 'People who consider themselves bisexual are really heterosexual, but are experimenting/playing around/trying to be cool/liberated/trendy/politically correct.' Connected to stereotypes 6 and 8.
3. 'People who consider themselves bisexual are really gay/lesbian, but haven't fully accepted themselves and finished coming out of the closet.' Connected to stereotype 7.
4. 'Bisexuals are promiscuous hypersexual swingers who are attracted to every man and woman they meet. Alternately, bisexuals are exactly fifty per cent attracted to men and women, and must always have concurrent relationships with one (or more!) of each to be satisfied. Bisexuals are never monogamous, nor do they marry or live in traditional committed relationships.

Under no circumstances could a bisexual be happy being celibate.'
Connected to stereotypes 5-7.

5. 'Bisexual men are AIDS carriers, picking up the virus while having promiscuous unsafe sex with men and spreading it to their (innocent heterosexual) wives and female lovers. Bisexual men represent the entry points of AIDS into the "heterosexual population".' Connected to stereotype 4.

6. 'Bisexuals are shallow, narcissistic, untrustworthy and morally bankrupt.' Connected to stereotypes 2, 4, 7 and 8.

7. 'Bisexuals are traitors to the cause of lesbian/gay liberation and justice in general. They pass as straight to avoid trouble and maintain heterosexual privilege, support heterosexism and the patriarchy, dilute lesbian/gay anger and power, and don't care enough about the lesbian/gay cause to work for lesbian/gay rights. (They are too self-absorbed to be involved in other justice struggles.) Or they want to take over lesbian/gay issues and environments and make them bi. In fact, they want the whole world to come out as bi. Bisexuals who call themselves feminists are hypocrites; bisexuals would revert all separate women's space and make it accessible to men.' Connected to stereotypes 2-4 and 6.

8. 'Bisexual women will always leave their lesbian lovers for men.' Connected to stereotypes 2, 4, 6, and 7.

9. 'Bisexuals are desperately unhappy, endlessly seeking some kind of peace which they cannot ever find.' Connected to stereotypes 1-4 and 6.

10. 'Bisexuals always have the best of both worlds, a doubled chance of a date on a Saturday night, and the serenity of being more in touch with their sexuality than lesbians, gay men or heterosexuals.' Connected to stereotypes 1-4 and 6.

While these stereotypes will be addressed separately, there is something basic to all of them which is worth mentioning at the outset: their grounding in a Western ambivalence about sex which comes down to us from the Greek philosophers and the early Christians. We are both sexophobic and sex-centred. At some level of our collective psyche, sex is still dirty and disgusting, but it is also a major advertising device, at least in the extremely consumeristic society of America. Sex equals both sin and success to us.

Homophobic and biphobic stereotypes succeed in dehumanising lesbians, gay men and bisexuals by overemphasising the sexual in 'homosexual' and 'bisexual' as though some people could be reduced to their sex drives. Sexual minorities thus join women and blacks (and Latinos in America) in bearing the brunt of the Western obsession with/abhorrence of sex. This is useful to remember when considering the stereotypes of lesbians, gay men and bisexuals. We know better than to ask what heterosexuals are like as a group, and we are learning that it makes no sense to ask what homosexuals are like as a group; why do we persist in making claims about what bisexuals are like as a group? If anatomy is not destiny, neither is sexuality.

'No such thing as a distinct bisexual identity' (stereotypes 1-3)
These stereotypes are based on an overly rigid understanding of sexuality and sexual identity. The person who believes them does not deny the reality of bisexual experiences or feelings, but rather denies them any meaning by locating them as a temporary aberration in an otherwise heterosexual or homosexual individual. Thus, a woman who happily identifies as heterosexual for forty years and (equally as happily) as lesbian thereafter, or a gay man who falls for a woman and marries her, are seen as either finally claiming their true identity or 'copping out' on it completely. A significant part of their sexual history is seen as false and meaningless. But we can ask, with Mariana Valverde, 'why do we have to rewrite our histories and dismiss experiences that were at the time extremely powerful as "just a phase"?'[2]

The understanding of sexuality at work here is called essentialism, and the essentialist claim of relevance in this case is that every person has an inner core or essence of sexuality, a sexual orientation (usually described as biological). Were essentialist thinking to include the idea of a bisexual orientation (which it generally doesn't), the above stereotypes either would not exist or they would play out quite differently, with contested claims about orientation in which bisexuality was one of three legitimate options. However, the great majority of people who have an essentialist view of sexuality believe that people are either 'naturally' heterosexual or homosexual. To an essentialist, someone who is 'really' a lesbian but who is involved with a man is not being 'true' to her sexuality. The possibility that the woman claims a bisexual identity is usually not even considered. If essentialism accurately describes human sexuality, if in fact all people have a basic heterosexual or homosexual core, then stereotypes 1-3 are actually true. How might we challenge this perception?

Research by the creators of various sexuality scales (Kinsey, Storms,

Klein)[3] show that a significant percentage of people surveyed are neither exclusively heterosexual or exclusively homosexual throughout their lives, if we take into account their attractions, dreams and fantasies as well as their activities. This is a surprising amount of bisexuality for essentially heterosexual or homosexual people.

Moreover, essentialism in its current form (the hetero/homosexual split) is a historically located understanding of sexuality, specific to modern Western culture. I mean by this that the West's way of understanding sexuality has only appeared within roughly the last century in countries whose culture is bound up with traditions of rationality, individualism, progress, industrialisation, the nation-state and other Enlightenment tenets.

Prior to the 1870s in Europe and the 1890s in America, a form of essentialist thinking did exist, but it was different in some ways from the essentialism which we see today. Certainly, people had been known to engage in same-sex sex acts for a long time, but the corresponding idea of a homosexual identity did not exist. Since all people were understood to be 'naturally' attracted to the opposite sex, engaging in same-sex sex acts was simply 'unnatural', and the idea that a person could *be* a gay man or lesbian was unknown. With the creation of the words 'homosexual' and 'heterosexual' and the growing understanding that same-sex attraction was part of some people's identity, we progressed to the point where only people engaging sexually with both sexes were (and are) thought to be acting 'unnaturally'.

Essentialism is also a strictly *western* concept; sexuality is managed quite differently in native societies of North and Latin America, Africa, Asia and other locales. Men who we might call 'gay' – such as the Native American berdache – do not have a gay identity as we understand it. We can locate essentialism even more specifically, not just in modern western culture but in the strategic agenda of early gay liberationists, when essentialism took on an 'ethnic' tone and bisexuality was rejected for political reasons.[5]

Thus, essentialism takes one particular cultural view of sexuality and elevates it as gospel. It denies the role which environment and socialisation play in sexuality, and it fails to describe the range and fluidity of sexuality beyond certain actions in certain societies. It denies the meaningfulness and validity of a great deal of sexual experience. These factors make essentialism an inadequate descriptor of human sexuality.[6] If we do not need to particularly honour essentialism's claims, there is no pressing *a priori* reason to deny the existence of a bisexual identity. Many people have bisexual thoughts or experiences. For some of these people, the most honest way to understand themselves seems to be as bisexuals, while others consider themselves heterosexual, lesbian or gay. Bisexual identity (as opposed to acts) is mainly a matter of self-definition, and all people have a right to define and understand their own sexuality as they see fit, including changing those definitions over time. Bisexuality is no less legitimate than homosexuality or heterosexuality.

Are bisexuals confused? Many may well be, living in societies where our sexuality is denied by lesbians, gay men and heterosexuals, but that is a problem of oppression, and does not indicate the non-existence of bisexuality as a human option. Are bisexuals undecided? Quite the opposite; we have decided to honour the full range of our experiences, fantasies and dreams in envisioning our sexuality. 'Fence-sitting' is a misnomer; there is no 'fence' between homosexuality and heterosexuality except in the minds of people who rigidly divide the two. The Kinsey scale runs along a continuum from exclusive heterosexuality to exclusive homosexuality; where on the continuum does a fence appear?[7] Many bisexuals are as 'settled down' as we wish to be – in relationships of various sorts, in solitude or in any number of lifestyles.

Special attention needs to be given to the idea of 'going through a phase'. It is based in the essentialism described above and fails to acknowledge a great deal of sexual experience. Even if some people identify as bisexual as a transition from heterosexuality to homosexuality (and some certainly identify as lesbian or gay as a 'transition' from heterosexuality to bisexuality), that does not make the transitional sexuality any less real or valid. Transitions are a part of life, not just a dress rehearsal for it. They count as much as any other part, and are just as meaningful.

When accusations about 'confusion' and 'phases' come from lesbians and gay men, some serious hypocrisy (or amnesia) is in process. Lesbians and gay men have been called confused, have been told that they were going through a phase, and have been urged to settle down for as long as they have resisted doing so. They ought to know better than to pass that bigotry on to bisexuals.

Given the degree to which bisexuality is a question of identity, whether an individual is an 'experimenting heterosexual' or is bisexual depends on his or her perception rather than on some external standard (since bisexuality does not have to involve a fifty-fifty split between men and women in feeling or behaviour). There certainly are people who are trying to be liberated or trendy by being bisexual, but they are generally not the people who come to a bisexual identity amidst pain and ultimately claim it with pride. That bisexuality should be considered politically correct is, of course, problematic in the sense that 'p.c.-ness' is not the same as true deep acceptance of diversity; at the same time, it points toward a greater acceptance of homosexuality even if the acceptance is coupled with a misunderstanding of how to respond to it. Just as whites have to learn how to be allies to people of color and men have to learn how to be allies to women, heterosexuals (and to an extent bisexuals) have to learn how to be allies to lesbians and gay men; and homosexuality as a means of solidarity is not likely to be the best way.

When bisexuals are said to be experimenting heterosexuals, the area of concern is not the 'unnaturalness' of our acts (as one might expect) but rather their effect on 'genuine' lesbians and gay men who are hurt by thoughtless trendy types wreaking emotional havoc. More on this later.

Many bisexuals are completely out of the closet, but not on the terms of the local lesbian or gay community. (It is worth noting that many lesbians and gay men are not completely out of the closet and *their* process is generally respected; it is also worth noting that the lesbian/gay communities whose 'terms' are in question here have tended to be white and middle class, and the terms may be quite different for working class lesbians, gay men of color, and so on.[8] The closet *is* a little different for bisexuals – in part because too few heterosexuals, lesbians and gay men understand it. Coming out does not involve a complete break with heterosexuality, but rather puts bisexuals in a position where the different social settings of gay and straight worlds must be negotiated regularly. Nonetheless, bisexuals in heterosexist societies share many powerful experiences with lesbians and gay men. Non-heterosexuality 'does not exist' (e.g. there are few or no positive role models who are not heterosexual) or is viciously maligned as sick and sinful. Bisexuals, as well as lesbians and gay men, are harassed, bashed and murdered, lose jobs, homes and children, cannot legally marry our same-sex lovers and must live under sodomy laws. With regard to the media (which shapes much of our cultural perception), gay men and lesbians are invisible, silly, evil or tragic; bisexuals are invisible, confused, pathologically promiscuous and – these days – AIDS carriers. In societies of compulsory heterosexuality and degrading, dehumanising, sometimes life-threatening sex roles, bisexuals are a lot more like gay men and lesbians than we are like heterosexuals.[9] We both have the capacity to challenge destructive social assumptions and patterns. It is this very similarity which makes it so important for us to work together against heterosexism.

'Bisexual sexuality is strange and excessive' (stereotype 4)
In most ways and for most people, bisexual sexuality is not somehow qualitatively different from that of heterosexuals, lesbians or gay men. People of all sexualities engage in a variety of lifestyles, sometimes remaining with one for their entire lives, sometimes trying out different ones over time. These include celibacy, marriage/committed monogamous relationships, nonmonogamous committed relation-ships, sexual friendships, concurrent relationships, casual sex and other options.

Bisexuals are no more attracted to all men than are gay men or heterosexual women. Bisexuals are no more attracted to all women than are heterosexual men or lesbians. Moreover, some bisexuals are never sexual with men. Or women. Or either. Bisexuality is about dreams and desires and capacities as much as it is about acts. There are, for example, celibate bisexual priests and nuns.

Bisexuals do not need to be perfectly equally attracted to both sexes to 'count' as bisexual. There are a number of people in the US bisexual communities who are primarily attracted to either men or women, but do not deny the lesser attraction, whether or not they act on it.

Bisexuals are people who *can* have lovers of *either* sex, not people who *must* have lovers of *both* sexes.

Bisexuals and AIDS/HIV (stereotype 5)
In America, bisexual men are particularly targeted as infecting the 'heterosexual population'[10] (their 'innocent' wives and children, primarily). This stereotype is primarily believed by those heterosexuals who still have not learned that HIV is spread by unsafe sex and drug practices rather than by a particular group of people. Many bisexuals know about, encourage and practise safer sex; bisexuals have been part of the fight against AIDS since its inception (some, for example, are active members of ACT UP). The infection rates among gay men have dropped since safer sex education became part of the urban casual sex scene; bisexual men in those settings have been educated as much as their gay partners.

America's targeting of bisexual men (and prostitutes) makes a great deal of cultural sense. As long as the populations affected are sexual minorities, drug users and prostitutes – the poor, the perverts, the people of color – America will not protest too loudly. Bisexual men and prostitutes are considered responsible for transmitting HIV to 'normal' people. Of course, the suffering of bisexual men and prostitutes with HIV/AIDS is completely discounted in the general alarm about the mainstreaming of AIDS.

The way to fight HIV/AIDS is – and always will be – with education, funding, creative research and compassion, not with bigotry, scapegoating and judgmentalism.

Personality traits associated with bisexuals (stereotype 6)
The set of descriptions (shallowness, narcissism, untrustworthiness, moral bankruptcy) listed here has a wide-ranging history. For example, we have heard the last two characterisations in reference to people of various ethnicities and races, the first two in reference to women, and all four in reference to 'promiscuous' gay men. In none of these cases have they been accurate, nor are they in the case of bisexuals.

This stereotype reflects our profound ambivalence, not just about sex but about pleasure in general. America, at least, is pleasure-phobic and pleasure-centred in addition to being sexophobic and sex-centred. We are guilt-ridden workaholics and irresponsible hedonists all at once. Bisexuals are envisioned as ultimate party animals (once again overemphasising the sex in bisexual) and turned into the repositories of the pleasure which our society enjoys so much and which troubles us so much. In fact, people of any sexuality can get caught up in an excessive lifestyle provided they have the money to support it; bisexuals are no more likely to do so than anyone else. The call of untrustworthiness would seem to be linked to the inability to be monogamous, but (a) there are monogamous bisexuals and (b) some proportion of the nonmonogamous bisexuals are honest about it and work out arrangements for concurrent relationships (e.g. triads) or otherwise nonmonogamous situations with careful communication and high levels of trust.

The charge of moral bankruptcy is linked to sex and pleasure, and raises the question of why morality language is still sex-centred when there is so much interpersonal and institutional violence in the world. Regardless of context, bisexuals are as moral and as immoral as anyone else. Bisexuality *per se* is not immoral, and the actions (sexual and otherwise) of bisexuals – like those of anyone else – must be considered individually.

Bisexuals as political traitors (stereotype 7)
There is no particular political commitment (or lack of one) which goes with bisexuality. People of all sexualities can be found everywhere on

the political spectrum from left to right, anarchist to state socialist, and apolitical to extremely political.

Obviously, there are bisexuals who pass as heterosexual to avoid trouble. There are also many lesbians and gay men who do this. The issue at stake is political awareness and integrity, not degree of homosexuality. To deny one's bisexuality is as painful and false as denying one's gayness or lesbianism when the sexual identity is an important part of one's sense of self (which, for some people of all sexualities, it is not). A few brave souls never pass, many do when they feel they must, and some do as a regular pattern. This is as true of lesbians and gay men as it is of bisexuals.

Politicised bisexuals remain aware of heterosexual privilege and are committed enough to lesbian/gay/bisexual rights not to just abandon lesbian/gay communities when in heterosexual relationships. Politicised bisexuals do not support heterosexism, sexism or other systems of stratification, and are active in organisations working for many different causes. Specifically, politicised bisexuals are active in lesbian/gay and AIDS organisations, recognizing that we share with lesbians and gay men the need to struggle for a world where all are free to love as they will. As noted above, bisexuals suffer the sins of omission and commission which make up homophobia and heterosexism, and many of us are committed to eradicating them. But bisexuals also encounter biphobia from lesbians and gay men. This gets in the way of bisexuals working for lesbian/gay rights and dignity. Politicised bisexuals want to connect with lesbian/gay groups, not to overthrow them, and to strengthen, not dilute, lesbian/gay anger and power.

Some lesbians and gay men have suggested that bisexuals form their own political organisations and some such organisations do exist (BiPOL in San Francisco, BiCEP in Boston, BiPAC in New York City), and are very useful. But it is not enough for bisexuals to work alone, especially since bisexuals can add energy, creativity and outrage to lesbian/gay and AIDS organisations. Where possible, we must work together; our collective strength and power increases as our numbers increase.

Many bisexuals do not believe that the whole world is 'really' bisexual (this would be the flip side of the essentialism described above, and therefore equally problematic), though a sizeable number do believe that each individual is born with some kind of capacity for bisexual feelings and experiences. This should not be read to mean that every person will (or should) have bisexual desires or experiences, or will (or should) identify as bisexual. Many people who *do* identify as bisexual respect the rights of others to claim whatever identity they are most comfortable with; it is unfortunate that the same respect is so rarely granted to us.

The idea that bisexuals make bad feminists seems to be based on the idea that only lesbians can be good feminists – a claim with which many feminists of all sexualities would sharply disagree. The idea that bisexuals cannot be separatists is as false as the idea that bisexuals cannot be celibate (one's sexual identity is not only based on one's current sexual activity). There are heterosexual and bisexual women leading separatist lives; the bisexual women may date other women or no one at all.

'Bisexual women will always leave their lesbian lovers for men' *(stereotype 8)*
There is so much pain behind this stereotype that it is probably the most difficult one to sort out. As with the other stereotypes, it does sometimes happen; one can find examples of bisexual women leaving lesbians for men. One can also find examples of bisexual women who have good long-term committed relationships with lesbians. There are bisexuals for whom bisexuality is a phase; there are also lesbians for whom lesbianism is a phase. There are women of every sexuality who are unable to make commitments, and there are bisexual women *and* lesbians who go back in the closet or never really come to grips with their sexuality. Bisexual women who truly accept themselves and their sexuality will leave a relationship with a man or a woman when it no longer works for them or is destructive in some way. The same could be said of lesbians who accept themselves; there are simply times when a relationship is over. As hard as it is to get clear about the reasons a relationship may end, and as many challenges as lesbian relationships in particular may face, bisexual women are not constitutionally incapable of handling lesbian relationships.[11]

Bisexuals and their state of mind (stereotypes 9 and 10)
These somewhat less widespread (thank goodness!) stereotypes share with those concerning our sexuality the image of bisexuals as ultimate extremists. Again, the reality of our humanity is forgotten. Bisexuals are people and are subject to the blessings, pains, ambivalences, drudgery and grace which all people encounter. To say that bisexuality makes people either exceedingly miserable or completely enlightened is to utterly misread its place as one of many factors in people's lives.

There are happier bisexuals and less happy bisexuals. Some bisexuals may be enlightened; if so, the rest of us would like very much to know how they got there![12]

The stereotype about bisexuals being unhappy should be extremely familiar to lesbians and gay men, who are also used to being told that they will live awful lives. Bisexuals can respond in the same way that clever lesbians and gay men have: much of the pain comes from oppression, so people concerned about the 'awful lives' of bisexuals should join the struggle against heterosexism. Beyond that, the best way to relieve pain is to live with as much integrity and self-respect as possible, something which many people of all sexualities are trying to do. As to the 'peace' which bisexuals are seeking, it sounds suspiciously like exclusive heterosexuality or homosexuality (depending on who makes the comment). Bisexuals are used to being told that we would be happier if we would only straighten out or come out for good. Self-accepting bisexuals are not looking to change our sexuality, and there is no reason why we should.

The stereotype that bisexuals have the best of both worlds may be the only positive stereotype about bisexuals, and we may not want to get rid of it in quite the same way that we want to get rid of the others. Yet like the other stereotypes, this one fails by being too all-inclusive and generalised. Does it refer to having more sex than others? Having more romantic relationships? Sorry, bisexuals don't especially qualify. Any given person, regardless of sexuality, has a limit on the number of relationships and frequency of sex, and being bisexual does not increase one's sex drive exponentially. Bisexuals are people, not raw sexual energy implanted in human bodies. For example, if a bisexual woman has a hard time meeting people, her bisexuality won't help much. If a bisexual man thinks the dating scene is a giant flesh market and would rather go birdwatching, his chance for a date on a Saturday night is not doubled. Moreover, since bisexuals can be found with the same range of enjoyable and less enjoyable personalities as lesbians, gay men and heterosexuals, there undoubtedly are bisexual men and women who are turned on by as many people as the stereotype suggests, but who do not find partners, due to their less than enjoyable personalities. A bisexual man may be considered unattractive, or may have a lover who demands monogamy. A woman who is open about her bisexuality and who falls in love with a lesbian may be rejected if the lesbian fears being left for a man.

No one has asked whether ever bisexual would *want* more sexual opportunity even if it were always available. Probably some would and others would not. Relationships, sexual and otherwise, are difficult, and 'the best of both worlds' can bring the worst of both as well. This stereotype is created and sustained in the minds of people who have some serious thinking to do regarding the importance of sex and who don't know very many bisexuals at all.

To claim that bisexuals are more in touch with their sexuality than anyone else is to claim that everyone has a core bisexual identity. Why should bisexual essentialism be any more valid than opposite-sex essentialism pre-1890s or contemporary homo-heterosexual essentialism? Jan Clausen is probably not the only person who has wondered 'about the astonishing malleability of my sexual inclinations: am I some sort of weirdo, or is it just that most people are a lot more complicated than the common wisdom of either gay or straight society encourages us to think?'[13] People are complicated indeed, and hopefully one day we won't need labels that simplify us and cut us off from one another. Until that day, bisexuals will continue to proudly 'flaunt' our sexuality as a legitimate sexual option in a sexually diverse world.

Notes

1 Lisa Orlando, 'Loving Whom We Choose: Bisexuality', *Gay Community News*, 25/1/84: 8. Let me make one point about this essay clear at the outset. Because I am an American, some of my perspective may not translate as fully as I would like to bisexual communities outside of the US, and I can only hope that others will address the gaps in this account, helping to provide a richer and more complete understanding of who we are and what prejudices we face.
2 Mariana Valverde, *Sex, Power and Pleasure*, Women's Press, Toronto 1985, p112.
3 See A.C. Kinsey, W.B. Pomeroy, and C.E. Martin, *Sexual Behavior in the Human Male*, W.B. Saunders, Philadelphia 1948; F. Klein, B. Sepekoff, and T.J. Wolf, 'Sexual Orientation: A Multivariable Dynamic Process', *Journal of Homosexuality* 11 (1/2), 1985, pp35-49; M. Storms, 'Theories of Sexual Orientation', *Journal of Personality and Social Psychology* 38, 1980, pp783-792.
4 I use 'opposite-sex' and 'same-sex' here because the words 'heterosexuality' and 'homosexuality' were only coined in German in 1869 and translated into English in 1892. Nor did the concept of heterosexuality as a sexual identity exist, for the reasons given above. Amusingly, the first use of 'heterosexual' in English described a sexuality which we now would call 'bisexual'. See Jonathan Katz, 'The Invention of Heterosexuality', *Socialist Review* 20 (Jan.-Mar. 1990), pp7-34.
5 See my essay 'Bisexuality in an Essentialist World: Towards an Understanding of Biphobia', in Thomas Geller (ed), *Bisexuality: A Reader and Sourcebook*, Times Change Press, Ojai, CA, 1990, pp51-63. This account, unfortunately, is limited to an analysis of political developments in the US.

[6] The discussion here is admittedly incomplete and extremely simplified. More complex discussions can be found in Edward Stein, (ed), *Forms of Desire: Sexual Orientation and the Social Constructionist Controversy*, Garland Publishing, Inc., New York 1990.

[7] This question is even more amusing when applied to Storms' and Klein's models. Storms presents us with an X-Y axis, with one axis indicating the degree of heterosexuality and the other the degree of homosexuality. Klein uses Kinsey's breakdown, but offers a number for each of seven different questions ranging from sexual activity to social setting, and in three different time contexts!

[8] San Francisco-based historian Alan Berube, the author of *Coming Out Under Fire: the History of Gay Men and Women in World War II* (New York: The Free Press, 1990), has recently proposed a 'queer identity' model based on a 'fitting in' narrative rather than the traditional 'coming out' version. Berube has indicated that the purpose of his model is to provide a way of understanding those people who are problematic in the more traditional coming out narrative. His examples of such people include people of color, people of working class backgrounds, *and bisexuals.*

[9] Bisexuals are not, however, in precisely the same situation as lesbians and gay men; our acknowledgement of this fact is a matter of integrity and should lead us to continue our work against heterosexism with lesbians and gay men, not to come up with a new twist on middle-class liberal guilt.

[10] This phrase is one of many condemned by AIDS activists and theoreticians for its inaccuracy and its contribution to an AIDS mythology in which some people are guilty and others innocent, some deaths horrifying and others (implicitly) deserved. The particular targeting of bisexual men (rather than women) in America is interesting, given the trend of lesbians castigating bisexual women as 'AIDS carriers' in England which has been brought to my attention. If such a trend is taking place in the US, I am not aware of it, though there are other tensions around lesbian caregiving and AIDS, and around AIDS and women's healthcare priorities.

[11] This stereotype exists for men as well and could be countered in the same way, but I have heard it almost entirely from women, for reasons having more to do with lesbian culture and community than with female sexuality; see my 'Culture and Community: Thoughts on Lesbian-Bisexual Relations', in *Sojourner: the Women's Forum*, December 1990, pp11-12.

[12] I cannot resist mentioning Ram Dass (formerly Richard Alpert) here as a self-identified bisexual who has undergone a long and intense spiritual journey ranging from hallucinogens to Asian religious traditions. His book *How Can I Help?* is a journey in itself, and one which I highly recommend.

[13] Jan Clausen, 'My Interesting Condition', *Out/Look* 7 (Winter 1990), pp14-15.

Bisexuality in the Arab World

An interview with Muhammed by Françoise Gollain

Muhammed is of Tunisian origin. He has lived in England for several years and became involved in the bisexual movement here. He was interviewed during the 1991 bisexual conference held in London.

F There is a current debate in the bisexual community, on the issue of what is a 'bisexual identity'? Is there anything like a 'bisexual identity' in the Arab world? In what way is it different from (the) bisexual identity in European countries?

M Firstly, I can say straightaway that there is not a bisexual identity in the Arab world. However, it is a very widespread practice. In the Arab world, almost all men are bisexual. Female bisexuality has very little existence – women who are, to an extent, attracted to men remain straight. This practice is not limited to a specific community, such as the 'closets' over here. It is a mass sexual practice.

F Present in all social classes?

M The lower the social class the more widespread bisexuality is. In the upper class, the pattern of behaviour is very similar to the Western one. But 90 per cent of the Arab world is deprived, and belongs to the lower class. Bisexuality concerns the man in the street. A bisexual is not someone who has been identified as such. Nobody points a finger at him.

Nonetheless, 'bisexual' is a very vague term. In my own experience, there are different degrees of bisexuality. Bisexuality doesn't mean men who fall in love with men, want to live with them, etc...

F How is bisexuality then expressed?

M Bisexuality is not what people understand over here: i.e. a bisexual man as someone who is committed entirely to both men and women. A bisexual man there is someone who is open to an experience with a man, not someone who wants to live with a man. In the Arab world, every man is more or less open to an experience with a man – at different degrees of involvement. Women are not aware of it. Women don't know about what is man's private domain.

F Do you think that they really don't know it or do they pretend not to?

M They know about gay people but they are not aware that, may be, their husband or son engages in homosexual practice. Bisexuality is men's world. But it is not mentioned amongst men in the family. A man would not tell his brother or his father. His father would beat him up although he himself did it well before his son!

F Do you mention it to friends however?

M Amongst friends, it is more or less acceptable, if it is the subject of jokes. You laugh about it and it is not important and is never mentioned as something positive. When two men have sex together it is very important to know which side each of them is: passive or active. The two positions are totally different. Like two different races in the same bed.

F Does the passive partner identify himself as a woman or is he considered as such?

M Here, we touch upon the question: why is bisexuality such a mass phenomenon in the Arab world? It is precisely because the active bisexual sees the passive gay whom he has sex with as an extension of the/a woman. The bisexual man who likes women derives his pleasure only from the thought that the gay boy he has sex with is not another man but a gay, i.e. a half-woman. A clear cut line is drawn between bisexuals and people who are a hundred per cent gay.

F Do 'relationships' develop – for instance, has an active man a relationship, lasting several months or several years, with the same passive man?

M If a relationship is developed it will be established because it is convenient. For instance, the man and the boy are neighbours and it is easy for the man to see the boy regularly. But there is no emotional commitment. Bisexual men are not repressed because being active is not degrading in the Arab world. It is why a man with big moustache and muscles can say to his neighbours: 'I fucked this boy yesterday, you know!' In those very terms. It is not badly considered at all to fuck, but to be fucked is a catastrophe. To penetrate a man is perfectly acceptable. However, if you are caught once touching or sucking a man's penis or getting penetrated you are damned socially, you are a queer. You are not allowed through these acts to recognise a man's virility. You are yourself a man if you deny the virility of the person you are making love with.

F Is the age relevant: do younger boys tend to be the passive partner?

M No. It is simply a preference. An active bisexual man prefers young boys with little hair and a soft skin and can feel more virile because he can see a woman in him. But a lot of boys fuck older men. In the Western world, the man in the street can't admit to himself that he is bisexual because even being active makes him gay i.e. gives him a socially lower status. If a part of yourself is straight, all your sexuality will be directed this way. You will deny your homosexuality because the straight option only is acceptable.

In the Arab world, on the contrary, you have two options which are equally acceptable: to love women, or to love men as the active partner. Now, these freely expressed bisexual behaviours can be graded from 1 to 10 as far as the emotional involvement is concerned: I have known men who refuse to have anything to do with you after sex; men who might stay for an hour with you afterwards; etc ... This goes up to the man who falls in love with you. Western tourists to Arab countries tend to meet up with people whose bisexuality is a minor feature and later comment: 'these Arab men don't like kissing; they are just interested in fucking' But these tourists in fact don't realise that these same people – a big group – would be straight if they lived in England.

F I am personally under the impression – and I would like to check my hypothesis – that bisexuality is so wide-spread in the Arab world because men have no access to women. I am referring to the fact you mentioned earlier that the virility of passive partners had to be denied.

M The very first cause of bisexuality is the cultural acceptance of bisexually active men. Over here, even in prisons, men without access to women find it difficult to express their homosexual instincts – as has appeared in conversations I have had with many of them. In the Mediterranean zone, this acceptance is deeply rooted in culture and historically very old. The second cause is that women are not available for sex, as they are protected by families. Because of an obvious sexual deprivation in the Arab world, men go for an alternative.

F Does it mean that as soon as someone is rich enough to get married he puts an end to his homosexual activity?

M The average man in the street, if given the choice, chooses a woman as a sexual partner first. The fact that women are not available contributes to bisexuality but doesn't explain it. The cause is cultural.

F How do individuals feel about their acts with men? Is there or not any guilt around? Is there a positive feeling?

M More than social this acceptance is a personal acceptance on the part of the individual concerned. This positive inner feeling allows the man to express his sexuality.

F At the bisexual conference going on at the moment, one of the main assumptions is that bisexuality represents being a political liberal. However, in the Arab world bisexuality doesn't appear to be a very positive thing. What is your feeling about both bisexualities, how do they compare?

M I find bisexuality in the Arab world is freer than over here. For me, liberation of any kind is not a matter of a group of intellectuals starting off a movement. It means liberation at the level of the people (the man in the street), of society in its entirety. Obviously, from the point of view of law and politics the movement is more advanced over here than in the Arab world where the issue is not raised in the media, not mentioned, even in intellectual circles.

F Does it mean that you feel personally more oppressed over here?

M From the point of view of society in general, yes. Of course, in my circle of liberal intellectuals, no. However, if I go to the pub or to work over here I feel much more oppressed than over there, where I can talk more openly.

F There is, at present, a bisexual movement being built up in England and some other Western countries. Do you see anything similar happening in the Arab world?

M It will never happen! One can always reckon with intellectual development, with social progress, etc ... but there is one thing which eventually blocks any advance: it is Islam. Islam will never change. I have very few hopes.

Roots of a Male Bisexual Nature

Guy Chapman

Imagine – I am three years old, an infant boy of people known as Asmat, who you class as of stone age origin, in a land you call New Guinea.

My family know I will find another infant boy with whom to explore our world and naturally also our bodies, sensual and extraordinary. We learn quickly and easily to give pleasure to each other; to touch, feel, fondle, stroke, kiss and suck. Our parents are glad, expecting this of all boys. They know this is the making of a life-long bond.

We are becoming 'mbi', exchange friends. Through our lives' joys and difficulties we will be there for each other; best friends and confidants. We become more sexual too; masturbating, sucking and entering each other. Always we know that the essential is reciprocal balance. In every exchange of friendship and love-making we give and receive the same.

As I grow I learn this same balance is sought between men and women. There is a balancing of the vagina and penis. The juice of our seed flows freely to protect and calm our daily lives and to keep our universe in symmetry. In special celebrations we men and women suck each others' genitals, absorbing the healthy essence and making oneness of all our differences.

If a man comes from outside, whom we feel to be one with us, we initiate him by sucking all parts of his body all together. Thus we are absorbed into each other and bonded. Do not think this is only what you call sexual or erotic – it is about harmony, essence, pleasure and the juice of life.

Later I partner with a woman and we have children. Sometimes I am with them and sometimes they know I am with my mbi; maybe hunting or making love. Mbis are for life.

I have here described something of the social and sexual relations of Asmat men recorded in the book *Where the Spirit Dwells* by Tobis Schneebaum.[1] It embodies much of what I have sought in my life – touch, bonding, sensuality, solidarity, change, freedom and celebration.

A war across the world is not long over; I am born in March 1947 in a coastal town in England. I am cared for lovingly and hygienically and this includes the assault of an unnecessary circumcision. My food comes in a bottle; not when I call out but according to a clock. I do not understand that my mother has been told she must break her children's will to bring us up well. My father means well but seems busy or angry.

I grow and delight in things of this world. On holiday age four I herd cows alone; what nomadic impulse? There is a wilderness nearby where I roam and collect snakes without fear; what possessed me? I am passionate for dance but there are only girls' lessons with me the only boy. My brothers and I seek sensual pleasure with each other but we know we are not supposed to.

Outer expectations grow. I am to sit and learn for years at school, compete at sports and experience the ways of men, as in the war movies of that pre-television period. I am gradually overpowered by the dominant ethos. The bible teaches me original sin and how I can be saved, but I'm not. It will be many years before I understand what was happening to me.

One view is that most original cultures were matrilineal, with shamanic forms of religion, and ecstasy the accessible experience of all people. Acts of pleasure and love were the predominant rituals and celebrations. Sexuality was a great unifying energy across gender, race and age. Bisexuality was more widespread where sexual taboos did not control the individual.[2]

In the western world this kind of culture was slowly overwhelmed and became a subculture to city and nation states. The standing armies of professional warfare, a comparatively late development in human history, subjugated the rural nature-based societies to support the centralised urban and religious powers, and their systems of property and class.

There was increasing repression of women and the female-associated aspects of life. Slavery, obedience and codes of discipline came to replace communal ownership, consensus and the relative absence of class and work divisions. Sexuality, and especially homosexuality, was subjected to control or distortion – for who would willingly make war rather than make love? Who would penetrate another's body with sword and arrow, with pain and death rather than mutual pleasure and aliveness?

In early times the primary spirit image was of a goddess of creation, celebrating women's miracle of giving birth and nurture, of sex and the lunar cycle of fertility. Usually she had a male consort for the annual cycle of life. He was virile, depicted often with hairy legs, proficient genitals and horns.

Church leaders wished to divert energy to male spiritual ends. The deities were confined to a male trinity with Christ depicted as the asexual hornless Lamb of God and promoted as the male role model. The goddesses, powerful and sexual women, were repressed and instead there was the virgin as a model of meek womanhood. The 'horny' consort of the earth goddess was transmuted into the devil – associated with the now denigrated sexuality and earthly life. The priestesses and priests of this old religion were to be condemned as 'witches'.

A moralistic approach to life was imposed with polarised dualistic ideas of good and evil, us and them, lightness and dark. Darkness had been previously associated with the magic of night, with the annual phase of dying down, with the planting of seed in the dark dampness of the soil or womb for new life to grow, and with the journey of self discovery down into the subconscious. Life, as in the yin yang symbol, was considered a creative and changing balance between dark as well as light.

With the rise of the church's obsession with otherworldly light, dark was no longer a principle to balance with light but something to be denied. The churches monopolised supposed 'good' and condemned non-adherent people or acts as evil.

The church has used the bible as its source for condemnation of male homosexual expression. But reading the bible does not support this.[3] The story of Sodom and Gomorrah is not about unbridled homosexuality. What took place at Sodom was an attempted ritual insult of two male strangers, by threatening to treat them like women, with sexual penetration. Lot, the biblical hero, offers his two daughters sexually instead of the strangers. Finally he impregnates his daughters himself! There is no biblical condemnation of this sexual treatment of women, but plenty for the attempted violation of hospitality laws by the planned humiliation of two men. This has been used as basis to condemn all male homosexual acts. The later retelling in the epistles emphasises the destruction of the cities of Sodom and Gomorrah not because of these events but simply because the peoples were unbelievers. In the case of St Paul, he considered homosexual behaviour as god's punishment of unfaithful idolaters, not the other way round.

Homosexuality was just one of a great host of taboos developed and exploited by the rising religious hierarchies and nation state rulers of the west. The taboos were generated to disempower people of their natural source of self-determination, pleasure and ecstasy. They were policed by priests placed between people and an elevated God.

Burning up with fear and guilt. Burnt alive to death. Flames rise higher. Pain beyond imagining. How many of my forebear faggots were burnt? How many of my sisters, bisexual woman, lesbians, healers, midwives, guardians of the old nature religion and witches were put to death? These believers in pre-christian ways had always celebrated their sexual freedom and were not subjugated to the codes of enforced 'normal' reality or 'normal' sexuality. They stood in the way of the church, rising, capitalism and male dominated professions of the fifteenth century. Across Europe alone the numbers of deaths runs into millions, some say ten millions over the next 250 years. Joan of Arc, who would not submit to the disempowered role of women, was actually sentenced to death for wearing men's clothes.[4]

The ongoing genocide of lesbians, gays and bisexuals reached a peak in the Inquisition and its Protestant equivalents but has continued in some places to present times. In Britain, after the church, the state took over the executing of men for homosexual behaviour right into the nineteenth century. No wonder people are so often 'scared to death' to talk about homosexual behaviour, let alone feel it or do it! The fear of death, of being burnt alive or tortured for same gender love has been obscenely programmed into brains and bodies. A mass aversion therapy of diabolical proportions.

In my story I am in my early teens. At school I am warned against homosexuality but have sex with other boys, fulfilling a powerful but suppressed longing. At home my mother transfers her own marital and social oppression into 'queers' and 'inferiors'. Well trained to carry out patriarchy's duty and correct 'unmanly' behaviour, she doesn't realise how deeply she hurts her two gay-oriented sons.

At eighteen, I have little self esteem, confidence or purpose. I work in London and begin a long climb out of a deep pit. Many help me. Some are lovers; men and women. With care and pain the layers of hurt come off, slowly I start to reclaim my powers of feeling, thought and body.

In my mid twenties, the early 1970s, I meet Ronnie. He is extrovert, confident, black, American and everything I am not or that I project on to him. I get fucked, literally and metaphorically. Two bodies, two personal and social histories intertwine, interpenetrate. Hard, liberating breaching of an up-tight-arsed spell. In those times before HIV, carrying within me, deeply moved, the seed of a man on to whom I pour love that I feel, have wanted and learnt not to feel for myself.

In certain indigenous cultures the initiation into manhood is 'impregnation' by an older man; a similar rite of passage with similar learning? I do not recall ever wanting to be, or to imitate, a woman but now I feel I know more about love with a woman by being penetrated myself.

I leave Ronnie carrying an infection. I go to the sexually transmitted disease clinic and have a cold metal tube stuck up my arse. An ultimate humiliation for a 'man'? But strangely it is not. The opposite of passion but done with such gentleness that it is healing, not only physiologically.

If each cared fully for self and body, would we then exploit and abuse others and the earth? The denial of earthly bodily joy and natural wonder haunts us with accumulated frustration and the present glare of consumerism. My need is for bonding when our alienating systems empty me and the earth of innate value. Whereas the strength of any sustainable system is diversity, of our individual natures as in outer natural ecosystems.

My late twenties, and I meet Jane from Eire. We share our joys and our knots, growing and healing, bonding deeply. I love as never before the softer finer flesh of body, breast and cunt. A trusting nest for seven monogamous years, but our limitations and challenges come poking through.

There is also Winston. We drum, dance, carve, rap to other spaces I've searched for. The otherness of his character, Jamaican Afro-European roots, 'blackness'; antidotes to my white frosted history. My interracial attraction a mix of excitement, aliveness, ignorance, projection, neediness, caring, solidarity, trust. I want closer but he is straight.

Jane draws away, pregnant. Laurie our son is born doing it our way; home-birthed and freely breast-fed; always with us giving love and freedom; vision of a different life; until finally overwhelmed we crumble apart screaming. Active parenting of my son remains vital for me; disappearance would be a betrayal of him and myself, but it's often hard to be a part-time single parent.

In the mid 1980s I start a new life in Mid Wales. On London visits to my son I find friends at the London Bisexual Group and work on the book *Bisexual Lives*. A new sexual self identity grows. Over four years I am lovers, in turn, with a man and three women. But as a rural-living active father, not on the gay scene, I become absorbed all too easily in heterosexual lives. I feel I've marginalized my gay self; have I always? I miss that part of myself, and choose to actively identify as gay. I return to city living. I search for gay friends but my way of life seems so dissimilar. I find the Edward Carpenter Community, a gay network based broadly on personal growth, socialist, non-sexist principles. Friends from there and bisexual meetings and conferences come into my life. But what models can I find that integrate my sexuality, my role as an active father and the importance to me of the raw natural world? I read about gay and bisexual people in different cultures.

The Native American peoples' ways of life have inspired me. The peoples revered all of creation, its diversity, the unusual as much as the more familiar in life. Everyone was considered born for a purpose, homosexual people generally for a particular and often sacred intention. They were honoured for their wholeness as a bridge between men and women. Gay men, the 'berdaches', were often the shamen, priests and healers, adept at going beyond the usual limits of everyday reality, and sexual and gender identities.[5] They were diviners, tuning into creation principally to heal. They took on the female social roles of crafts-people, potters and weavers. Similarly lesbian women could adopt male social roles as hunters and warriors and 'take a wife'.

Section I: Theory and Representation

Some current anthropological research points to the origin of certain ritual practices of early indigenous cultures in the lunar bleeding cycles of women.[6] In those close rural communities women ovulated and menstruated synchronously and in phase with the moon. Thus they were manifestly connected with the changing patterns of the heavens whose movements of sun, moon and stars marked the cycles of life. Women gathered to retreat for bleeding and a time of introspection and intuition. They evolved rituals celebrating the cycle of the miracles of birth, death and rebirth, all associated with blood.[7] Men eventually took over these practices, adopting the ritual dress developed by the women. This cross dressing can be seen in the berdaches of North America and shamen of other cultures, and survives even in the skirted dress of Catholic and Anglican priests and bishops. Spiritually, same gender sexuality and cross-dressing continue closely entwined throughout our human history despite all attempts to draw them apart.

NB. In Britain the Celtic cultures had sophisticated social structures, with women independent, highly appreciated and respected, and free to choose their sexual partners. There were many forms of relationships which could be entered and left; with commitment from short to long term. Their religious rituals were often fired by the ecstasy of sexual celebration.

At different historical times and places male homosexual behaviour has been variously: universal, 'unheard of', marginal and oppressed, as for the last millennium in Britain. My journey out of that oppression has been informed by the struggles of gay feminist, men's and other liberation movements. Learning of same gender erotic love amongst other peoples, from earliest to present times, I now have a broader sense of belonging, and commitment, to the assertion of a diverse queer people. For six years I have been actively involved in the bisexual movement, including the collective preparation of this book.

However much homosexual identity is presented as a post-nineteenth century phenomenon, homosexual desire and acts are not products of modern urban society. Queerness, in more than 40,000 years of human history, has frequently been prominent and celebrated. Modern societies are more complicated, with sexuality often a common ground among diverse people. For me the experience, politics and direction of sexuality are expanded by having the widest queer historical background; one that explores present definitions and further unravels the creative roles and destructive knots of our past.

68

Notes

[1] Tobias Schneebaum, *Where the Spirits Dwell*, Weidenfeld and Nicholson, 1988.

[2] Pat Caplan, *The Cultural Construction of Sexuality*, Routledge, London 1990.

[3] John Shelby Spong (Bishop of Newark), *Living in sin?: a Bishop rethinks human sexuality*, Harper and Row, 1990.

[4] Arthur Evans, *Witchcraft and the Gay Counterculture*, Fag Rag Books, Boston 1978.

[5] Will Roscoe (ed), *Living the Spirit: a gay American Indian anthology*, St Martin's Press, New York 1988.

[6] Chris Knight, *Blood Relations: menstruation and the origins of culture*, Yale University Press, 1995.

[7] Starhawk, *Dreaming the Dark: magic, sex and politics*, (Mandala) Unwin, 1990; Siobhan Kierans, *Riding the Snake: women celebrating menstruation*, unpublished 1992.

Further reading:
Walter L. Williams, *The spirit and the flesh: sexual diversity in American Indian culture*, Beacon Press, Boston 1988.
Mark Thompson, *Gay spirit, myth and meaning*, St Martins Press, New York 1987.

Annie Sprinkle Interview

Loraine Hutchins

I spoke to Annie Sprinkle at the time of the release of Monika Trent's film *My Father is Coming*, in which she stars as herself. Annie Sprinkle is a former porn queen from the 1970s who has, with an impresario's skill, built herself multiple personas, as porn queen, photographer, writer, teacher, comedian, video producer and performance artist. Having transformed herself out from under the porn bosses' control, she continues the transformation process by constantly recreating herself as an artist and teacher. Using the skills she learned in the sex business about fantasy and arousal, she has turned them around in a real way, to teach people about how to improve their sex lives and heal themselves in an age when more and more people are becoming afraid of sex.

A My Father Is Coming is an important film because it has all the sexual varieties – gay guys, lesbians, straights, kinky people, transsexuals – all in one film, which is the way the world is, a mixture of things. It's very sex positive. That's such a rarity in the world.
L And it's inter-generational too. Is it the kind of film a woman could take her father to see?
A Why not? My father asked me would it be OK if he went to see it. I usually say no. But I said yes, see *My Father Is Coming*. So they're excited that they're going to see a film I'm in.

The female-to-male transsexual in the film is based on my ex-lover Les Nichols, who was a woman who became a man. Transsexuals fascinate me. One of the women's workshops I host is Drag King For A Day, which is taught by a friend who's a female-to-male transsexual. He's very good at making up women to look like men, because he's spent his life trying to look like a man. They learn to walk and talk and act like a man. Then we all go out afterwards to a club. One night, when a lot of the women who'd come were ex-strippers, we went to a

Topless Bar. I felt like such a sleazeball being a 'man' in that place, I felt like we were being so disrespectful to the women. Here are these goddesses on stage and you're waving a dollar bill, looking like a jerk.

L Did you all pass?

A Yeah, but after a while things became a little suspicious. A few of the men were kind of whispering to each other, and looking at us kind of weird, but it was a lot of fun.

My apartment is a centre for women to explore their sexuality. Shelley Mars, the male impersonator who was in Monika's film, *Virgin Machine*, taught an Erotic Massage workshop there, and we do Ecstasy Facials and Oceanic Tantra workshops. I'm just really happy to offer my space for women to explore their sensuality and their sexuality. It's like my gift to the community I guess.

L Your community – is that a community where there are sharp divisions between women who identify as lesbians and women who don't?

A Certainly not when they come into my space. Pretty much all these events have both. The lesbians work right in with the hets, it's so hot, it is so incredible. I did a Sluts and Goddesses workshop in Australia with 24 women. This woman who used to have a fetish clothing store brought baskets full of the most gorgeous fetish clothes. It was so fun and erotic to see 24 women running around in these fetish clothes. That was the slut part, right before we got into the breathing. There was a fireplace, someone threw a bunch of wood on the fire right before we got to the breathing part. (Usually we wear goddess costumes, colourful loose wraps.) There was this raging fire, so of course everyone took everything off. And there was this sea of naked women undulating and breathing, coming all over the floor. I said, I can't believe my life!

L These were straight women?

A Yes!

L Were they straight when they left?

A Some of them did mention that they were interested in being with women, exploring that possibility.

L What's this new video you're editing?

A Oh, *Sluts and Goddesses*, it's so exciting, women of all shapes, sizes, colours and ages, all safe sex, very hot, very fun, it just expands the concept of what sex is.

The main thing I'm interested in now is teaching women's workshops, it feels so good. I worked with men for a long time. As a prostitute I did a lot of educating, a lot of giving, although it was more subversive. Now I've accepted the role of teacher.

I try to get people in touch with their own stereotypical notions of sex workers. Just like we're all in some sense racist, we are all in some sense conditioned to think a certain way about sex workers. I have it myself. If I hear someone's a prostitute, there's a little part of me that says, 'How can she do that?', that looks down on sex workers. If *I* have it, being as sex positive and pro-sex-worker as I am, I know that a lot of other people have that prejudice. And it's no different than racism or being prejudiced against someone's religion.

L Because why?

A Because you aren't going by the person. It's not the person, it's your idea of what that kind of person is.

L You mean, because there's nothing wrong with selling sex?

A Why should it be wrong to sell sex when it's right just to give it away? It's just absurd. It's perfectly fine, well, better than it's been in a long time, for a woman to go out and have sex with three guys in a day for free. But if she takes money for it she's liable to get her children taken away, liable to be put in jail. Now to me, that simply says that society's trying to control women so that they don't make money.

I had my first *real* lesbian sex with another woman I worked with in a massage parlour. I mean, I'd done it in movies, but this was my first time just for fun. There's a lot of lesbian prostitutes. More and more young women now.

L Do they identify as lesbians?

A Yes, totally. I'm hardly ever with men any more, unless they're gay or bi men. As my friend Shannon Bell (she did that film *Nice Girls Don't Do It* about female ejaculators) says, 'I can't figure out who's having sex with hetero men anymore!'

L So women do ejaculate?

A Yes. I do, not all the time. In the beginning I didn't know really it was ejaculation. I'd have these really giant orgasms. I would gush fluid but I was also real into golden showers so I thought, well, maybe it's just urine, but it was definitely different. It was clear, and it felt real different, totally different. It only happens with a vibrator or with being fist-fucked, for me. Fluid builds up in the glands around the urethra. If you push out it'll squirt.

L You're pushing out like peeing?

A Yes. I'm really into the idea of women ejaculating because I'm into women being sexually knowledgable and powerful, if they want to be. We're just in kindergarten when it comes to sex. (I'm in sixth grade because I've been studying this more.) I love the idea of women ejaculating and men not ejaculating. I'd like men to learn how to have orgasm without ejaculating, which is what good male lovers can do.

When I do my performance I do a Questions and Answers part. I always say, 'How many of you women out there ejaculate?' and there's always 2, 3, 4, sometimes 10 women who raise their hands. Women are again starting to ejaculate. Which is really exciting, because when you ejaculate with orgasm, it's very intense, it's very pleasurable.

There are many kinds of orgasms and they all have different uses. Every four months or so I have a therapy orgasm, with breathing and kegels. There'll be a certain amount of built-up emotional energy. I'll use the vibrator and someone's got to midwife this orgasm by finger-fucking me. It has to be someone who can handle intense energy, intense emotions and is going to be supportive. It's not about connecting or intimacy, it's about midwifing my emotional release and clearing out all my chakras.

It looks like you're in pain but to me it's beautiful. Most people can't handle it, just the way most people can't handle female ejaculation. Most people can't handle women's orgasms, including their own, themselves, though gay people are often better at this than others. So I'm interested in building up our capacity for pleasure and intense orgasms. And you know, we're capable of hour-long orgasms. A lot of people hate it when I say that because there's women who don't have any orgasms.

L And it's hard to get beyond the fear sometimes; women feel inadequate because they don't ejaculate or aren't multi-orgasmic, men feel inadequate if they're told they need to learn how to come without ejaculation when they're still afraid they can't even keep it hard with a rubber on.

A And a lot of people who enjoy sex aren't aware of the higher levels, the spiritual, therapeutic levels, healing levels. We're not taught about sex in this society. So my job is to teach about those things.

Each summer I teach a four-day women's Sacred Sex workshop in upstate New York with my tantra teacher, Jwala. It's so fulfilling.

L What do you teach about breath?

A Most people hold their breath and focus all their attention on their genitals, so that's where the orgasm is, just in the genitals. If you want to have a more full body experience you learn to work with your own breathing. And when you take deep breaths it pulls the energy up to your heart, your throat, then the top of your head. You go on to much higher states of ecstasy. The more you breathe the more sexual energy you're going to have, the more it's going to go throughout your body. And it's totally safe sex.

Again, it's not for everyone. It's just a technique, but simple techniques do work when you practice them.

L Have you ever done an all lesbian workshop?

A I run some workshops probably half lesbian, half het.

L If I were there I'd probably tell you some of the lesbians were also bi and some of the hets too.

A That's probably true. I'm sure a lot of the women come to my workshops because they want to be erotic with women, it's an all-women's group.

L It's safer.

A And there's no actual sex, yet it's totally ecstatic. In the four-day one it can get pretty wild though. But people don't consider that sex because they're not going down on each other, it's just breathing on the floor.

L But they come.

A Well to me that's sex, to me everything is sex, but, in their terms, it's not partner-sex. To me, the television is sex, the bed is sex, the sky is sex, you're sex, I'm sex, everything is sex.

Divided Heart, Divided History: Eighteenth-Century Bisexual Heroines

Emma Donoghue

So far, books on bisexuality have offered personal stories, sociological statistics and psychoanalytical theory; fine as far as they go, but the reader gets the distinct impression that bisexuality is a twentieth-century invention. A culture without tradition will always be a thin one; how can we know what bisexual choices mean until we discover some of the many and varied ways they have been lived? It is not that we lack evidence on bisexual women throughout the centuries and nations, nor has that evidence always been censored. The real problem is that it has been divided. Split into the component facts which are used in a bitter scholarly tug of war to prove that, say, Virginia Woolf was either a placid wife or a Sapphist rebel, but never both. And bisexual readers who have to hunt down their heritage in separate, conflicting histories will feel similarly split.

The main blame must be put on wilfully ignorant, lesbophobic biographers who erase the evidence of a woman's love for women, and play up any interest she showed in men. Lillian Faderman exposes their techniques of 'bowdlerisation, avoidance of the obvious, and *cherchez l'homme*' in her sharp essay 'Who Hid Lesbian History?'.[1] But the next question is 'Who Hid Bisexual History?' As a lesbian and a feminist I feel disloyal in insisting that some of the blame must go to lesbian feminist historians; the sad fact is that pioneers like Lillian Faderman have used those same strategies of distortion and avoidance of the obvious. By omitting any mention of a woman's male lovers, or assuming that she was forced into a loveless marriage of convenience, they pressgang clearly bisexual women like Mary Wollstonecraft into the all-star exclusively-lesbian history pageant.

Many lesbian feminist anthologies refuse to even include bisexuality in the index, and others skip over it, for example by acknowledging 'bisexual patterns' in the lives of some Modernist authors but insisting that their works are 'about lesbianism'.[2] Even when the occasional woman is mentioned as bisexual, her choices are given no theoretical framework.[3] She will be treated as a deviation from the lesbian norm, a heroine who didn't quite make it. Discussing a late eighteenth-century novel, Faderman notes with distaste that the heroine is 'not without some heterosexual feeling'.[4] This kind of ploy could be defended as 'redressing the balance', but the time for such tit-for-tat is over. Of course wishful thinking, or what pioneering lesbian historian Jeannette Foster called 'conjectural retrospect', has been useful to fill the gaps made by censorship in the history of sexuality, but we will never get anywhere if we replace old lies with fresh lies, heterosexist fantasy with lesbian feminist fantasy, letting bisexuals slip down the crack.

What we need is a kind of history that looks at bisexuality head on, rather than footnoting it as a deviation from a main topic. As an example of the kind of thing I mean, I want to look at four very different bisexual women in eighteenth-century English literature.

Feminist historians often ignore pornographic/satiric evidence for bisexuality, seeing it as merely phallocentric fantasy. Certainly such well-known stories as *Fanny Hill* are not really about bisexual lives at all; they tend to introduce a lesbian episode only as titillating training for the young woman before she discovers the bliss of heterosex and gives up what Fanny calls 'this foolery from woman to woman'.[5] But some texts are worth a second glance, because they escape from this cliché.

William King's *The Toast* (1736), a bizarre mock-epic in four books of English and Latin verses and footnotes, was written by an Oxford don as an attack on the Duchess of Newburgh who had bested him in a court case. She is characterised as Myra, a voracious bisexual hag and sorceress who is turned into a hermaphrodite at the end of the poem. Not the most inspiring role-model, you might think, but actually Myra is a figure of peculiar glamour, ironically celebrated for 'Changing the Sex, to try alternate Joys.'[6] Her bisexuality prioritises women: as her libido grows with age, she needs both heterosexual and lesbian sex, but it is the latter which pleases her best. Her favourite lover is Ali (Lady Allen), a Black Dutch Jewish lesbian dwarf (King likes to pile on the prejudices), who, a footnote admits, 'gave Myra more Pleasure than all the rest of her Lovers and Mistresses'.[7] Far from being titillated with lesbian 'foolery' before moving on to real men, Myra warms up each day by paying male 'Gallants' for sex, then summoning her favourite for final satisfaction. When Ali, in the form of an imp, is sucking Myra's nipple, Myra can desire nothing else:

> In a Rapture she stroak'd it, and gave it the Teat,
> By the Suction to raise sympathetical Heat.
> Then by *Hecate* she swore, *she was sated with Men*,
> Sung a wanton *Sapphoic*, and stroak'd it agen.[8]

But she continues in her flexible bisexuality, using one kind of sex to supplement or outdo the other: whenever her male gallants are 'few, or not made to her Mind', we are assured, still 'her Joyance was full, if the *Jewess* was kind.'[9]

This lifestyle is no barrier to her holding an honoured position in the powerful tribadic subculture; there is no suggestion that '*Tribades* or *Lesbians*'[10] are obliged to give up sexual relationships with men. Nor is bisexuality seen as milder, or politically tamer, than exclusive lesbianism; in fact, King seems to reset it as a wider spreading of immorality, since he makes Apollo punish Myra by limiting her 'wayward Amours' to relationships with other tribades, 'her kind'.[11] Despite his hostility, then, King's poem glamourises bisexuality, and suggests how an aristocratic female libertine could have got away with having as many lovers of both sexes as she happened to want.

A less knowing observer, King explains, would only notice Myra's affairs with men; like other eighteenth-century bisexual women (and, to a lesser extent, men), she minimised exposure by letting it be assumed that her bonds with women were friendships. At the height of the cult of romantic friendship, middle-class women could sleep together, kiss each other's throats and behave with possessive frenzy, all without arousing any suspicion that their relationship was sexual. An early example of a text of romantic friendship is a play first performed in 1695, *Agnes de Castra*. It was written at sixteen by Catherine Trotter who was rumoured to be a lesbian before she turned to religion and married a clergyman.[12]

An analysis of the play by Katherine Kendall provides yet another example of how lesbian scholars sometimes dig up the evidence they want and drop the rest back into obscurity.[13] Kendall's essay is all about Agnes, the 'lesbian heroine' and devoted friend of Princess Constantia; she ignores the character of Constantia, who can be read as a remarkably self-aware bisexual. The Princess loves her husband and her longtime companion Agnes simultaneously and ecstatically. She explains in the first act:

> You are both so equal dear to me,
> So closely wove by Fate to my fond breast,
> That neither can be sever'd from my love.

Agnes and the Prince, she tells them,

> … share my divided Heart
> So equally, I cannot tell my self
> To which I have given most.

They don't split or tear her heart, they share it; this is not the tabloid cliché of an angst-ridden bisexual triangle, but a story of three people committed to sharing each other.

Trouble comes from outside: jealous of Agnes, the villainess Elvira tries to fracture the triangle. But Constantia remains utterly loyal to her friend and her husband; even when she discovers that the Prince has fallen in love with Agnes, she refuses to blame him, since, as she explains, she feels the same way about her.

> For I myself, prefer her to myself,
> And love her too, as tenderly as he.

When Agnes, horrified to be the cause of grief in their marriage, asks to leave court, Constantia tells her that she cannot do without her; Fate having taken away half her blessing, she refuses to lose Agnes, 'the other half'.[14] Constantia's dividedness has now become a doubleness, giving her emotional stability, since even though she has lost the Prince's erotic focus, she is growing closer to Agnes. A servant reports to the wicked Elvira that her plot is backfiring, having seen

> The Princess leaning on her Rival's Neck;
> They mingled Kisses with the tend'rest Words,
> As if their Rivalship had made 'em dear.[15]

Elvira has to resort to murder. Slowly dying of a stab-wound, Constantia begs Agnes to marry the prince and be a foster mother to the child. In the play's rather ambiguous ending, Agnes talks herself into a half-consent before she too is murdered. She promises the Prince

78

that she will consider him as a future husband, but mostly for Constantia's sake.[16] Katherine Kendall reads this as a conventional cop-out; just as predictably, heterosexual critic Edna Steeves assumes that Agnes has been motivated by a secret passion for the Prince all along.[17] But both of these are distortions of what the play actually says, which is that Agnes, like Constantia, gradually finds in herself the potential to love both a woman and a man.

Another fascinating set of documents for bisexual history are women's transvestite memoirs from the eighteenth century. Julie Wheelwright's *Amazons and Military Maids* (Pandora, 1989) uncovers a surprising number of such publications; in most cases, the women's stories include both marriage or affairs with men, and flirtations or passionate relationships with women.

Mrs Christian Davies was a happy Dublin wife until her husband was pressganged, whereupon she dressed as a man and spent ten years looking for him in various wars. Having found him, she insisted on living as soldier comrades, until her sex was discovered and she was commanded to give him his 'marital rights' again. It seems to have been a loving, though turbulent partnership. On his death, she tells us, she reacted with appropriate frenzy: 'I bit out a great Piece of my right Arm, tore my Hair, [and] threw myself on his Corps'. Although the motive Christian gives for her transvestite travels is wifely devotion, the story includes several lesbian flirtations. 'In my Frolicks, to kill Time, I made my Addresses to a Burgher's Daughter, who was young and pretty', she mentions casually. Davies admits that when she tried to take an 'indecent Freedom' with the girl, and was virtuously rebuffed, she grew fonder than ever of her, though she puts in the traditional disclaimer that 'mine, you know, could not go beyond a platonick love'.[18]

It seems that Christian Davies's relationships went with her clothes; the opportunity to switch gender allowed her a flexible sexual preference too. She mentions no conflict between these roles, and can switch them at will. Nor does she expect the reader to be shocked; it is as if wearing men's clothes gives her the temporary right to woo women, so long as the game ends when she puts her dress back on.

The last text I'm going to deal with is *Mary*, a classic of romantic friendship – but not, as it has been read, just between women. Feminist pioneer Mary Wollstonecraft published this semi-autobiographical novel in 1788. Its simple story concerns the heroine's total emotional commitment to one woman and then to one man. This is not the old cliché of female friendship being replaced by mature heterosexuality;

in fact, this novel gives both platonic loves equal weight, but suggests that Mary's first choice would be a partnership with a woman.

The young heroine, neglected by her parents, decides to look elsewhere for what she calls 'an object to love'; freedom of feeling is what matters to her, not the gender of the love-object. She forms an instant passionate bond with Ann. They are physically intimate, though this is carefully justified in case any readers are suspicious.

> Mary always slept with Ann, as she was subject to terrifying dreams, and frequently in the night was obliged to be supported, to avoid suffocation.

Unfortunately, Ann has an 'exhausted heart', being still preoccupied with the man who jilted her.[19] But this actually increases Mary's compassion, and she becomes addicted to helping her consumptive beloved, going so far as to marry a man she loathes just to be financially secure enough to take Ann away to a warmer climate.

To begin with, Mary has no interest in men: we are told

> her friendship for Ann occupied her heart, and resembled a passion. She had had, indeed, several transient likings [for men], but they did not amount to love.

But Henry, the dying musician she befriends in Lisbon, slowly begins to matter to her. At first it is an intellectual friendship: Mary tells us that in his company, her mind expands. Far from being jealous of Ann, Henry tries to entertain her, and is in awe of the women's friendship. Mary begins to find conversation with him a welcome relief: 'This divided attention was of use to her, and prevented her continually thinking of Ann'.[20]

At this point we expect a crisis of jealousy, but Wollstonecraft refuses to do the usual thing. The relationships are cleverly paralleled, rather than contrasted, and one gently follows the other, rather than clashing with it. When Ann dies, Mary needs someone else to love: 'Her heart longed to receive a new guest; there was a void in it'. Sometimes she feels guilty for forgetting Ann even for a moment, but at other times her love for Henry dominates. Wollstonecraft is realistic about Mary's motivation: 'had Ann lived,' she explains, 'it is probable [Mary] would never have loved Henry so fondly'. But the fact is that she loves them both. The relationships are similarly platonic, and she nurses Henry to death, just like Ann. She tells him that her only comfort will be 'in heaven with thee and Ann'.[21] Wollstonecraft never makes her heroine choose between female romantic friendship and heterosexual romance; in a sense Mary loses them both, but in another sense she has it both ways. This must be one of the earlier texts in English to offer an idealisic vision, almost a philosophy of bisexuality.

So where does the future lie for bisexual history? I am not making a case for complete segregation, as in parallel gay, lesbian, and bisexual studies of each era; our sexual cultures have always overlapped and we would lose so much if we tried to cut them apart. Nor do I look forward to compulsory integration, with every 'lesbian and gay' book title adding the lip-service of 'and bisexual', or a quota of bisexual themes in every critical anthology. But what I would like to see is the real tackling of bisexual issues in what is coming to be known as 'queer theory', and much greater honesty about bisexual lives in all histories and biographies, as well as the publication of studies written from a specifically bisexual viewpoint. Biographies of such women as Queen Christina and Emily Dickinson could present their loves for women and men fairly and thoughtfully without diluting the issues of sexual politics. None of us is neutral, but a book written from one angle can welcome others; a study of bisexual ethics in the Bloomsbury set would include some women who were exclusively lesbian, for example, while a history of lesbian social circles could not ignore the bisexual lives of many of the members.

Already there are beginnings of this sort of careful piecing-together of the sexual jigsaw. Jeannette Foster's early classic *Sex Variant Women in Literature* is an excellent source for researching texts about bisexuality, since although she focuses on the woman-to-woman element of female 'variance', Foster is scrupulous in naming bisexuality when she sees it, and her index gives over seventy references, neatly categorised into 'men preferred', 'no preference', and 'women preferred'.[22] The recent anthology *Hidden from History: Reclaiming the Gay and Lesbian Past* may have an old-fashioned subtitle, but in fact many of the essays question traditional definitions of heterosexuality and homosexuality, and give close, fearless analysis to bisexual lifestyles from classical Athens to seventeenth-century Japan to Jazz Harlem.[23] It is impossible to read such anthologies right through and feel completely comfortable, and that is their excitement. Far from being apolitical, this kind of sexual history challenges the bigots in us all.

'Divided Heart, Divided History' is adapted by the author from her *Passions Between Women; British Lesbian Culture 1668-1801*, Scarlett Press, London 1993.

Notes

[1] Lillian Faderman, 'Who Hid Lesbian History?', in Margaret Cruikshank (ed), *Lesbian Studies: Present and Future*, Feminist Press, New York 1982, pp115-21.

[2] Gillian Hanscombe, 'Katherine Mansfield's Pear Tree', in *What Lesbians do in Books*, Elaine Hobby and Chris White (eds), Women's Press, London 1991, pp111-33 (112-3).

[3] Lillian Faderman's *Surpassing the Love of Men*, Women's Press, London 1985, mentions bisexuality only a handful of times (mostly in connection with hermaphroditism), and does not give a single example of a bisexual woman between Mary Frith in the sixteenth century and Kate Millett in the 1970s.

[4] Faderman, *Surpassing the Love of Men*, p113.

[5] John Cleland, *Fanny Hill; or, Memoirs of a Woman of Pleasure*, first publ. 1748-9, ed. by Peter Wagner, Penguin, Harmondsworth 1985, p71.

[6] William King, *The Toast*, 4 books (London, 1736), poem by 'Knapp', 1, lix.

[7] *Ibid.*, p53.

[8] *Ibid.*, pp106-7.

[9] *Ibid.*, p101.

[10] *Ibid.*, p56.

[11] *Ibid.*, p116.

[12] Catherine Trotter was portrayed as 'Daphne' in the lesbian 'New Cabal' section of *The New Atlantis* [1709], in *The Novels of Mary de la Riviere Manley*, ed. by Patricia Loster, 2 vols, Gainesville, FL, Scholars Facsimiles & Reprints, 1971, 1:584-8.

[13] Katherine Kendall, 'From Lesbian Heroine to Devoted Wife: Or, What the Stage Would Allow', in *Historical, Literary and Erotic Aspects of Lesbianism*, Monika Kehoe (ed), Harrington Park Press, London 1986, pp9-22.

[14] Catherine Trotter, *Agnes de Castro*, in Vol II of *The Plays of Mary Pix and Catherine Trotter*, Edna L. Steeves (ed), Garland, London 1982, pp5, 6.

[15] *Agnes de Castro*, p20.

[16] *Agnes de Castro*, pp40, 45.

[17] Edna L. Steeves, introduction to *Agnes de Castro*, pxxvii.

[18] Anon, *The Life and Adventures of Mrs Christian Davies, the British Amazon*, Richard Montagu, London 1741, 11:48; 1:27-8.

[19] Mary Wollstonecraft, *Mary* and *The Wrongs of Woman*, ed. by Gary Kelly, Oxford University Press, Oxford 1976, pp5, 23, 18.

[20] *Mary*, pp19, 27, 30.

[21] *Mary*, pp35, 49, 61.

[22] Jeannette Foster, *Sex Variant Women in Literature*, first publ. 1956, Naiad Press, Tallahassee, FL 1985.

[23] Martha Vicinus, Martin Bauml Duberman, and George Chauncy Jr (eds), *Hidden from History: Reclaiming the Gay and Lesbian Past*, Penguin Books, Harmondsworth 1991.

Section II: Personal Stories

Introduction

Sue George

It can be a long time between our first doubts that we are really and solely homosexual or heterosexual, and a full acceptance of our bisexuality. For some, this process was easy; for others it was hell, calling into question everything they had ever thought about themselves. For everyone, they had to find out what bisexuality meant to them, which has been difficult in the absence of a bisexual community, or many openly bisexual individuals.

All this was as true for me as anyone else. It was 1973, and I was 16, when I first identified as bisexual. This was a feeling I kept to myself, knowing full well that it wouldn't be well received at my conventional grammar school. To most people, I appeared entirely heterosexual for at least another six years – but I knew better. I had an intense, sometimes desperate, fantasy life with women during those years, which continued during several good, long relationships with men. I knew I wanted a relationship with a woman, but had no idea how to find the woman for me. Thankfully, I went to university, where I did meet like-minded women. But, a two year lesbian relationship later, I returned, very reluctantly, to heterosexuality. As the lesbian community had dropped me like a hot potato, I seemed to have no choice. Thank God I found a bisexual women's group to go to, where, if I didn't find a girlfriend, at least I could talk about what I was going through, and know I was not alone. I would say it took me fifteen years to 'come to terms' with my bisexuality and be as out about it as I am today.

This section includes the personal stories of a range of bisexual people. Reading about other people's personal histories is essential for us, to know we are not alone, particularly if we do not know many or any other bisexuals. This is especially true for people who are just coming out, but it always remains true to some extent. There simply aren't enough images of bisexuals, openly bisexual people, bisexual groups and clubs – or even openly negative bisexual representations of us in the tabloid press – to meet the need for us to know about other people.

Whether or not we choose to go public about our sexuality, whether we have personal difficulties in 'coming to terms' with it, even if we live in an already 'supportive environment', our bisexuality is something we have to think about and our sexuality has to be questioned before we can be at home with it. Like lesbians and gay men, bisexuals cannot just slip, unconscious, into bisexuality. Indeed, moving towards a bisexual identity can involve considerable pain and struggle – as some of these articles show. Also in common with lesbians and gay men, some people have 'always known' they were bisexual, and others came to realise it in quiet or dramatic ways at various times in their lives. Other people find the way they feel actually changes.

So one reason for this section is to help to create the knowledge that we are not alone. Another crucial role for this section is to enable us to identify with other people's feelings. We can connect with this person or that person's struggle, pain or joy. Reading the articles gives us all cause for optimism. Paradoxically, this is in stark contrast to the feeling which many of the contributors express – that there is no place for bisexuals. While this has been true, now we are creating it ourselves, slowly but surely, and this book is part of that.

The contributors include people with a wide range of experience, and from many different backgrounds. *Bisexual Horizons* has made a particular effort to include as many different sorts of people as possible, so this section includes the personal stories of a number of people from traditionally marginalised groups, whose stories do not usually find their way into books on sexuality. But there are still gaps: people of colour, for instance, are greatly under-represented. Perhaps not surprisingly, there are rather fewer men than women in this section. Men tend not to want to talk about their deepest feelings in a way which is true and honest, and the men who do so here should encourage others to emulate them.

These articles are written by many different types of bisexuals, so although it would be hoping for too much to think that everyone reading this book will be able to identify with one of the contributors, everyone should be able to find at least some personal points of reference. It also seems there are some situations that have happened to large numbers of bisexual people. One such situation is that of feeling strong same-sex attractions for the first time, when in the middle of a heterosexual relationship. Micky Fargo and Eileen O'Connell deal with precisely this in their pieces.

In terms of the way they are written, and the issues they raise, the articles also vary widely. Not all of the stories included in this personal section are directly about the experience of fancying men and women. Some of them take that as given – and move on to show how bisexual identity or experience has been the filter through which other things are seen. McKenzie Wark and Kelly Drake both do this in their stories, which look at popular culture and spirituality respectively. Other contributors address a particular subject, looking at how their bisexuality has shaped their feelings about it – for instance, Felicity Cade and Sharon Rose talking about their different perspectives on marriage.

Personal stories flesh out the theories, the need for political change. Our feelings, how we behave, our experiences, our lives, our coming-out stories are the starting point for everything else. Ultimately, we all read these stories to know that we are not alone, and that other people, like us, have fought and won.

Double Agency

McKenzie Wark

> What is interesting about people in good society is the mask that each one of them wears, not the reality that lies behind the mask.
>
> Oscar Wilde, *The Decay of Lying*

This man speaking, this man who has the conference floor, I want to suck his nipples. It's nothing personal, it's just that he's been speaking for an hour now about 'pleasure' and 'resistance' and 'consumption' and 'everyday life' without giving himself away in any way. I secretly imagine walking down the aisle, through the auditorium, to rip his sweaty shirt open. Maybe it's the heat. It's summer in Sydney, all sultry air and diamond light. He is talking about Madonna now. I want to suck her nipples too.

This is the trouble with academics – they talk so casually about other people's pleasures, draw diagrams of the various subject positions, as if their own preferences and positions didn't figure in the analysis at all. To them, the pleasures of the text are something *other people* feel. Cultural critics spy on other people's pleasures. We like to watch. We watch TV and it doesn't please us. So we imagine how it pleases others, and *that* pleases us. A curious perversion, a sort of voyeurism of the second degree.

The thing which made me what I am was not the theatre of Oedipal drama but the *Mary Tyler Moore Show*. Endless hours, sprawled luxuriantly on the carpet, prostrate in front of the box. The flicker of its luminous blue-grey rays on my body in a darkened room, the comely murmur of its voice, the soft swell of its musical scores, the teasing play of its pictures, scintillating on my skin! Television impressed upon me the various and variable geometries of desire when I was at a very impressionable age. Now and forever, between me and the bodies of others, lies the inky blue balm of its images. I am countless heroes with firm hands, magnanimous hearts; countless damsels waiting to be conquered and possessed. I am endless longing glances in shot reverse-shot. I am infinite instant love in the commercial spot.

I owe it all to my first lover, the one who seduced me with a knowing glance. The one who turned me aside from the antique law of patriarchal desire. The one who turned me on to the artfully modern game of beautiful ruses. My darling television, with your wicked eye that hides more than it shows in its glimmerings. With your nightly ritual of transubstantiation, turning a base lusting into a promiscuous glint of images. An alchemy abstracted from my body, set loose in diagrams of ambivalent, versatile love. Television penetrated my body, sexualised my surfaces, long before Edmund, who likes to think he was my first lover, got his hands on me.

Television is supposed to put us in our place, show us what we can and can't have. It doesn't always work that way, though. Just as we can twist the social law of desire to suit our tastes, so too we can twist its representation, on television. All that is required is a slight recoding of its cyphers of desire:

1. I look at her: I want to have her.
2. I look at her: I want to be her.
3. He looks at me: I want him to have me.
4. He looks at me: I want to be him, projecting his desire.

These are of course only the most basic codes, but they are as old as the silver screen itself. The close-up of the star in old black and white movies still stirs in me silvered memories of my first great loves: to be the adorable Audrey Hepburn; to be loved by Cary Grant. Later I came to realise there were more complicated vectors of seduction playing across the screen of my body. For example:

5. He looks at her; she looks at me. I want to be her, to feel his desire.
6. He looks at her; she looks at me. I want to be him, to feel she is mine, all mine.

I can recall these triangulations at work in the youthful crush I had on *The Avengers*. Dashing John Steed, elegant and always proper in his English suits and bowler. Luscious Emma Peel in her zip-up boots and jump suits. They were super secret agents, fighting not the cold war but the cool. In the opening credit sequence, he holds up a bottle of champagne, which she shoots the top off with a bullseye hit. The wine spurts, and he pours them both a glass. The music swoons. They draw close. I look at Emma. I want to have her. I look again and I want to be her. I feel Steed's eyes upon me. He wants me. I feel his desire. It makes me desirous too. I want Emma. I look at her longingly. Steed looks at Emma. That he wants her too makes me want her more. Glance upon glance, the luscious tendrils of electrolust brush their gentle fingers against each other and against my gaze. Here there is nothing certain about desire. Here fascination peels away from the supposed laws of nature. Here, in uncertainty, it is free. At this point, a commercial break.

These interruptions were a bore until I discovered that the same logic worked in the ads as well. In commercials the transubstantiation of sex into images passes by way of the magic product, a brand of lipgrease or grog, that appears to make it all work. A fetishist's delight! But I had to be disciplined. I had to ignore these entreaties to cash in my cravings for mere things. The banal attempt to pass off some useless object as the secret of seduction is the laughable side of advertising. The joyful side is the play of figments, freed from nature and the law. This is advertising's queer promise of possibility. Here all that is solid melts into images. The black box of desire, the little object of want which makes these visions play upon me is not some product, but television itself. The love spot of television, with its endless transactions of flesh for flesh; touch for touch.

Of course, these tantalising codes of love lack not only tangible form, but symmetry. To want or be wanted; to be the subject or the object of desire are not the same. One is coded in this particular transactional logic as masculine, the other feminine. I learned this from a lecturer I had at university who made quite an impression on me. I forget her name, but she looked strikingly like Mary Tyler Moore. Anyway, she used to quote from that wonderful book, *Ways of Seeing* by John Berger:

> Men act and women appear. Men look at women. Women watch themselves being looked at. This determines not only most relations between men and women but also the relation of women to themselves. The surveyor of woman in her self is male: the surveyed female. Thus she turns herself into an object – and most particularly an object of vision: a sight.

Berger's book was a puzzle to me back then. It made me feel like a bit of an oddity. It gave me the curious notion that when, for example, John Steed looked at me, and I felt myself being watched, there was a woman inside me being watched and a man inside the woman inside the man watching us being watched. Presumably when I got the hots for Emma, they all changed places. The noughts became crosses and the crosses noughts, like on *Celebrity Squares*.

It took me years to figure out that it was John Berger and Mary Tyler Moore who had got hold of the wrong end of the stick. It isn't quite right to say that in this society 'men act and women appear'. The asymmetry that Berger discovers in the codes of the gaze are there alright, but they don't neatly map onto our bodies like that. Berger was being a fetishist, focusing only on the butch side of men looking and the femme side of women, desiring to be looked at. Like that man at the conference, Berger doesn't quite connect with the real perversities of our image culture, where we are all double agents, masking and dissimulating even when we least suspect it. Somebody should have sucked on Berger's nipples, long and hard and maybe both at once.

What Berger didn't quite figure out about these codes, which the media inscribes as its secret writing all over our bodies since we were born, is that it doesn't make nice het citizens out of all of us. Sometimes we learn to float in a free space between identities, to be spies in the house of love. Thanks to television, the transubstantiation of the body into a tissue of seductible surfaces, once just a dream of the decadent poets, is complete. The logic of the signs of sex separates out from the crude facts of biology. The codes of love reconfigure the erogenous zones of the body, subordinating the body to the image. This is why it is pointless to look for the hidden logic of bodily drives and desires in television. It all works the other way around. Television is an enigma machine that showers us in endless honey-shots of mutable images; its transsexual lexicon; its blueprints of yearning. It holds no secrets, yet it secretes in liquid form the masks for a double game of hide and seek with ourselves and the other.

Televisual codes of lust and longing nevertheless have a logic to them. They are not polymorphously perverse, they are inflexibly binary, rigidly heterosex. Yet the way we can make those heterosigns of sex play on the surface of our bodies cannot be controlled by television, and herein lies its glorious perversity. Berger's diagrams of desire classify images like suspects in a file, whereas the actual dynamic process of television, of popular culture in general, is endlessly seductive, endlessly subversive.

I thought about all of these things at the Gay and Lesbian Mardi Gras, Sydney's great contribution to the global polysexual culture. A million people are in the streets! For hours the floats shimmy and cruise up Oxford Street with their gaudy colours, fabulously peopled by queers and queens, leathermen and dykes, femmes and fairies. There is a float for every kind of scene – except mine. Absent from this grand procession are the double agents, the ones who do not let their identity fix on one image long enough to get hooked on it, even for an evening. I imagine a float for us, peopled not with bodies, but images, a great cut-up of every image of desire, blasting from a dozen TV screens, fashioned from nothing but the static-charged rhythms and white noise of manicured light.

I mention this to my lover. We are standing in the crowd, where for the moment at least, the queers reign over the street and the straight couples, unconsciously on the defensive against their own impulses, hold hands. We decide to skip the big party at the showground. Picking our way through the litter of empty bottles, we wander home to a showground of our own.

Quiet now, under the mosquito net, we lie. It canopies us like a cone of silence. We draw the black box close. Turned on, its inscrutable electronics sends out strange beams. They reach through the gauze to scintillate on our skin. Its serene blue rays, cool and remote, reflect like tiny eyelets on the beaded sweat that clings to the pores of our screens. We become a moist commingling in the dark with beaming, cyclic stories. We come to become what we behold.

'And Then She Kissed Me'

Micky Fargo

I never knew. For all those years, I never knew. And then she kissed me.

She was my best friend at school, from the first day to the end of High School, and then we went to University together.

We had helped each other with homework, played together after school, camped in each other's backyards, become obsessed with horses, then with boys. We congratulated each other on the loss of virginity and consoled each other at the loss of boyfriends.

I was bridesmaid at her wedding and she was bridesmaid at mine.

At Uni. she studied Art and I did Biology. She became a well-known artist, and I became upwardly-mobile in a big national Laboratory.

We still saw a lot of each other. With our husbands we made a foursome for occasional dinner parties and camping trips.

She kissed me on my tenth wedding anniversary.

We were in the shed, getting out the trestle table for the party. I walked into a spider-web. She put up her hand, brushed the web out of my hair, and then she kissed me.

It was months later that she told me she and Todd were getting a divorce.

I asked her why, of course. It was quite a shock.

She said, 'I'm a lesbian.'

After a while, I closed my mouth. I said, was she sure?

She said, yes, she and Todd got on well, like friends. They hadn't slept together for about five years. After she told him, they had worked out what they were going to do. There would be no apparent change, she had no deep relationship at the time and neither did he. She had no desire to strike out on her own yet, and Todd was free to have discreet affairs. If she formed a lasting relationship or he wanted to remarry, they would get a divorce. With this possibility in mind, they quietly divided up everything they owned together and got separate bank accounts.

Now that Todd wanted to move interstate and remarry there, it was

91

time to get the divorce. And so they did.

'And what are you going to do?' I asked.

She looked at me, surprised.

'I mean, after the divorce. Aren't you going to go away or something?'

'No,' she said, 'why should I? Everything I love is here.'

We had a brief affair. I was ridden with guilt at cheating on Geoff and uncomfortable with the idea of being a lesbian. It wasn't for me, I thought. I like men, I'm married to one. But I like women too. I came to realise I'd always liked women, but in the past I'd just ignored it as no more than idle fancy.

One day, she told me she was leaving.

'I thought everything you loved was here.'

'It is,' she said, 'but you'll never love me, so there's no point in staying around.'

She was right and she did the best thing. I missed her, I still do, but only as a friend.

When Bronny kissed me she woke up all the sleeping desires in me. All my thoughts about women came welling up to the surface. I couldn't ignore them, though I tried. I was so confused. I knew I couldn't be a lesbian because of the way I felt about men. I even had an affair with a man to prove it to myself. That just left me feeling as confused as I was before, and even more guilty about cheating on Geoff. People were beginning to notice something was wrong. Geoff asked if I was sick. I said yes, and told everyone I had yuppie flu. My work began to suffer, I snapped at colleagues and friends. I was losing sleep. I didn't want to sleep. My dreams were full of women, kissing me, touching me.

Eventually I got help. I booked in to see a psychologist. I was very nervous. I was going to have to tell her about my dreams.

I told her the whole story.

She laughed and smiled at me.

'Don't worry, you're not a lesbian. You're bisexual.'

I'd never heard of bisexuality before. She told me what it meant. I was so relieved, I cried.

She gave me a book to read, written by bisexuals, other bisexuals, and some contact numbers.

In the book were stories very much like my own. I cried and laughed. It was like getting a letter from someone you thought was dead.

✣

I rang the numbers she gave me. They were for bisexual networks, sort of like clubs. At the first couple of meetings I felt like I was at Alcoholics Anonymous. 'Hi, I'm Ellen and I'm bisexual.'

After a while I stopped feeling nervous. These people were just like me. They took me onto the gay 'scene'. As soon as I walked in the door I saw Danielle and Danielle saw me. I didn't know what to do. I just stood there as though I was going to be shot. She smiled at me and said, 'Relax, no-one here is going to tell on you.'

My new friends were great, my sense of freedom in the gay places was terrific. But still I felt something was missing.

It was time to tell my husband. He had a right to know.

Geoff had always listened to what I said and considered it. He had never run me down as just a woman or anything like that. He wasn't violent or whatever.

But when I told him I was bisexual – well, it was a different matter.

He accused me of being too chicken to say I was a lesbian. He said I'd ruined his life and his friends' wives. It was so stupid and horrible, so I left. I just packed a suitcase with him shouting at me and telling me I was a dyke and he was better off without me.

I booked into a hotel. The next day I found a flat, hired a removalist and moved out while Geoff was at work.

A few months afterwards, my mother gave me a letter from Geoff. He didn't know where I was, so he gave it to her.

The letter said he was very sorry, he didn't know why he'd acted like that, he still loved me and wanted me to come back.

I agreed to meet him. The meeting was not successful. He said he wanted me to forget all this dyke business and come home. I pointed out that I was bisexual, not a lesbian, but he said it was the same thing.

I love Geoff, but what he did and the way he still thinks about my bisexuality hurt me very deeply. I don't know if I can ever go back to him.

A couple of weeks ago I met a nice bisexual woman and we are going out together, but it's not serious.

I'd like one day to meet a nice bisexual man and get married again. I guess that means I've got a heterosexual tendency.

Today I told my mother I'm bisexual. She said, 'Really, dear, what does that mean?' When I told her, and told her what had happened with Geoff, she said she hoped I found someone nice to take Geoff's place, for my sake. But if it was a woman it might make things awkward at the office party.

My life is so different now. Only my work and my mother are the same. Most of the friends Geoff and I had won't talk to me. I don't know what he told them. It's easier now to tell who my friends really are.

On Being Bisexual
and Black in Britain

Paul

At age 13 or 14 I was going through 'who am I; what am I; what could I be?' I accepted then the possibility of being in a same sex relationship. I was always open, attracted to men in a way of being warm, loving and caring; and wanting that. But there was never really appropriate spaces for that in school, family networks and so forth.

I suppose my same sex relationships came from discos and clubs when I was about 22. I was with a man who was a pre-op transsexual. He'd come around to my home. My Mum couldn't believe it when I told her that this was a man, not a woman and I was having a relationship with him. She almost disowned me, but settled with changing the sheets and fumigating the room. She'd have put quarantine signs up if she'd thought of them.

My mother fully expects me to have children. I have always expected children to be a major part of my life. My preferred parenting arrangement would've been as a single parent. But practice does not always make perfect, so I've given up trying. Although the practice was fun!

However, having a child with a woman would only happen when she was fully aware of my desire to be within other mutually loving and respecting relationships, whatever the sexual orientation; monogamous, moi? – non! I suppose if I am honest, my preference would be for loving friendships, which are less defined by one's gender, but by our ability to set each other free, give hope and foster the challenge of our possibilities together.

My working life had been a little skew-whiff, in that I tend to see work as a hobby that I do in order to acquire dosh so as to pay for courses which I may find of interest. I've also chosen never to work unless it really interests me as well as challenges. So the moment the 'hard work, but phew' aspects supersede the 'hard work, but rewarding' aspects, I've tended to resort to the DSS until the next interesting and always part-time (so I'd have enough time for adult playtime), post arrives.

Some of my posts have included: working with children and adult survivors of abuse; male victims of rape; TV agony uncle; a creche worker/play leader; an all round (show-off) entertainer, a dancer. I was also one of five consultants who produced a report on behalf of the Health Education Authority on 'HIV and Bisexuality'. I had specific responsibility for related black and ethnicity issues. At present I'm a qualified counsellor, training to be a psycho-sexual psychotherapist.

One of my greatest challenges has been facing and celebrating my sexuality within the 'black' community I term 'home'. This is because within my limited personal experience, home has been a little cluttered with the ills of society which have oppressed us for so long. These are racism (internalised, as well as the usual run of the mill kind), sexism, homophobia, and other phobias which afflict other oppressed groups *and* the so-called non-oppressed majority (we are all, I feel, diminished by the negation of another). I suspect that this is symptomatic of trying to be accepted into a hostile environment.

You still hear of situations where people get stoned back home for venturing to talk about, or be proud of their gay/other sexuality. I feel it's the influence of many things, like the church and colonialism, inciting people's fears. Traditionally persons of different sexuality were probably held in much higher esteem. I want to explore and challenge this belittling of other sexualities much more, because I am finding it increasingly frustrating to not be able to communicate with persons of my colour, because of some of their erroneous beliefs.

On the day of the Pride March, I came out of the Brixton tube station and saw a lot of youths, ranging in age from 11 to 18, pretending to be shooting obviously identified gay, lesbian or bisexual men and women as they walked out. They were using words like 'anti-man', meaning the reverse of man, 'bottom hole lover', 'shit fucker'. I went up to three guys and said, 'Why are you doing that? No one's intruding into your life'. They said, 'It's wrong, it's sick, it's nasty, it shouldn't be allowed'. I said 'Don't you remember that many moons ago when our people were first "discovered", or when we first came here, we were classified as being animals or sick or not worth anything? So why are you turning around, now that we've found a voice? You can't belittle us in this way. We have the right to be respected as equals, as human beings! You're turning around and oppressing other people for the same sort of reasons that we were oppressed – fear, ignorance – and that's no reason at all'. All this young chap could say, turning his head to the side and looking away from me throughout the conversation, was 'If you don't go away from here I'm going to cut you'.

I find that, in terms of an awareness of sexual diversity, it's almost too late when people are going through their teens and they want to say 'I am definitely this and this'. Awareness really has to happen earlier in childhood, or sometime later when people are more relaxed about proving themselves.

There is a need to challenge things here. There's a top layer of conservatism, Christianity and respectability; beneath that all sorts of things go on, everything imaginable, irrespective of what it says in the Bible. What they don't see can't hurt them – unless you get found out. Then you apologise profusely and say 'the devil got me', or something like that. You get patted on the shoulder, for it's a good show to admit you were wrong and get back on the straight and narrow. Then you can carry on doing whatever it was because they don't want to expose you twice. The church and I aren't too good a bed fellows. Stepping out and saying 'I have the responsibility for my own actions' is negated by the church.

I feel rather confused here, for although I'm not a religious guy, I love the rhetoric which the religions emit – love, tolerance, justice, hope, trust, reconciliation and others. But more often than not, religions become intransigent. I've come to see this as their incongruent posturings.

In the context of gay, lesbian and bisexual peoples, there's great cause for concern at the moment about linking with each other. The lesbian and gay worlds seem reticent about accepting bisexuality as a fact. This reminds me of some black people belittling other people: lesbians and gays experience similar oppression and persecution to bisexuals, for daring to express a sexuality other than what has come to be imposed as the 'norm', and yet they themselves reject others.

Bisexuality doesn't tend to have a clear and simple definition of what it is or isn't – for me; whereas many lesbians and gays feel they are not supposed to move and flow in sexual orientation. In truth, many gay people I know have had, are having, or would like to have, good experiences with the opposite sex, sexual as well as the platonic relationships they may already have. But they feel threatened to express that openly, and have to pretend.

That's what the gay movement was originally about – not having to pretend. But it now seems like another group trying to survive, be accepted, taking on more of the negatives of general society. I can't be a party to that. I've been brought up in a society that's sexist, racist, homophobic, ageist, the whole gamut. So I know those things are in me. Unless I'm willing to face that, I'm not going to be able to address them. You can use the right words, but if it's not in your heart and soul you're not really being honest; you're a hologram. It's a process of living, learning and changing. So some people think I'm fickle for changing my mind, but I'd rather that than become entrenched. I want to breathe and stretch. Hence I don't really like the term bisexual, because at times I'm gay, at times heterosexual, and at times bisexual, whilst most of the time I'm me, myself and I.

A while back I experienced a sexual encounter that was challenging, stimulating and empowering. He was athletic, intellectual, very sensual. Whilst I was athletic, intelligent and very sexual. Together we'd pursue a roller coaster of carnal pleasure, which felt like heaven and earth. It tasted of sugar and spice with nowt taken out. In short, sexually we kicked arse. Until that is, two very important things became apparent. Firstly, he became more and more uncomfortable with our public show of affections. This did little to enamour him to me. Secondly, during one of our more tactile, inquiring, exploratory 'love ins', he quite literally made contact with Nirvana. Before my very eyes he experienced a series of mind, body and spirit orgasms. He even seemed to levitate! Bastard!! However, the first aspect became more profound, and it moved onto his denial of his same sex side, so we parted. But, the second aspect set me off on a journey of discoveries about my sexual/sensual self.

One thing many oppressed communities do is to try and get respectability. Many television programmes I've seen on bisexuality seem to play down the sexual aspects. For me, sex plays a large part in my life. It's very therapeutic. I'm a very 'safe-sexy' lover; most of my partners don't know when I've put on a condom – I learnt that from reading an article on prostitutes who can put a condom on clients without them even knowing. I love practising this and making it into an artform. Safer sex can be fun and joyous. It's taken me time to learn that. Sex is a place where people can feel sated and soft afterwards, and feel that they can communicate in a way that everyday talking doesn't include. Sex is about the intuitive sense, and all the senses.

I'm a member of the bisexual centre collective which is developing 'Kaleidosphere', a freedom of sexuality resource centre. I hope it will have a broad remit for people to explore their sexuality with both genders. There will always be differences. It's when people say others can't explore and express their differences that I object. The bisexual centre will be a secure place for our communities to say, and get, what we need; a place to explore our sexuality, for people of colour to identify, for women to have a space for themselves.

I think men and women need to explore our sexuality separately. But this must not be done in isolation from each other. Two-way communicating pathways are needed so as to exchange learning. In the collective we'll be attempting to understand what we've taken on board, and what we need to change in ourselves, and then coming together as people, as human beings, with different histories and desires. There's a need for more self awareness – and there's a need for much more awareness in our 'black' communities. The political powers need to help with this process, otherwise it's always on the back-burner. We need to think more about how to utilise the political structures. Indeed, the personal is political, but we live within our community of societies as well as within the inter/intra-personal – and as independent persons, with all the intricacies that entails.

Being black and bisexual, every day is proving to be more of a blessing in disguise – the disguise being my and others' collusion in a denial of the freedom for me to be who or what I may be. I am particularly implicated as I'm more able to drop the disguise (appearing in the *Voice* newspaper, *Boyz* and *Options* magazines) and to be more real in the world – I commend it.

Support for a tapestry which at its core expresses that love has no colour, but that the colour of love abounds both around us and within us ALL, is a bias I'll admit to.

From a trainee apprentice human(e) being to other trainee apprentice human(e) beings:

I wish you, and one 'n' all L.O.V.E.

This article is based on an interview with Guy Chapman of the Off Pink Collective.

Coming Out

Eileen O'Connell

My initial reaction when I first came across lesbianism was 'Arghhh, how could my female friend have slept with a woman? How could she possibly have touched another woman's private parts?' Catholicism and sexism certainly had me brainwashed. I'd always seen women's bodies, including my own, as dirty and not very nice. I could never understand why men loved touching them. Luckily for me, my strong sense of curiosity overcame these prejudices, and I got to thinking and wondering what it would be like.

At this time I was married with two children, and wanting my freedom from the restraints of matrimony. I was very friendly with another married woman called Jenny. Jenny had two children and we both were childminders. Every Friday, Jenny would come over to my flat, leaving her husband to mind the children, and we would sit and get pissed together. Having opened my mind up to the possibility of sex with a woman, I began to realise that part of the bond between Jenny and I was of a sexual nature. Jenny also knew the friend that had come out to me, which meant we were both realising at the same time the sexual aspect of our close friendship. Soon there were sexual vibes flying all over the place. Looks and body language were rife, even when our respective husbands were around. It was very exciting, but also rather scary.

Nothing was ever said, but Jenny and I planned our escape from under the watchful eyes of husbands, to a caravan by the sea. We took our four children, plus two minded ones, all aged five and under. Once in the caravan I claimed the double bed as mine and Jenny's sleeping space and although she blushed, she did not object. We bought bottles of Vodka and Bacardi, and once the children were in bed we sat and drank, as was our way.

It was a strange week. We touched tentatively, both very innocent and shy in this new experience. Jenny was very frightened. I think she had always known that she was a dyke, but had desperately tried to conform. She knew that once she had experienced a woman there would be no turning back. She was right, and she and her husband split up in the next year.

Our relationship continued for a few more months. In the afternoons, we would try to frantically settle all the children in our care to go to sleep, and squeeze in a cuddle or two. One day we both looked at each other and said in amazement and unison, 'we have never kissed'. We soon broke the taboo and it was the most wonderful kiss I'd ever had, it was like I had never been kissed before.

Once Jenny had come out as a lesbian, she began to lay a lot of pressure on me to become one. I couldn't cope with this as I was splitting up from my own husband – although my marriage break-up was not about my sexuality, but my freedom to explore and grow as a person. My ex-husband just wanted me to be a housewife and mother, and I knew I could not stay in that role.

I split from my husband and went on to have more heterosexual relationships. I actually thought at this time that perhaps I was straight and that my relationship with Jenny had been a one-off. This seemed okay – and preferable – to me, as I knew being gay was not an easy choice. There was of course no obvious bisexual movement that might have helped me feel good, and supported my 'dodgy' sexuality.

I was wrong about being straight, and I went on to have another short-lived lesbian relationship with Cath. Then I met Jason, whom I lived with for two years. I was very confused about my sexuality around this time. When I was with a guy I would think I was straight and when I was with a woman I would seriously consider the possibility of being a lesbian. I knew nobody else who was bisexual, and consequently there was no support or validation, just an attitude from both gay and straight friends that I wanted my bread buttered on both sides.

My relationship with Jason came to an end, at least as a live-in lover, and he moved out. Just before he moved out I found myself feeling attracted to Cath again. We started to go out, even though I didn't want a commitment with her and she agreed to that. Jason stayed out of my life for a while, but then reappeared. I started going out with him again, but it was an open relationship. This did not suit Cath at all. I mean, I was really having my cake and eating it. I was being the true practising bisexual. I could not help but feel guilty, but what could I do? I was fond of both of them. I had not planned it. I did not want to make choices or long term commitments to either of them. Jason on the whole was quite reasonable about it, although I felt that it was partly because he found it erotic and a turn on. Then I really put the cat among the pigeons by unintentionally double-booking them. Unfortunately I was not there when they turned up on the doorstep together. You can imagine Cath's face. She apparently just turned and walked off. Cath made my name mud, and my sexuality. She also played on friends' negative attitudes about bisexuality. I was reeling and did not know which way to turn, especially as I had other problems to contend with at that time. I fled to Sheffield, relieved to leave the entire mess behind.

Once in Sheffield I resolved to join a bisexual group and sort this business out once and for all. I wanted to find the support of like-minded people. Luckily for me a group was just starting up. It was the saving of my sanity, as in London. I had begun to feel very isolated, and was beginning to seriously think I was abnormal. Now I am out to all my friends and family and am really proud. I feel really good and think bisexuality is the best thing since sliced bread.

Since then I have begun another relationship with a woman and I am currently still with her. There were problems initially, as she is a lesbian and had at one time been a separatist. She found the idea of my bisexuality threatening, and was sure I was really a dyke. However, she has come round to accepting my sexuality and even marched in the bisexual section of Gay Pride.

My children have always known about my bisexuality, as I have always been honest with them. They accept it and are very supportive, but I live in an area where many people are bigoted. Their school friends live locally and this means that when these friends are there, my partner and I have to be careful about how we act with each other. I am torn between wanting to be out and comfortable in my own home, and the awareness that this will cause problems for my sons at school. It does not seem fair to inflict this battle upon them, especially since they are 'mixed race' and already have to deal with racist attitudes. I have spoken to them, and they would prefer not to have to deal with homophobic attitudes at school, so in a sense I feel I have no choice.

The whole process of coming out has taken me twelve years. There is now a growing and more visible bisexual movement and I hope, as a result, that nobody will ever have to feel the isolation and negativity I went through before I came out. I was so proud and inspired to see so many of us on the Euro Pride march this year. Let us hope that next year there will be even more of us opening the closet doors.

My loving Mum

I have no memories of Eileen being anything but bisexual. It has made my life different in some ways. I feel that if all my friends knew that my mum was bisexual I would have no rest, especially if it got out in my school. I have to lie to some of my friends about when her female partner comes round to sleep, like where they sleep and who they are.

But I love my mum a lot and she can do anything she wants – apart from a few things like taking drugs, committing suicide and smoking. My mum is very kind, forgiving and peaceful. She lets me talk to her if I've got problems and she will always listen no matter what. She is firm but kind with it. I really love my mum so I'm not really that bothered she is bisexual.

Written by Casey Farquharson (age 12)
Eileen O'Connell's loving son

My Mum, for who she is

I am writing how I feel about my mum being bisexual. It has never affected or given me great reason for concern as my mum has always been open to me and my younger brother, showing us there is nothing wrong in what she is. I accept it is part of my mum's life and if she is happy about it, then so am I.

In brief, my mum has brought me up in an open caring way and given me a good start in life and taught me not to put people down for what ever they happen to be.

So I love my mum the way she is.

Alex Farquharson (age 16)

A partner's view point

When I first met Eileen, she said that she was bisexual and opened what I thought would be major complications. I felt unsure because of the word. I thought she would want a man as well, which was part of the myths that I associated with this word. I wanted Eileen to be a lesbian.

So we talked more and I listened to Eileen. I knew she had the scope to love female and male. My fears of Eileen going with a man or another woman began to fade. I have found that bisexuals can and do have monogamous relationships with either female or male. Through listening to Eileen I found a new understanding, and that my fears have been based upon prejudice. Being 'mixed race' and an incest survivor I know about prejudice. So I tend not to turn away or bring my prejudice with me. I have had enough of those to last a lifetime.

I am a lesbian and I am proud of having a relationship with Eileen; the warmth that I feel and the understanding we have makes it worthwhile. We get along like any other couple. We have our rows and laughs like any other. The only difference is we are both women, and one is bi and the other lesbian, no big deal except for other people. Talking to Eileen has made me look at myself and also look at issues which she has to face from other women and men.

To Eileen I give my love and support.

Goanita Jacques

It Could be Either

Marie King

Having lived my life for a number of years as a heterosexual and then for an equally long period as a lesbian, I have lately arrived at a kind of bisexual synthesis.

When I was growing up I didn't really know if I was a boy or a girl. I knew I was supposed to be a girl but somehow it wouldn't wash. I first became aware of this as a problem from the age of about five. I would stare anxiously at myself naked in the mirror, trying to convince myself that this was a girl's body. I worried that I didn't feel inside how other girls felt – not that I knew how they felt, but I was sure that I felt different. Perhaps it was something to do with the soppiness of other girls and the way they liked dolls and the colour pink. I was frightened because I knew that other children took their gender for granted and that this was expected.

I am the youngest of three daughters, so when I went to school I mixed with boys for the first time. I saw their penises and was fascinated by them. At home my sessions in front of the mirror took a new turn: I stuffed hankies down my knickers and strutted about, sexily thrusting my bulge out. I have never completely lost my taste for cross-dressing and even now wish I was rich and reckless enough to splash out on a man's made-to-measure three piece suit.

As I approached adolescence I got the idea that this would be a turning point and that it would become clear one way or the other which sex I really was. I got scared that I would actually turn into a boy, that I would grow a prick and my voice would break. How on earth would I explain this to my family? It was a great relief that this didn't in fact happen. However I did grow quite hairy and my periods were never regular, my hips not as wide nor my waist as narrow as a proper woman's are meant to be. So my uncertainty did not end, because I put this freakishness down to a lack of true womanhood.

Throughout childhood I had a series of close relationships with other girls. When I was eleven I went to a girls' grammar school in the nearest town and my best friend was Louise. I often went to Louise's house after school for tea. Afterwards we would go up to her room. One day we decided to emulate the fucking of adults that we had recently got very interested in. So we undressed and took it in turns to lie on top of each other and rubbed our cunts together. I learned much later that this act goes by the strange name of tribadism.

Louise and I enjoyed our experiments with tribadism and would no doubt have continued were it not for my wish to appear respectable. One break time we were hanging around with a group of girls when the talk turned to the subject of lesbians. I knew what lesbians were from my homophobic older sister, so was not surprised to hear my schoolmates discuss them with similar contempt and ridicule. It made me uncomfortable but I didn't know why, until Louise whispered horrifyingly loudly in my ear, 'That's what we are!' 'No we're not, no we're not', I hissed back. After that I refused to go to bed with her in spite of her entreaties. At fourteen, Louise left the school, but I didn't mind, because I had grown out of her by then and already replaced her with someone else.

Throughout my teens, I suffered daily the dread that no man would ever want me, because I thought myself hopelessly unattractive, as well as not being a proper girl. By night I was in the grip of a powerful longing: I would run my hands over my body, imagining a lover's hands, the empty aching feeling relieved only temporarily by masturbation. But much as I yearned for sex I was frightened of the prospect, and even after leaving home and spending three years at university I was still, to my great shame, a virgin. I would have given myself to a boy called James, but my love for him was unrequited. However whilst at university I met Maggie who was to have a great influence on the development of my sexuality.

I first saw Maggie sitting near the front of the lecture room that I entered at the beginning of my second year. When we met she had a steady boyfriend, but she had a chequered past and was to have a promiscuous future. She told me early on that she had had a baby at fifteen and also that she was bisexual. I admired her openness and wealth of experience, and hoped that some of it would rub off on me, which it did, thanks to Maggie's encouragement of my efforts to get laid. This culminated in her pushing me up the stairs at a party after a boy called Eric, slipping a packet of Durex into my jeans pocket as she did so. It was to Eric that I finally lost my virginity on the bottom bunk of the bunk beds that I shared with Maggie at that time. I later discovered that earlier in the evening Maggie and Eric had been screwing on the top bunk, but I didn't mind. On the contrary, in those days of making love not war, I was happy to have entered the adult world of sex at last. I was 21.

I felt I had a lot of catching up to do, so for the next few years I slept with any man who would have me. In spite of the discomfort of relationships going awry – which mine, being so indiscriminately chosen, frequently did – I was high on the knowledge that some men did, after all, find me attractive. But this happy discovery could not compensate for the fact that none of my affairs developed into the serious relationship to which I aspired.

During these years, my early twenties, I began to get involved in the women's movement. The second wave of feminism was sweeping the country and women's groups were springing up everywhere. I had always been politically minded (as a libertarian sort of leftie), but never politically active and now I welcomed the chance to work for something that I could really believe in: my own and my sisters' liberation.

I started attending regional and national women's conferences, where I first saw openly declared lesbians flaunting their sexuality or pouring their passions into political speeches on stage. I admired these women and felt drawn to them. Maggie and I took to wearing identical clothes and walking round holding hands. I wore a badge that challenged passers-by on their presumption of my heterosexuality (although in the circumstances they probably presumed no such thing). I allowed my affairs with men to fizzle out and spent a celibate year trying to decide what I wanted sexually. Of course, I wanted to sleep with a woman. But who? I didn't know any lesbians personally. In my women's group there were two or three women who identified as bisexual (the rest being heterosexual) but I ruled out those, like Maggie, whom I had known for years and whose friendship I did not want to disrupt. This only left a shady character called Paula, whom none of us knew much about. And it was Paula I propositioned one evening in my twenty-sixth year, while we were sitting on my bed getting stoned. We got into bed and my initial boldness immediately evaporated. I was so scared that sex was the last thing I felt like. Who was this woman anyway? Did I want to make love with her? I did not. But Paula was not a person to be put off easily. She spent most of the night grabbing at various bits of my body while I tried to fend her off. It was an inauspicious start to my sexual career with women, but strangely I was not daunted. In the morning I felt almost euphoric because I had overcome a major hurdle and somehow I knew that when I met the right woman everything would be all right.

And it was. Shortly afterwards I met Anne and embarked on what has so far been the happiest sexual relationship of my life. It didn't last long, but triggered a time of great change for me. Anne was an out dyke and a staunch feminist. She had no interest in men to speak of and through her I got more involved in feminism and met other lesbians. I felt the pressure to come out as a lesbian. Not that anyone said anything, but didn't I, after all, have a female lover? And wasn't anything else a cop-out? People whom I met as Anne's lover assumed, reasonably enough, that I was a lesbian, but this was unsettling as it did not correspond with my idea of myself. So I went through another period of confusion about my sexual identity, during which time I slept with an ex-boyfriend, Lenny.

I found that I preferred sex with Anne and I also found that I was pregnant. I was delighted: I was going to give birth to my child and love it and bring it up, hopefully with Anne's help. What was more, I at last had incontrovertible proof of true womanhood and this gave me deep satisfaction. However, at twelve weeks I had a miscarriage. I was very sad and cried a lot, but Anne was enormously supportive and I got over the loss. Although I knew miscarriage was common, I privately suspected that I was after all deficient in some magic female ingredient necessary to sustain pregnancy. During this time of transition I wondered if I should call myself bisexual, and scrutinised my own and society's prejudices against lesbians. This period lasted no longer than six months, and by the end of it I was calling myself a lesbian.

I moved with Anne to another city where there was a large lesbian ghetto and I worked in feminist groups and socialised almost exclusively with other lesbians. As a new girl in town I wanted to make friends, but the lesbian scene, especially for lesbian feminists, was riven by factional in-fighting. There were a number of political groups, each of which believed that their line was more feminist and therefore more politically correct than the others. It seemed socially necessary to align yourself with one of these groups, otherwise people tended to suspect you of being sympathetic towards their political rivals and to steer clear of you at best, attack you at worst. This usually took the form of character assassination, occasionally supplemented by attacks on property. It was a threatening atmosphere but I told myself that now I was a serious politico I couldn't expect a cushy life. I was at the forefront of the revolution and bound to get a few knocks. So I knuckled under, aligned myself with the 'radical lesbian feminists' and worked hard at my political correctness.

One idea that we thought a good one at the time was

non-monogamy. Anne and I both professed to believe in it, but when the crunch came I found I was on my own. I was approached by another woman, a mutual friend of ours, and because I was in the habit of sleeping with anyone who asked me I started an affair with her. This led to a painful break-up with Anne. Not long afterwards my affair with the no longer mutual friend also disintegrated.

In the ensuing years I slept around with women much as I had done with men in my heterosexual days. At this time I thought of myself as a true lesbian and couldn't imagine going back to men. I didn't want to: women were my whole world and with them I lived, loved and worked. Work centred around the local Rape Crisis Centre where I was a volunteer counsellor. Here I met Cass. The first time Cass and I sat down to talk we didn't stop till 4 a.m. and I wasn't even particularly tired. We seemed to have a reviving effect on each other, based on an immediate and profound rapport such as I have never experienced before or since. Cass wanted to sleep with me, but I didn't fancy her because she was fat and I thought she was ugly. I felt sorry for her, so I did sleep with her a couple of times, then I intended to stop. But somehow I couldn't extricate myself. During my feminist apprentice-ship I had learned what seemed to be one of the central tenets of feminist belief: the general theory of the moral superiority of the oppressed, which now became the justification for my relationship with Cass. She impressed upon me how much more oppressed than me, being fat, she was, and that I was at fault, because my vision was twisted by patriarchal notions of beauty, currently thin. Clearly it was my duty to stay with her until she no longer had need of me. This turned out to be two and a half years later, when Cass emigrated to America to join the Fat Liberationists. By the time she left I was severely depressed: I had lost my sense of will and, in part, my sense of self.

I moved down to London and from here I viewed the lesbian ghetto as my prison and my relationship with Cass as the cell in which I had been chained. I rejoiced in my new freedom, but carried the scars of bondage. I was terrified of any further sexual involvement and during the next ten years I had only three brief affairs. During this time I steered clear of anything resembling politics and was drawn instead to a more spiritual outlook on life. In my efforts to recover my lost sense of self I came to question the most fundamental aspects of my existence, and this of course included my sexuality. I gradually became aware that the lesbian me was no more definitive than the heterosexual me and that I encompassed both these aspects. Now, approaching forty, I say if asked that I am bisexual. I feel ready now for a committed relationship but as to the sex of any future lover of mine, it could be either.

Bisexuality and Spirituality

Kelly Drake

Bisexuality has been liberating for me, yet to assume that this is 'it' stops the journey. It reminds me that it is unwise for me to sit on my laurels and believe that what I have done is ever enough. When we move from the conventional script we are developing ideas for our 'quest plot' – our life journey discovering and unveiling our personal truths, values and beliefs.

'Quest plot' may have the ring of Star Trek, and boldly going where no wo/man has gone before. However it seems to me that is important to analyse what this might have to offer us.

The notion of a 'quest plot' relates to the idea of recreating ourselves from scratch; to develop individual and collective thinking, ethics, values and culture. For me this has been a process of stepping out and away from my conventional bounds, going to a place I have never been before.

What I contemplate when I make this great leap of faith into my quest plot, is a void, a space. I do not necessarily know where I am going, or how to get there, but I feel and know that I do not want to stay where I am. This notion can be attached to any situation – political activism, sexuality and the erotic, relationships, community building etc.

What we are doing, is daring to have a vision of what we would like our lives to be, what we want for others, and the planet. The notion of a bisexual vision is as wide as the multitudinous answers to the question of 'what is bisexuality?', and in this quest plot lifestyle we are going to be faced with challenges to our vision; our courage, endurance, and faith will continually be called into question.

For me, it was through the yearnings of my spirituality, that I saw bisexuality as a path to explore. Somewhere, very deep inside myself I felt that the possibility of being able to create erotic, intimate, personal, sexual, political – indeed *any* relationship – whatever the genders involved, was the basis of my sexuality and spirituality. In this deep level of faith, awareness, knowing – whatever the label – I have believed that way back in the past, men and women were able to arrange their lives just how they wanted. Inherent in this faith is my belief that people were bisexual, and not so split within themselves as we are today. My vision, as a bisexual feminist activist, is one where our sexual energies can flow freely around an infinite spectrum of possibilities. My vision is one where we do not have to waste our very precious energy suppressing our or other people's sexuality, and acting out pre-ordained gender roles that we did not ever have a hand in choosing!

I need to feel good about my daring to have a vision of the way I would like my life to be, but I have noticed that I have often felt alone and a fearful intimacy with the unknown. This feels like being deserted, and going on a journey into darkness. It is my belief that my faith or vision keeps me in this space, and binds me to my journey. Somehow I have known that the fear in me is part of the journey, the path to be travelled, and even when I have wanted to stray off or back, I have not been able to do so. My vision has taken over from the fear, and led me gently through the rocky parts. My faith in me is a candle that glows very bright at times, and sometimes is only a faint dot, and very often I have felt that She has left me. This has felt like the cave experience – trying to navigate a path in darkness with no map, just relying on my senses that I was born with, and trusting with my heart.

On this journey, I think that it is very important to create my own labels for myself as references, at different times. Some bisexuals reject labels; however, it seems important to me in 90s Britain to re-claim labels and names and turn them on their head. This has always been intrinsic to feminist activism! To me, being *queer* is something to be proud of. It signifies that I am different, while simultaneously I am the same as everyone – I am a human being. I use labels as a sign-post to challenge and compare experiences I have, and those that happen around me. Obviously identity is never static – the Kelly that wrote yesterday, is not necessarily the Kelly that reads today – but understanding this helps me to cope with the dilemmas of a fluid identity, and a co-existing fluid sexuality.

As a bisexual woman, I often feel very hopeless and helpless about the way I am treated and victimised. And of course, this is exactly the way 'they' want me to feel. I am always trying to subvert this feeling, and it is a hard process to wade through at times. I am trying to connect and network with others, I am going to bisexual, lesbian and gay gatherings, political action, groups etc. I am writing this paper and thinking my passionate thoughts about politics – all this subverts the system. I am trying to turn my disappointment into a force that does not feed off me and other allies, and I am trying to use it to liberate, rather than incarcerate.

All of us bisexuals are rocking the boat, just by being who we are. Some of us choose to do this within the system, and live with the inherent dilemmas this brings. Bisexuality is not new, nothing under the sun is, however it is a powerful place to be in to challenge the 'authorities' that seek to bind us. I believe that we are all in this one together, whatever our differences, and in re-creating a bisexual movement, you and me are being passionately subversive.

Afterword, February 1995: My journey continued ... and three years on I'm a proud dyke; powerful, passionate and excited about who I am today.

Marriage and Bisexuality

Felicity Cade

Marriage has been defined as 'a solemn state of holy matrimony binding one woman to one man ... for richer for poorer, till death do [them] part'. It sounds a very long way from freedom-loving bisexuals, promiscuous, unsure of the gender of their next lover. Both are stereotypes of course; most marriages and most bisexuals are not like this in 1990s Europe.

I am a happily married bisexual feminist with other lovers of both genders, and playmates whose gender I would not dare to predict. I got married because I loved the man I had been living with for the previous few years, and we trusted each other not to change our attitudes towards monogamy and housework on account of a piece of paper. I wanted to prove to myself and to him and to the world that I wasn't going to 'come to my senses' and go off with a richer man, as he thought I should, or become a lesbian, as some lesbians thought I would. One lesbian tried to tell me that bisexuality was just a phase I was going through – she'd seen it loads of times before and I'd end up a lesbian. I pointed out that I found it offensive to be told my sexuality was only a passing phase, and that lesbians had been told the same thing themselves, being offended in their turn. She assured me she was right in her prediction and gave me a job in a women-only building. Still, I can't believe all men are the enemy, every single one of them, all the time. Equally, I cannot accept the converse, that all women are on my side – though this is not so widely heard in these post-Thatcher times. I find good and bad in each gender, and an a-mazing (i.e. de-mystifying, following Mary Daly's usage) amount of similarity between heterosexual and homosexual relationships – jealousy and possessiveness, caring and wanting to belong are not confined by sexual orientation.

Marriage for me is not about faithfulness to my spouse, or joint bank accounts or children. We don't have any of these things and that seems to be at the root of our success as a partnership. His recipe for

114

happiness in marriage is for a man to get a wife with the same taste in women as himself. Now we share female lovers and live in a house of eight people and five cats. One of our lovers is married too, has four children and thought she was heterosexual, now she's not so sure. I explained to her that I'm a heterosexual-identified bisexual, and I'm not the only one.

According to the state and my biological family, we were married in a registry office. I am Jewish, with Pagan leanings. My husband is of no fixed religion, though he has been known to pray to 'The Occupier'. According to us, we were married a couple of days later than that, in a ceremony devised by a friend of ours, a Pagan priestess. She married us in her garden with cakes and ale and sacred rope to bind us, surrounded by our friends. She conducted the service in the name of the Old Religion, calling on the powers of the four quarters and five elements, and not in the name of a particularly deity. She removed vows on monogamy from the ceremony at our request, replacing them with vows of openness, honesty, respect and friendship towards each other. The very idea that one person would be sexually fulfilling enough for the rest of our lives was as unthinkable as the idea that one person could supply all our needs in any other area of life. On the other hand, we loved each other and do so still, and see ourselves as a couple for the rest of our lives.

It was not always this way. People were not expected before to sever all ties with family and friends, buy a new house and move to a new area when they got married. The extended family was their safety-net and we have created our own around us, fellow computer-nuts and cat-lovers, older and younger people, a whole group who have chosen to live together and relate to each other in various ways. I recognise that this may not always be right for me either; communal living does have its drawbacks, and I may move back to just living with my husband as a couple, now that we both use electronic mail and computer conferencing from home to keep in touch with the wider world. Most of my other lovers live outside my household, staying in touch by visit, post, phone and increasingly by electronic communication. My marriage is a bedrock, a firm foundation from which I can explore the world. I don't depend on my husband financially. I retain my independence, secure in the knowledge that I am loved. It does not restrict me in who else I choose to love. I can explore different facets of what I want from relationships with different people. For example, an interest in sado-masochism can be treated within several relationships without leading to the demise of any, unlike some rigid couple structures, where one person wanting to play a role that a companion could not reciprocate has been a real problem. I have several people that I play SM scenes with, sometimes taking one role, sometimes another, without feeling that it *has* to be always one way. Starting from a baseline of being happily married, I know and make it clear to others that additional relationships are secondary to our marriage, not a replacement for it. I find it easier to explain to third parties that we are committed to each other by our vows and by our love for each other, but this is truly not exclusive, for either of us. As I heard one newly-wed remark, 'I know my wife has enough love for more than one person.' This is how we are too. Many people presume that only one of us is free to seek other partners, or that the 'open marriage' is a much-touted theory, which does not carry through into fact, but it has done so for us.

I should not like to give the impression that all bisexuals want relationships concurrently with men and women and will feel unfulfilled with one partner. This is not the case. Many of us call ourselves bisexual because we feel some attraction to both men and women, and are quite happy with one person, just as a heterosexual does not desire all people of the opposite sex. Nor do I believe that marriage is right for everyone. Many people are happier in larger groups, or looser bonds, or on their own, and this should be respected and sanctioned by society at large. I value my unmarried friends and lovers as individuals, and as an alternative to the couple-clique which society tries to impose on us.

As someone attracted to people of both sexes, a feminist, and an activist for the rights of people with disabilities, I have been a member of the bisexual community in London for many years, attending meetings and conferences in London and elsewhere. I remember especially a bisexual women's conference in 1992 with a workshop for married women. Primarily, there was a sense of relief that there were others like ourselves. Many of those active within the bisexual community come from the lesbian and gay communities, and as the majority grouping, certainly in terms of visibility, they can be rather overwhelming, leaving others feeling isolated. At a previous mixed bisexual conference in 1991, which had a workshop for women only on feminism, a married woman got upset, as she thought she was the only one in the room. In fact, many of the women present were married, but it is easy, in such a diverse movement, to feel as she did, that our issues are not being addressed and that we are not visible.

The general consensus at the married women's workshop seemed to be that same-sex relationships did not affect marriage vows in the same way that different-sex ones did, that to 'go with' another man was adultery and could seriously affect the marriage, depending on prior agreements, whereas heterosexual husbands regarded another woman as different, even welcome. Understandably, bisexual husbands were the most likely to be happy about non-monogamy, as it also opened up opportunities for them to have relationships with other men. However, many women feel anger and pain that relationships with other women are not taken seriously by men, who expect the threesomes so common in pornography. Some bisexuals may want this, others find the idea offensive and maintain separate relationships with male and female lovers.

Most of the women at the workshop agreed that marriage does not necessarily affect our politics, or cause us to support the state in everything it does in our name. We can still be resolutely opposed to the oppression of women and minorities. To me, those who are different from the crowd are my people. As a tiny minority within a minority it would be strange if it were otherwise. As sexual minorities, we have many areas of common interest, not least the efforts of government to intervene in our lives. The very idea that I can marry a man but not a woman is offensive to me. I believe that people should be allowed to pair-bond as they choose, and I have friends who have conducted their own Pagan ceremonies for their homosexual relationships. The fact that these unions are not recognised by the state does not lead me to conclude that I should stay away from state marriage. It does encourage me to show what can be done within it, so that its benefits can be available to all.

People think married bisexuals can vanish within the heterosexual community any time we choose, and to a certain extent this is true, but only at the cost of burying our true selves. Many people can 'pass as normal', but this can cause more distress than satisfaction, for example, when people deny that others are members of a minority group on the basis of appearance. I know people who think I am not a feminist because I have long hair. Others tell me, 'You don't look Jewish, you can't be Jewish.' People are a lot more complicated than the simple stereotypes. I worked in a voluntary group putting books on tape for blind feminists and lesbians for many years. This work was necessary because statutory authorities could not believe such people as blind lesbians and feminists existed.

At the 1994 bisexual conference, which was mixed, it was clear that the space for married bisexual feminists within the feminist movement had still not been established. One woman at a workshop on marriage said she found it harder to come out to other feminists as married than it was to come out to them as bisexual. Within the bisexual community there is not the same hostility, it is more a question of invisibility. Whereas, within the community at large, a bisexual is commonly seen as a married man 'cheating' on his wife, among bisexuals in the movement, the stereotype is lesbian or gay-identified, but still recognising the possibility of a heterosexual encounter. The married bisexual tends to be the converse of this – heterosexual-identified but recognising the possibility of homosexual encounters.

It is my belief that marriage answers a need within people, the need to find rites of passage and rituals that affirm our lives, to ourselves and to those around us. It does not have to be tied to a particular lifestyle. It is up to the individuals concerned to make it fit them, rather than the other way round. To paraphrase Hillel: 'Were people made for marriage or marriage for people?' To abandon the whole thing because we do not like what others have done to it is to lose the opportunity to remake it in our own image, and show others how it can be expanded.

Against Marriage

Sharon Rose

For three years after joining the Women's Liberation Movement and calling myself a radical feminist, I lackadaisically thought that I would probably get married one day, if only to keep my parents happy ... if only there were a suitable candidate, which there never was. Then gradually I began to realise that I couldn't be against patriarchy, against the state, and against religion, and still be prepared to go through a ritual which represents the summit of patriarchal, religious and state interference in peoples' lives.

I was brought up in a religious Jewish family where even the most commonplace actions – eating an apple, buying new shoes – are accompanied by religious ritual. I was confused about my sexuality as soon as I was aware of it. Perhaps as a result I developed, at an early age, a burning resentment of any demand for unquestioning obedience. And make no mistake, society's demand that we should all be married is very heavy indeed. When my partner and I had our child 'out of wedlock', as it is so appropriately called, my 85-year-old uncle did not speak to my father (his 75-year-old brother) for a year, because, not only was he unable to 'exert his influence on us' to marry, he was also unwilling to do so.

I fail to understand how supporters of marriage can argue that marriage is no big deal, and does not make a difference anyway, when all I hear from them is the many benefits of marriage. Sorry folks, you can't have it both ways. I know people who have got married to please their families (lots), to secure family inheritance (which is what it was all about in the first place), to keep a partner in the country (understandable, but in this case try and marry someone with whom you are not involved), or to prop up a fading relationship. (How many couples do you know who have been co-habiting happily for years, who suddenly announce they are getting married 'to affirm our commitment to each other', only to split up not long after? I know several – and they never send the presents back.) All of these reasons, and many others, illustrate the fact that marriage is a very significant institution in our society for keeping individuals in their place. If it were not, why would the state prosecute bigamists? It doesn't prosecute the married man (they always seem to be men) who maintains a mistress, sometimes with children, in another abode, even though the situations are structurally identical.

Of course there are good human reasons for wishing to make a public statement of your love for another person, and though I have been thoroughly inoculated against ritual myself, it obviously plays an important role in many people's lives. But in that case, why do almost all the pagans, humanists and secularists who organise their own ceremonies, also find it necessary to nip down to the registry office for a quick (average 8 minutes) rubber stamp from the state?

I don't believe the answer lies in a desire to get entangled in a bureaucracy from which it takes a minimum of two years to get disentangled. Rather, I think that what motivates people to get married is their desire, however subconscious, to equip themselves with possibly the most important accessory of the modern marriage ceremony – a certificate of straightness. Getting married is a very public statement of your heterosexuality, and indeed of your intention to remain faithful to this one particular individual. Looking at the issue from this perspective was what finally allowed me to make the connection between my opposition to marriage and my bisexuality. For years I had been arguing the anti-patriarchal, anti-religious, basic radical feminist line against marriage, arguing also that it was a betrayal of my lesbian and gay comrades, who had no such option of having the state acknowledging their unions, as they could never present themselves as heterosexual. (I understand why some lesbians and gay men sincerely believe that state recognition of their relationships would be a benefit, but I disagree politically and strategically with this position. Civil and legal rights should be available to everybody as autonomous individuals and members of society. And it is surely not wise, anyway, to seek legal status for oneself by reference to one's relationship with somebody else. In seeking recognition for lesbian and gay relationships from religion and state, people are seeking dignity; but you cannot demand of others to grant you dignity, you must claim it for yourself from within your own heart and mind.)

Having argued the intellectual position for so long, I eventually realised that, in my heart, I could never make myself get married. The very thought of it made me feel ill, because, even though I currently live with a man, and look forward to doing so for many years, I do not, and never have, felt myself to be heterosexual. My first loyalty is to women, and the biggest betrayal of all would be to myself, if I were to publicly deny my deepest identity in favour of tying myself officially to a man, any man, even one so lovable and kind as my partner. We will stay together as long as it makes sense for us, not because of any artificially applied external circumstance. I appreciate the irony that to many people my lifestyle looks rather conventional (though this was certainly not of my choosing, but the result of 15 years of Thatcherism). All I can say is that I feel as if I am passing, anyway, which is not a situation I feel at all comfortable with. It would be so much worse if I were openly denying the most fundamental part of who I am.

The Hasbians

Meg Clarion

My lesbians-coming-out-as-bisexual support group started in April 1988 with a meeting in my living room. There were five of us at that first meeting, nine at the last, with many faces seen only once and several anonymous inquiries over the phone from lesbians who hesitate to leave the fold, with good reason.

Vanessa's first sexual experiences were with women. She came out as a lesbian at age eighteen, about ten years ago. She wasn't interested in men or attracted to men until recently and now her whole world's turned around. She feels very little acceptance from her lesbian friends and is angry about it.

> This is my first relationship with a man ever. It's a blast. I'm having a great time. I'm kind of afraid I'll just go live a straight lifestyle now. If I'm interested in having a long-term monogamous relationship, then I feel like I'm forced to choose whether I'll be straight or gay, one or the other.
> I'm feeling really cynical about the lesbian community lately. If my friends can't be there for me any more because I have a male lover, then who needs 'em. I'm still the same person. I haven't changed. In fact, I'm really happy in this relationship. But the non-acceptance hurts too much. I don't want to be around lesbians at all right now because it's hard for me to accept myself when the people I thought were my friends are being so judgemental. It's too painful seeing the community I can't be a part of.

Rene identified as a lesbian for about six years. She met and became involved with Miguel about three years ago and spent time with him separate from her women friends.

> I became pregnant and knew that I wanted to have a child. Miguel and I were clear about not wanting to live together or get married, but to continue our relationship and to coparent Daniel.
> I looked into joining a lesbian mothers' support group because I was

122

still very connected to the women's community, but that didn't feel quite right. Many women there were looking into how to get sperm or find positive male role models for their children. Since my relationship with Miguel was intact my concerns were elsewhere. I'm now involved in a single mothers' group that better meets my needs as a parent and where I don't have to explain myself.

Ellen was a very politically active lesbian feminist for over ten years. Her whole life was politicised. But now coming out as a bisexual she feels like hiding.

I just want to be. Be myself, do what I want to do because I want to do it. No deep meaning. No justification to anyone else. I feel interested in certain men. I think I may want to be sexual with them. I can't get into flirting though and it seems expected. I want him to like me for me. Not because I can be sweet or cute or flirtatious. I want to be taken seriously.

She went to Mexico for a few months to study Spanish and hoped to explore sex with men. Leaving the community where she lives seems to be the safest way to test the waters. This way her lesbian friends can't see what she's doing and no one in Mexico knows her history. She can just be herself and do as she pleases. Sandy kept quiet about her relationship with Joel until he was killed in an accident. Through her grieving she came out to her lesbian friends, some of whom were critical or judgmental. Several times she fought the urge to become involved with men in order to keep her place in the lesbian community.

I told myself 'You don't really want to sleep with him. You're a lesbian, remember?' and I'd stuff down my feelings 'til eventually they went away and I'd say 'Phew, I got over that one. It was just a phase.' But how many times have I done that? After a while it just didn't make sense anymore. It's been two years since Joel died and I haven't been sexual with a man since then. I know I could still call myself a lesbian and think 'Okay, so I slipped up once, but I don't want to live like that.'
Calling myself bisexual is as political as calling myself a lesbian was. I want all my close friends to know that I'm bi and I want to be accepted as I am. If someone can't handle that then I'm not going to put a lot of energy into a friendship with them. No more hiding. I refuse.

Fran identified as a lesbian throughout most of the 1970s, then decided that the label bisexual fit her better. As a feminist, whether lesbian or bi, she likes her independence, freedom and rebelliousness. She's rebellious against society at large and men in particular, in that she's not here to make men happy.

I'm independent of what asshole men want from me and think about me. You don't like my hairy legs? I don't care. I'm not making my life miserable trying to please you.

The men she dates aren't interested in her for her clothes, her make-up, her legs, her jewellery or her hairdo. They're interested in her as a person.

I've always felt like an observer among straight people – not fitting in, not conforming. I've felt like an imposter among lesbians. This isn't quite me, but it's a lot closer than the straight crowd. When I'm seeing a man I still go to parties with my lesbian friends, but I don't bring him along, don't mention my relationship and keep my thoughts to myself when remarks are made about women who sleep with men.

Meg: I came out as a lesbian in 1980 because I'd had it with men. Some of those I'd trusted I'd found were untrustworthy and I couldn't seem to figure out how to tell who was and who wasn't. In my anger I was emerging as a feminist activist and soon discovered that many of my new friends were lesbians. One of them came on to me. I came out with a bang. I was 21. I began organising in the lesbian community and instantly found 200 new friends welcoming me with open arms. I considered myself a separatist. I wore proper 'dyke attire'. I became a vegetarian. I discovered women's music. I organised women-only events. I put down women who called themselves bisexual. I went to the women's bar. I went to the Michigan Womyn's Music Festival and to the Women's Pentagon Action, to the Peace Encampment and to Gay Pride. I moved in with my lover after three months. We were sexual for another three months then trauma over the abuse in my past caught up with me. Bang. I had hoped that because my lover had no penis that sex would be easy. It wasn't. When after two years she left me, partly because we hadn't had sex in a year and a half, I decided it was time to take a look at this. I found out that having women lovers wasn't the solution to my original problem.

In the lesbian community I found a safe place to express my anger and I found the support I needed to discover a love for myself and other women. I also found out that my feminism was strong even when I wasn't angry. It was the foundation for my way of moving around in the world. And I found out that women's culture was my culture and the women's community was my community. The four years I spent as a lesbian were happy and empowering. I gained a lot of strength during that time and knew what it meant to have a family again.

Rene: I had been part of a women's community long enough to know that bisexual women weren't always trusted or welcome, were trashed and put down and if they had any sense they hid the fact that they slept with men, were attracted to men, 'left you for a man'. I have felt guilty and like a traitor for deciding to be sexual with men.

Sandy: It wasn't an easy decision. I can fight the urge to become involved with someone in order to keep my community and maybe that's okay the first time I meet a man I'm attracted to, but how many times can I do that? After a while it just doesn't make sense anymore.

Vanessa: It's not just sex with men, it's intimacy. Can I be a feminist and still like men? You wrestle with that some when your whole life has been lived in lesbian space for some years. Sure, plenty of lesbians know men, have male friends, but a male lover – that's taking things a bit too far.

Meg: For me it's not just any man who I'd consider sleeping with. I'm pretty picky. There are very few men who I'd let get that close to me. He's got to understand feminism and be committed to equality before I'd even consider a relationship. And he has to communicate well and be willing to cry. That's where I am around intimacy with men. Sex with men is something else altogether. There are men I know and trust who I might be sexual with once in a while with no commitments and no obligations. That can be fun. There are things I like about sex with men although fucking isn't one of them. I like being with someone who's bigger than me and solid. I like men's hairy chests and beards. And I like gentleness in a man. Sex with my male lover is really different from sex with my woman lover.

Ellen: My own radical politics were shaken a lot when I first came out as bisexual. There's not just a pro-female message in lesbian feminism. There's also an anti-male message that I started rejecting when I became open to men again. The transition was hard to reconcile.

Fran: I feel that sex and passion lasts longer in relationships with men. There's no room for femininity or being sexy in politically correct relationships. That really gets in the way of pursuit or desire. I got tired of lesbian bed death.

The group recently celebrated its fourth anniversary. We've seen each other through so much. We're all in very different places now than we were when we started to meet. Talking with other formerly lesbian identified bisexuals has helped us grow in our friendships and relationships, and has fostered clarity and self acceptance around our bisexuality.

Living with the Janus People

Dave Stone

Life as it is lived cannot be described in sequential terms. Memory is chaotic by its very nature; image and incident impacting, interacting, resonating in new and unexpected forms ... so that the recollected wet crunch as a leg shatters under motorwheels can leave you pretty much unaffected, while the way the sunlight shines through a certain window can have you shaking and jerking and slamming your mouth into a wall.

Autobiography is just the act of putting the pieces in the right order and shining the best possible light upon them ... and that's a game I'm not going to play. The following slices can and should be read in any order: each composite leaving a different impression, some new emphasis, just like real life. The appropriation of the Janus head as a metaphor for bisexuality tends to miss the point that rather than being a simple duality, Janus has two, or four, or any number of faces.

Pick a number. Any number.

Sticky Labels

I never really thought of myself as anything: I identified as bisexual in a general sense, I suppose – but that was something people like David Bowie were, something that had nothing to do with people like me no matter how much one liked dragging up for the Rocky Horror parties. And I certainly wasn't gay: why, I fancied *women*!

After breaking with Jacqui and a few minor flings with no one in particular, I took up with a Telecom technician, Susan, in the sort of unforced and utterly natural progression where you wake up one day and realise you're living with someone you love, without ever quite knowing how it happened.

I was still seeing men: like the way cigarette smoke feels in your lungs, there's nothing quite like it and you *miss* it when it's gone. After we were living together things became more circumspect – an occasional boys' night out while she went off with her own friends. I got my comeuppance, of course, when said friends decided to check out a disco-pub for a laugh ...

Things fell apart. My duplicity was a major factor, but we limped along for a while and it was more my depressive mood swings that finally put an end to it.

I was oscillating between design work and writing and abject unemployment, finally finding a job as an ad creative in Norwich. There, I lived for a while with an older, cloney gay, Michael, in what I gather is a pretty standard arrangement: the initial intensity devolving into a sort of loose, friendly partnership where we both mostly did our own thing. Strangely, sleeping with other men was never an issue; trying and failing miserably to pick up women *was*.

I couldn't see why. I'd never developed a gay sensibility, and was entirely uninterested in acquiring one – looking back, there was an element of denial in this, a flat unconscious refusal to accept that I was gay, rather than someone who just sort of slept with men.

The recurring death dream; I've had it before – lying on a sofa under an eiderdown, pneumonia gritty eating my lungs:

A black iron machine hanging in a hot red sky: the machine is me and as I try to comprehend its vast internal maze of conduits I go crazy and I start to scream ...

Sand dunes under a big summer sky. A blonde and beautiful child, a girl, reaches out to me, offering a clump of tiny, pale blue flowers.

Big white light blasts over me, filling my whole field of vision and –

Big Light Coming Down

The victim inside me gives me something that I need, in the same way as I need food or air. I have confused teenchild memories, miraculous flare-beacons in a cold black past, of a couple who used me – contemporary photos show a timid, bemused, girlish boy now lost and gone: a sense of wounded vulnerability that I can only assume triggered some predatory hunter-reflex. It certainly wasn't anything to do with *my* matchless charm.

It's happened with others since (just occasionally and God alone knows how) but the depth of surrender is diminished: the loss of some inner visual purple.

My fantasies are rich in mutilation: immobilised and powerless I am shredded by some purring savage force. Something inside cries out to be abused: I *need* to be abused, to freefall into that calm and silent state where the fight and the flight and the fear go away, and everything is still.

I'm incapable of taking a dominant role; I've tried and failed miserably. In the submissive, I've found basic but satisfying scenarios. I don't know why I want this now. I don't care. I dream about it. And I think about it. And it's what I want.

Fuck These People!

I've always had a soft spot for the bastard Don John. In his definitive speech: 'I cannot hide what I am ...', he effectively sticks a couple of fingers up at the saccharine piety of Leonato's court, and subsequent events are more the result of the hypocrisy of others than of his own frankly villainous involvement. (And for the literately-challenged, we are of course talking about Shakespeare's seminal tragicomedy, *Whoops, There Goe my Pantaloons*.)

Like that nifty Beatrice/Benedick sub-plot which has served as the template for every will-they-won't-they scenario since, this is as relevant now as then: we are all of us forced into roles we don't want, must walk the walk and talk the talk or must necessarily take a villainous stance.

Bisexuals, to hear some tell it, far from being the slavering libidinous monsters of popular report, are generally sophisticated and kind, with a relaxed and open attitude to non-hierarchical, non-gender-orientated relationships in a mutually-supportive environment and stuff.

Oh what a relief. Heaven forfend that sex might be dirty and humiliating and fun. This is the sort of superannuated hippie shit that makes us the laughing-stock of the gay world, and quite right too. Am I alone in having to bite back howls of derisory laughter as some laid-back New Age twat goes on about his 'rainbow politics' all the while making that little quote-mark gesture with his fingers? Probably.

We do not do this thing through choice; we do this because we are driven. Unlike Scientology, or Stalinism, or Radical Lesbian Separatism, which are other-directed and negate the self, Bisexuality is an *expression* of self.

We are all of us equal and different and existing – and any putative movement must be founded upon that fact, rather than an attempt to impose some arbitrary set of social values. Empathy is not the specious mouthing of the right noises learnt by rote, it is the natural product of a generous heart.

In the narrow terms of the intolerant we are perverts – and to protest that we're not is to accept those terms. Might I instead suggest the considered and reasonable response of: fuck off and die.

We are the people people warned us against, and we should be revelling in it.

Alphomega

We moved to Suffolk when I was six: a field with a housing estate in it where chartered accountants came to die. When I was fifteen, the second-nearest pub was the local gay bar, run I think by a transsexual and her partner ... and until about eighteen I was, I suppose, a sort of H.O.-gauge rent boy.

That sounds more intense than it really was: I just had a lot of drinks and food and cigarettes bought for me, and I was too dumb and gauche to say no. There was no particular trauma or pleasure: things happened and I coasted without much caring either way.

Simultaneously, I was going through your basic adolescent mill of peer-pressure and desperation and sweaty, clumsy fumbling, culminating in a miserable two-year engagement to Jacqui, who was pretty near as neurotic and bleakly depressive as myself – a relationship sustained only by my knack for faking nervous breakdowns at the drop of an ultimatum, and which fell apart spectacularly one Christmas eve when I broke down for real. (Years later, incidentally, when I was out as gay and we met again by chance in Romford, she was a happy and enthusiastic dyke. I would never dare draw any conclusion from this.)

Nineteen now, going through a Mickey-Mouse provincial art college and sleeping mostly on long-suffering friends' floors, I found myself gravitating towards the minimal gay scene. These people were utterly different from the predators I'd encountered before, more-or-less my own *age* for one thing ... and found myself sweating and nervous and tongue-tied. It had started mattering.

GROWLP!

I first came rubbing against my mattress, animalistic – a particularly dense child who hadn't worked out the mechanics of masturbation. Fantasy idealised images of the cousin I was determined to marry when I was old enough (and later, tongue-tied at family get-togethers, I would sit between splayed plump thighs and press my neck into warmth while shuddering adults tried to work out how to stop me without actually *saying* anything ...)

She had straight and jet-black hair, I think, in my mind.

My first real stand-up get-down actual **SEX** happened about six years later: a pub and flush with Saturday-job beer, and fifteen years of heterosexual programming went out the window.

Stubble and a transit van, spit and cool-cold cold cream and apparently I had a big fat cock and that's good and so so good but I didn't have much to do with it.

For months I stuffed wads of toilet tissue up myself on a two-hourly basis. I still do it, occasionally.

Descending

Twenty-five was almost ridiculously late to be coming out as Gay with a capital, and for a while I went a little crazy making up for lost time – and here, dear reader, we draw a discreet veil over the proceedings: self-honesty has limits, and so does propriety ... It didn't last. The price, the subsumation of self, was too high and by twenty-seven the basic sense of ambivalent alienation had resurfaced with a vengeance: the dawning realisation that I'd just painted myself into a corner yet again. Trapped in a profit-driven, image-orientated sub-culture that was anathema to me: I'd treated too many people like shit, run my *ingénu* routine one too many times, and nothing enough. Nothing was *ever* enough.

Those who truly tend towards the suicidal know that it isn't about jumping out at people with a couple of carefully-slashed wrists and shouting: look what *I*'ve done. It's more a sort of bored, Sunday-afternoon feeling where you think: yeah, well, maybe it's time to switch it off. It's no big deal. You don't really care much either way.

It was in this general frame of mind, on a Tuesday, idly flipping through a two-week-old *Time Out*, that I came upon a listing for Bisexuals at Partners. Yeah, well. I wasn't doing much else, so maybe I should check it out.

And sometimes people wear their scars lightly; people who are healed and well, who know how to deal with frightened children who find themselves turning into monsters and don't know why. Who take in strays, and feed them until they can run again, and then they let them go.

Miracles happen. Miracles happen all the time, and most of them are other people.

It's like gazing absently through a train window as you pull out of the city in the dead grey rain. Sunlight bursts through a gap in the cloud-cover, briefly illuminating a landscape with a hard-edged, coruscating clarity.

Nothing has changed, but suddenly, in spite of everything and against all expectation, it can just be a beautiful world.

Endpoint

The problem with running the edited highlights is that it distorts the picture: you don't get the breakdowns and the crying-jags and the long nights in, let alone the tedious business of eating and sleeping and working for a living that makes up the vast majority of any life.

Re-reading this, the main impression is one of abject confusion, the desperate search for some emotional Grail, something other and outside that will somehow make the pain go away and make us whole. Be warned: grailquests come to nothing. They're metaphors for the futility of life with a capital F, or the process of finding the light inside yourself.

We must shift the emphasis, focus not upon the end of life – which is just death, after all – but upon the act of living. We must delight in the infinite, exuberant variety of those around us rather than fixate upon the specifics any of one variation.

This is what bi can be, both as a movement or a state of being. In any given gathering of bisexuals you'll find gays who aren't fanatic about it, straights dragged along by their girlfriends, physical lesbians, transvestites, transsexuals, SM doms and subs, ambis, andros, the married and the single, the monogamous and the indiscriminate and the celibate, fetishists, freeloaders, the crazy and the sane, parents, shrieking queens and closet cases, and someone who just wandered in for a packet of Silk Cut ... and more and more and *any* combination. A kaleidoscopic collision of human sexuality in all its many and varied and coruscating facets – unified only by simple mutual tolerance, a celebration of our basic, immutable individuality, a joyful celebration of raw *life*.

It's in there all the time: a big light machine. All you have to do is switch it on.

Trade Secrets

Nicola Field

'What does it mean when lesbians and gays are attracted to people of the other sex? Is it a betrayal, evidence of letting the side down? Politically, is it a step forward, back, sideways, on top or in the missionary position? A pragmatic extension of the Queer Nation? Or a sad case of sexual dissidents lost to the mire of heterosexuality? Why is there so much guilt and secrecy surrounding other-sex love amongst lesbians and gays? Are we all bisexual really? Should it all be put away until after the revolution? Or should we call for a right to choose, exercised by individuals with their own bodies and desires?

Although research on 'straight' sex amongst lesbians and gays is scarce and findings hard to come by, the following extract gives some idea of the potentials of 'transgender gay sex':

> Project SIGMA, a research programme linked to South Bank University in London, produced a paper in 1990 which analysed through interviews the heterosexual practices of 930 homosexually active men. The paper concluded that over 60 per cent had had at least one sexual experience with a female. Of this number, 90 per cent had had vaginal intercourse. 12 per cent of the whole group (111 men) had had sexual contacts with females in the past year and 5 per cent (47 men) had had sexual contacts with females in the month preceding the interview ... In 1991 SIGMA collaborated with *City Limits* magazine on a questionnaire survey about the sexual attitudes and practices of people in London. There were 472 respondents. 78 per cent of the women polled who said they were lesbian had had sex with a man at some time. 68 per cent had had intercourse with a man and 12 per cent had done so in the past year. 18 per cent of women who said they were bisexual had not had sex with a woman compared with the 27 per cent of bisexual men who had not yet had a sexual relationship with a man. 5 per cent of bisexual men had not had sex with a woman. 17 per cent of gay men admitted to having had sex with a woman during their current gay relationship.

Similar conclusions were reached in 1993 by researchers on the National Survey of Sexual Attitudes and Lifestyles, a massive study of

133

19,000 people in the UK. As one researcher put it: 'we did not ask people if they identified with particular labels such as gay, straight or bisexual – we just asked them about their sexual history. The findings really blow the whole idea of having separate homosexual and heterosexual boxes apart – from our results that is clearly not the case.'

The following article, consisting of interviews and a fictional narrative, explores the ideas and feelings of four lesbian and bisexual women who have experienced sexual attraction towards gay men. The names have been changed in order to preserve confidentiality.

Hilary: Because coming out as gay is a cultural and political step, if men continue to feel attracted to women, or start to later, I don't think they're going to say they're bisexual. A lot of gay men are attracted to women, particularly dykey women, because of the boyish image and maybe a softness they think they wouldn't get in a man, but they suppress how they feel, that it's sexual. They say things, innuendos, like: you're looking really good, really dykey, really groovy, but not: I find you sexually attractive. Whether or not the sex would work, I suppose, that's a different matter. You could look at it negatively and think that a lot of gay men are attracted to boys, literally, and they know they can't have that, either because it's not available or they're frightened of being paedophiles. The dykey woman is a representation of that. Or you could look at it differently. Because there is a lesbian/gay look, if you get into that culture you find it attractive.

Years ago I hung out with a group of gay men in South London, going to their pubs and clubs and staying over in their flats and learning the meaning of words like trade, slag, fag, cock and drag. I was a mascot, a pet dyke. I made them feel better about not being interested in other women as people. And I went along with it, willing to pay any price for affection and belonging, although of course I didn't really belong because I wasn't one of the boys and I wasn't boyish either. I was fem and chubby and didn't suit a flat top. I was the only one in the gang who wasn't openly desired or whose body parts, haircut and clothing weren't the object of blatant erotic interest. In our world I was the only person whose sexuality was not interesting.

Most of them I fancied at some point, perhaps just for a moment, for a night, or a few days. A couple, though, were focal points of my sexual desire for many months, right the way through the endless affairs and one night stands I was having with women. I would never, never let on how I felt because I was ashamed and thought they would be disgusted. The men loved it when I had a girlfriend and would constantly try to match me up with other women. Maybe when I had a girlfriend it maximised my exchange-value as a lesbian hanger-on and doubled their credential. During these periods, one or two of the men, the ones I was more physically close to and the ones I was more passionately keen on, used to ask me very blatant questions about the sex I was having. One asked, 'Does her clitoris swell up?' I would gape, shocked, horrified, uncomprehending. Why on earth would he want to know? I was ashamed, especially, because clitoris-size was something I hadn't even noticed. Another told me confidentially that they had discussed whether I was a fag hag and not a proper lesbian because I was hanging around a lot with them. Did that mean they hated me more than they hated themselves?

Hilary: I've had sex with men who are having relationships with other men, who go to gay places and go out with gay men. I know some who say they are attracted to women, they'd like to have sex with women, but they're afraid to. I think lesbians' sexuality probably intrigues them, they don't quite understand it. On the other hand, I don't know if they think about it much. To some extent most men, straight or gay, aren't interested in what women like. Maybe gay men, because they sleep with men, think they no longer have to think about women's sexuality. So maybe when they go to a club, and there are lesbians there who are very openly sexual ... some think it's disgusting, but a lot of others might find it erotic. A lot of men I know like the mixed clubs where you get a lot of women wearing leather, they find it exciting. You also get a lot of women who play up the gay male role, the strap-ons, the moustaches. But I think women are more interested in male sexuality than men are interested in women's.

Sandy: When I had just left school in the 1970s I met a guy who was 34 and I was only the second woman he'd been out with. Most of his sexual experience had been with men. He was very upper class, unconventional and sometimes arrogant. He took me to a lot of gay clubs in Earls Court like the Coleherne, a leather pub. I was often the only woman there and I got a tremendous kick. The men were really nice to me. They used to say things like 'it's almost enough to make you go straight' about me. I used to find the atmosphere really erotic. Another pub had an upstairs bar – now I suppose it would be described as queer. Everyone was trying to get off with each other but nobody was sure, it was exciting. My boyfriend was still sleeping with men and he would tell me about this in graphic detail. I found it an incredible turn-on. I felt really envious.

135

Alex: My first boyfriend was gay. He had girlfriends when he lived in the same community as I did, but when he moved away he became gay. That was his attraction to me, he was different and he didn't fit in. I was able to talk to him, he was able to listen. He treated me as a person and respected what I thought.

I think I may be rejected because of the perfection that men can often look for in other men that women often fail at. I feel I would fail. They want hard muscular bodies. Yes, I do a lot of fitness training and I'd like a muscular body but I don't know whether it would be to attract gay men. I think the majority of my men friends see me as lesbian-identified, which increases the gulf between us. It makes us closer on a friendship level, but on a sexual level ... maybe they prefer to think of me as totally lesbian because it's safer for them. Socially, it's nicer to have gay people around than straight people. And bisexuals throw in some confusion. To make the *concession* to have sex with a man it would have to be a man that was really worth it. I'd have to feel very sure about him and very attracted, so we're talking wonderful man who can communicate, body perfect and someone who's not going to run away, who's going to be there. Well, I wouldn't have all those expectations of a woman. Or fears either.

Sex Thoughts

Hilary: I think gay male sex is really exciting. I think a lot of it is quite imaginative. You haven't got the taboo areas a lot of straight people and women have around the body, like the anus or certain sex acts. I've got a few gay male friends who'll tell me stories of what they're doing and I'm going, 'Oh why can't we do that!' It's not because it's not possible for us, it's just because women don't. I'd like to be a gay man, just for a little while, to have sex once as a gay man. The one-off men I've slept with have been a bit heterosexual really. The sex is quite pumpy, they expect you to lie on your back while they do it to you. Bisexual women I know go on about how wonderful sex with men is. I'm sure it's true but it's damn hard finding it. It's the images men have of women or the images women have of themselves, cos I find myself falling into those stereotypes as well. Maybe you've got to be quite assertive. Even with bisexual men, who mainly sleep with women, if you try to initiate something you end up in a battle and he's trying to take control and you give up and think, is it fucking worth it?

Hilary: The kind of men that like to be fucked will think: what's the point of sleeping with a woman? Maybe they think being fucked by a woman isn't possible, maybe the idea hasn't aroused them. A woman fucking a man is really reversing things a bit too much, though I'm sure it goes on. I know people who have worked with prostitutes say that a lot of male fantasy is being dominated by a woman but they can only do it with a prostitute, someone they don't consider to be more than a sex object.

There was something going on with Christopher. There was a lot of unspoken feeling, sexual tension, intenseness when I would think 'why is he staring at me?' And I think that something made him fly away from me. I think he's frightened of commitment, or demands. He calls himself gay but he still looks at women and fancies them. Bill, he's a very close gay friend, used to hold my hand and read me French poems. Recently, when we were out, he kept pointing to women and saying, 'Oh, what about her for you, she's really attractive and what about her, what about her?' I think it was suppressed heterosexuality on his part, why was he so anxious that I get off with one of these women that he found attractive?

Sandy: I think some gay men deny that they are attracted to women. A friend said, 'If I started having straight feelings I would hate it, I went through so much grief being gay that if I thought I was bisexual I would just die.' Other men I've spoken to have said, 'If I was straight I would really fancy so and so.' This reminds me of girls at school who used to say: 'If I was a man I'd really fancy you.' I think ideally, sex between lesbians and gay men could be very exciting, a very different way of having sexual relationships. Some gay men have said to me that if they had any sexual contact with women they would feel that they were compelled to re-enter straight society and conform.

Fantasy

Sandy: I saw some gay men's pornography and I just found it a complete turn-off. What I wanted was beautiful young men gently caressing each other rather than what I perceive as the worst excesses of male sexuality. I might like to be involved with two men sexually. I've never slept with more than one man at a time, but I have done other combinations and it's tricky. It's much more enjoyable as a fantasy.

I am in a lift, a bed, a cottage, an alleyway, a rooftop with this man/boy who, in me, is discovering, disclosing at last, his fascination with cunt. Other women have interested him sexually in the past, but I am the catalyst. We are both attempting to unlearn the codes and pressures and rituals and powerplays of early heterosexual conditioning. We try to forget them and to remember only the selves and sex we found with our own gender. This sex liberated us because we were fucking bodies like our own. We knew those bodies. We read and explored them like maps we had been studying since childhood. We found our own pleasure through another person assenting to and conspiring with our desire, inch for inch.

Hilary: Sometimes I really want to be a gay man. There's a place in Manchester called Rockies where they have a thing called the Mineshaft downstairs which is men only. I managed to get down there with no-one noticing and I spent about half an hour just wandering about. Nobody noticed and I was part of it all. Even though I really wasn't. I've got a fantasy about going cottaging and pretending to be a boy and having a strap on and having sex and then still not knowing whether I was a woman or a man. I'd really like to have sex with two gay men. They would have sex together but I would be involved, in a sense not as a woman, more neutral. Maybe I feel there would be expectations of me as a woman, there would be things I would have to do that I wouldn't be into.

Alex: The safe sex adverts or the party boys at clubs when they take their shirts off, they're the sort of gay men that can be fantasised about. If I wished to have sex with them it would be purely on a body basis, I would want to play with their bodies and not have any feedback from them at all; to use them purely as an experiment. One man I know, he's sweet and he listens and he talks and he's vulnerable. He's as scared of women as I'm scared of men. And he's prepared to admit that. But I don't think that heterosexual men aren't scared or heterosexual women aren't scared – it's just a huge act: 'We're heterosexual and therefore we're going to go out and fuck each other because that's what we're meant to do, but we won't communicate and tell each other how we feel about it.'

Sexpol

Hilary: I don't think sex is innately different for men or women. It's constructed differently. Men are very centred on the penis and pumping and finding an orifice, and female sexuality is defined as somehow subverse to that. I think men and women can have equal sex, not in the sense of no power relationships at all, I don't think that's possible, but each having as much control over things as the other.

Good sex won't develop until we're no longer fucked up about sexuality in general. Occasionally barriers between individuals are broken down, but not the whole thing. Women aren't able to feel comfortable about their sexuality, whether they're lesbians or not. There could be a sexual environment that no longer sees who you have sex with on the basis of their gender or anything about them apart from sexual, emotional or physical attraction. A kind of sexuality where passive and dominant roles are played out but women can be dominant, women can fuck men. There are still rules about sexuality within each community. And there are things that we can learn from everybody. Strap-ons are brilliant for safer sex. Imagine how many men would love to be fucked by a strap on, but wouldn't because it was a woman or not a 'real' man. Or because nobody feels comfortable enough to say it. It can go on for however long you want it to, avoid the mechanics of willies going floppy. A lot of people could be interested if it was seen as OK.

Him doing it on her, her letting him in to her. And each time she is fucked by a penis that only feels its own pleasure she is annihilated. She can have no anticipation of pleasure for herself. And she wants him to do it because it will bring him close to her, he will need something from her, she will become necessary to him. A woman's right to choose: be fucked or don't be fucked. Make yourself available to be fucked then regret it, or feel unsure again so that you need to be fucked again to be reassured. Sex is the only way he proves he likes her and wants to be with her.

Alex: I think his fear is to do with women not being able to say what they want from him and him not knowing what's happening when he's having sex with women. If I have sex with a man, I can't always tell what his reactions are, because I don't know how it feels, I don't know what a male orgasm feels like. Whereas if I'm having sex with a woman I understand what she feels and identify with that feeling. But it seems almost alien with a man, because they make different noises and have different reactions and unless you feel one hundred per cent safe you aren't going to ask someone to explain what's happening.

Sandy: For me it isn't any more conformist to go to bed with a man than to go to bed with a woman. When I was having sex with the man over the road, there was no way we were going to go out or go courting or watch TV together. That did give it a lot of edge sexually. I've never liked being in a couple. I've felt completely sucked in and that the whole thing was out of my control. I really hate the idea that I would be dependent on anybody. Being in a couple is so much the image that everybody is bombarded with, growing up in the nuclear family. I was one of those girls that always looked at their mother and thought 'I am not going to be like that!' But there is always a real pull to persuade us that we are wrong.

To fuel his desire I am careful about my appearance. I check my words, the way I stand/walk/sit, my clothes and make-up. Checked for the male gaze. Sex addiction. Constantly looking for it compulsively. The only way to be liked or valued is to be sexually attractive. Be irresistible, intoxicate, baffle, seduce. Led by his erection, the man feels weak. She is the destination of his desire, she is the place where he regains his power. He will say or do anything to reach into her. Bodysnatch. I write all these words and begin to understand the trap I am in, child/girl/woman. I want to be identified as the source of his pleasure so that he will desire me and give me the pleasure of being desired. Will this pleasure be mine or his? Where is my sexuality in this scenario? I fear that my real desire is the monster that will suffocate and crush him. He has taken refuge from woman cavernous sucking sex in being homosexual. But my vagina is a road, a journey. It is not a hole with uniform sides a pad of flesh for landing on.

Hilary: A lot of men don't use their hands with women. They might just to make sure where the hole is ... where is it, is it big enough yet? Is it wet enough? A friend of mine who is quite sexual towards women sometimes, although he's very gay, said, 'I'd quite like to have sex with a woman but I'm just scared of the hole. It's about the black hole and will I lose myself and worries about teeth inside and things.'

Alex: I don't know whether the way I achieve orgasms is all that different when I'm with a woman from when I'm with a man. With women it tends to be more clitoral than vaginal but with men it tends to be with hand or tongue or penis outside my vagina. I couldn't come just by being fucked by a man's penis in my vagina – I would have to be extremely turned on by him. All the men I've had sex with have had to be told how to make me come.

So when I am desiring this man, in this bed, lift, alleyway, rooftop. I can't separate him from what I want from him and for me. I keep my desire secret because it's too powerful to be allowed out of the house. Like a madwoman in a Victorian novel or a secret brewed in a laboratory. I live my life soliciting at the mouth of a cave, offering trips inside to interested tourists.

Sweet faced and gentle exterior. People comment to me on his exceptional niceness. But I lay down on a bed with him and felt my self fading away as his sexuality marched onto the battlefield. This sweet kind gentle and nice man's hidden brutality. As an object of desire I became for him an object of contempt and hatred. What images are filling his head of who I am, what I am like inside, what I will do to him? Men believe that women wish to control them, emasculate them, take away their power, make them weak. I am tempted to act passive so as not to frighten him away. I sense that he dreads I will ask for a commitment. He dreads I will require his time. If I trespass I will be punished. On shifting ground: with his men lovers the erection is celebrated. With me his erection is a reminder of power. It changes from physical tissue to abstract agent. The erect cock is ready for a fight; like a soldier trained up for a battle, desperate to be in there, slugging it out, like dogs or horses of war, harnessed and foaming at the mouth. The penis is like Oedipus: I have a rudimentary and vague idea of his/its meaning and function, but I do not know the significant details of his/its potential impact on the action. I am afraid of misunderstanding it, enraging it. What pleasure will it get from my body, how can I give it pleasure? How can I offer anything comparable to the ultimate sex, sex between men, where power and hunger are freedom? How can I help making this comparison? I am reminded of the dream where I had a penis and was fucking my girlfriend with it. What does he feel about my clit? Is it a tiny button he may never find or keep losing? How will I communicate to him how I want him to touch it? How can I break through his fear when I can't break through my own? How will I touch his cock? I am wary of his power but is he wary of something in me? Have the lessons of liberation we learnt with our own sex become another wall of silence to prevent us from loving each other? Can we only retreat from our affection and desire, claiming to have bypassed it anyway by our superior homosexualities? What are our (homo)sexualities while we love one another?

Note

[1] Nicola Field, *Over the Rainbow: Money, Class and Homophobia*, Pluto Press, London 1995.

This is Me

Joan

When I was younger I didn't have any feelings of being bisexual; women didn't interest me in that way although I had close friendships with women. Then around 1975, when I was twenty-eight, I began to realise that I found some women attractive. I didn't reject this feeling. I thought it's obviously a part of me, how nature made me, and there's no use in trying to fight against it. I was comfortable with it, and am quite open to talking to people I know well about it, although I still can't discuss it with my family.

I have been disabled since birth. I was born spastic, as was my husband. We met one another in 1970 when living in a hostel: we both worked in the Halifax workshops for spastics. When we left there in 1973 the wage was only £5 a week, and we had to put off getting married until we could afford it. I saw nothing wrong in being sexual before marriage, as we loved one another. However my husband can't maintain an erection long enough to make love to me, so according to the church our marriage hasn't been consummated.

We have an open relationship. It's a matter of trusting one another. My husband knows that I have other sexual partners but he knows how we trust and love one another after being married for nineteen years. We're both happy this way. If he happens to meet another man and wants to learn more about male love, I wouldn't mind because I trust him. I think unless you really trust somebody you can't really love them.

In 1975 I joined GEMMA, an organisation for disabled lesbians, and advertised in its magazine. Unfortunately it has meetings mostly in London, so I can't get to these. One woman replied to my advert. She was lesbian but married, and lived near Newcastle. At that time I was steadier on my feet and decided to go up there. We made love in her bedroom with her husband asleep in a small room. He was very good about it. She told me that one of her fantasies was seeing her husband making love to another woman, and soon that was how it worked out with the three of us. We were all happy with the arrangement and they came to stay in Christmas 1975.

I've only met that one woman, though I've written to others that I've contacted through the magazine of The Outsiders Club (a social club for disabled people) and GEMMA. Only a few answer. I've been writing to one woman for a number of years but there's no chance of meeting because of the difficulties of travelling.

I suppose really I'm only slightly bisexual. In the main I prefer men. Most of my contacts through my adverts in Outsider Magazine have been men. I don't contact them first, because I don't really feel it's a woman's place to go chasing after men. I know that may sound old-fashioned. The way things are with me now I can no longer travel, so they have to come to me.

Many of the men I've met this way have been quite naive sexually, or inexperienced, and they find my own directness intimidating. One man visits regularly and he usually brings condoms but recently he forgot. I haven't had a period in three years so there's no chance of getting pregnant, but that doesn't mean it's safe. He said he didn't know whether he was clean. I said, 'If you're not sure, how is anyone else supposed to know? I can't even suck you off because I'd be taking sperm into my body, I could catch something'. He was very apologetic …

With my husband I joined Outsiders in 1973. Its main purpose is to help disabled people to meet socially because otherwise we can get very isolated. Some of the men involved are simply looking for sex, and complain that women members just want to use it as a general social club, and don't want any mention of sex. My own advert says that I wish to make friends and that if the sexual side does crop up, all well and good if we're sexually attracted. If not there's nothing lost! My relationship with my husband is very strong. There's trust and love between us, and this gives us a lot of space.

Deaf Bisexuality

Louis Hamilton

I will start by explaining the difference between profoundly deaf people and hard of hearing people. I cannot explain all the subtleties of the differences among deaf people, but I will define the two main groups. Profoundly deaf people are those who are either born deaf, or become deaf very young, before they acquire spoken language. Usually they are brought up with British Sign Language (BSL), which is different from English, a separate language. It has its own structure and grammar. It is a language in its own right, a very rich language – it is visual, like pictures in the mind. It is not based on English words.

Hard of hearing people, on the other hand, are people who have been brought up hearing, gone through a hearing education and lived in the hearing world, and have then become deaf, maybe slowly, any time between teenage years and old age. Most of them are elderly; seventy four percent of elderly people are hard of hearing. Because of how they have lost their hearing, they still have English in their minds; that is how they think. So they do not start to sign when they become deaf, unless maybe they are very young when they lose their hearing. Generally, they rely on lip reading and talking one to one. It is important to make it clear that there are these two different groups.

So, with hard of hearing people, others do not always spot that they are hard of hearing – perhaps they have been at bisexual conferences and no-one has realised, because they have not come out as hard of hearing. Usually, hard of hearing people find it hard to accept their deafness because they have been brought up in the hearing world. They often feel embarrassed and unsure of themselves. They need to mix with the right people and talk it through to get to the point of self-acceptance. Often hard of hearing people do not say they are deaf, but say, 'I can't hear very well,' or, 'Would you repeat that?' and try to cover it up. Hard of hearing people have been to hearing schools, so they have had sex education and have a better understanding of sexuality and the issues involved. A hard of hearing person who is bisexual may be 'invisible' – you cannot spot them, and they may speak English fine.

I am profoundly deaf, but in the past I used to identify as hard of hearing because of social pressure. I now understand why that happened. I can both speak English and sign – I am bilingual, bisexual and proud!

Now as regards the profoundly deaf, the deaf community; when I was growing up, in the 1970s, sex education was non-existent. We never had health issues explained to us – STDs, AIDS, women's periods, protection using condoms. In schools there was nothing about all of that. When AIDS started spreading, we did not have any information and it was a very difficult situation. Until the 1980s, there was no health promotion of any sort in any part of the deaf community. No information was passed on. Then through the 1980s, HIV awareness started, and AIDS Ahead was set up as an independent organisation for deaf people. Later on it linked up with the British Deaf Association (BDA), and now things have started to improve a bit. But progress is still far too slow, and although there is now some sex education for deaf people, it is not at a good level. In terms of being open about sexuality, it is still very much taboo. Yes, there have been some developments, but the situation is still not at all as it should be.

At the time I am talking about, a lot of deaf schools were boarding schools. People from all over Britain were placed in residential schools, and they were really like the private 'public' hearing schools. You stayed there all the time, except for a few students who came on a daily basis, so you can imagine what it was like. As in the 'public' schools, there was a lot of same gender sex on the quiet. In the 'public' hearing schools there would be some sex education, and then you could understand to some extent what was going on as you developed, and then left school. But in deaf schools, which were always separate boys' and girls' schools, it was like prison. The boys and girls did not have any sex education, so how could they develop an understanding or sense of their own rights? People in same sex relationships would be taunted, put down and belittled, and a lot of very cruel behaviour would be directed at them.

When deaf people left school they came across words like homosexual, lesbian, gay, bisexual and heterosexual and they did not understand what they meant. But hearing people leaving school probably understood the words because they had better access to the media – TV, radio and so on. When people left the deaf schools they would go out without any sex education and would feel forced into conforming – getting engaged to a girl or boy friend, getting married and having a family. Some went through it and were happy but others became frustrated by it, unfulfilled and trapped.

The problem with answering questions like, 'How did you come to define yourself as bisexual?' is that deaf people have had inadequate or no sex education. This word 'bisexuality' did not mean anything to me in the past – nor to the deaf community. When they did find out what this word meant exactly, most of them kept their mouths shut. Partly it was fear, or a taboo, or misunderstanding the information about sexuality.

Nobody in the deaf community knew what bisexuality meant. I did not know. I had heard of gay and straight, but even when I was 30 and I came across the word, it did not make sense, though I had a vague idea what it meant. Then through friends who were bisexual, and particularly Rachel, I found out about a bisexual conference, so I went to it, and I realised that I was bisexual myself. I originally decided to go to get information for other deaf people, I really was not sure of myself.

All deaf people have had very limited information about sexuality, because society pathologises it so much, and thus people are forced into the closet. I wondered why deaf people were prepared to fit in with the straight world, then I worked out why. Deaf people rely on their eyes – and straight sexuality is all out there, all the time. Everything else is hidden away. All that heterosexual imagery is very powerful, so deaf people feel they have to be 'normal' to fit in with what they see around them.

I was engaged to a woman when I was about 18. I loved her and we had sex. But it did not feel quite right, because of things that had happened to me at school. I finished with her, because I felt I was not being fair to her – I knew there were problems that needed addressing, but I could not sort it out then. She is a lovely woman. She eventually married someone else, and we are still friends.

I thought I must be gay, and other people's view was that I was gay. I was depressed because I had no access to proper information. I still sometimes find it awkward to talk about my experience of my sexuality, and why I identify as bisexual rather than heterosexual or gay. It is hard for me to explain. People in the deaf community have all sorts of sex, but they do not realise what is meant by sexuality. People have sexual feelings without knowing and understanding exactly what is going on, because they are not given the information. This is why people feel bad and get stuck, and have a lack of understanding of their own identity.

Gradually I found out more about sexuality and bisexuality from sitting around chatting with hearing friends. And that is how I found out about the conference. I got involved in the bisexual movement because hearing people passed on information. I was extremely lucky that one of my hearing friends happened to be bisexual. I started to go to my local hearing bisexual group – deaf people get important input from hearing friends, from formal meetings, but just as much from chatting. I definitely feel part of the bisexual movement, although I do not go regularly to my local group any more – where there is now both a mixed group and a women's group.

I am setting up groups about sexuality for deaf people. I am slowly encouraging the doors of awareness to be opened, and educating people, mostly through informal gatherings. Hearing people are very welcome to be involved with this work, for example in helping to organise meetings and acting as interpreters. I do not want to be a deaf separatist. I think it is important to keep the relationship with hearing people alive.

Hearing people could make deaf people feel welcome in the bisexual movement by doing things like providing interpreters at all gatherings, or by getting someone in to do deaf awareness work with their group. This covers topics such as the range of deafness, communication, and the use of language – did you know that some deaf people are *tri*lingual, being fluent in, for example, Punjabi, English and BSL? This work is really taking off now, and even becoming quite fashionable. You can find out more from the British Deaf Association (BDA) or the Royal National Institute for Deaf People (RNID). You could also invite deaf people to your groups as speakers, to share their experiences and information.

One exciting development is that a deaf-only bisexual group, called Biscuits, has set up recently in London. For their address, see contacts section at the end of the book. There are lesbian and gay deaf groups across the country. There's the Triangle Club in Manchester, covering the North, the Brothers' and Sisters' Club in London covering the South, and the Dragon Club in Wales. The Central Rainbow is in the Midlands, based in Birmingham, and the East-Central Rainbow is in the Nottingham area. The Punch and Judy Club is based in Brighton. Bisexual people are welcome. You would not feel the odd one out.

It is also interesting that profoundly deaf professionals, including some bisexuals, are starting to talk much more about their sexuality. They are gradually coming out about it more, which is good. Another good thing – in 1991 at the London National Bisexual Conference there were quite a few deaf people, which was a really good first step, and I know that deaf people have been to conferences since, although I haven't myself. I hope those people will spread the word in the deaf community and we will get more and more deaf people involved in the future.

This article was translated from British Sign Language to English by Fiona Durance.

The Making of an Australian Bisexual Activist

Wayne Roberts

I was born in Brisbane, Queensland in 1955. Since I was about eight years old, I have been involved with other boys as well as having girlfriends. In those days it was the boys and girls at my school. It was usually confined to touching and life drawing; and with the girls, kissing and playing 'family' games. My interest in both sexes increased with the onset of puberty, but in different ways. With the guys it was more physical and visual, but with the girls it was more emotional and hormonal. My biggest discovery was masturbation at the age of fourteen.

I was still rather sexually naive, even during my late teens. What I class as my first true gay experience occurred when I was 21, and working as a laboratory technician in Townsville at the Teachers College. I lived in the residence with the students, and had a girlfriend there. One night I was seduced by Bruce, a student at the college. It was my first experience of oral sex, and by a fellow bisexual. The year was 1978 and I started to question my sexuality like never before. I knew I couldn't be homosexual, but couldn't be heterosexual either. I started thinking of myself as bisexual, but at the same time denying my gay side. I was in the closet.

In 1979 I met Debbie, the sister of my new best friend, Barry. We fell in love, had sex – my first time heterosexually – and eventually became engaged. However, this did not last, and after several affairs with other women, my gay feelings emerged even more strongly than before. Initially, my gay sexual activity was confined to isolated experiences with male friends, but then I discovered beats (meeting places for men such as toilets, parks and beaches). I even found the courage to go to one of Brisbane's gay night clubs. Under Queensland's National Party Government (the renamed Country Party) all forms of homosexual behaviour between men were illegal.

Police often used entrapment to gain convictions.

As a laboratory technician with some medical knowledge, I knew AIDS, the media's 'Gay Plague', could not be confined to gay men. Having been sexually conservative with men, I had already been practising safer sex. Later that year, at a beat, I met Ian, who worked at the Queensland AIDS Council and was to show me some new safer sex activities. By 1987 I had become increasingly involved with the Queensland AIDS Council, doing home care and peer education in the gay community. I was still not out, but my family, work and friends knew of my involvement with QuAC My relationship with David, whom I had met on a trip to Perth, flourished, despite the 4,000 kilometre separation. I was becoming more involved in the gay community, going to venues, parties and beats, and less with the het community. Then at the 1987 QuAC New Year's Eve Party I met Esme, and started a three-month relationship. As a bisexual man with QuAC, several other women also took an interest in me, which renewed my belief in my bisexuality.

Moving back to Perth in 1989 to commence studies and be with David, I became involved with the Western Australian AIDS Council (WAAC) and various gay groups. I could be out in Perth, and was. I became involved in the new political struggle for gay rights in Western Australia. With the break up of my relationship with David, I took on work as a volunteer with the WAAC again. The Council had only recently established a beat patrol team. After a small induction course, we would go out to Perth's beats, where men, many bisexual, go to have sex with other men. It was my job to approach these men in their parked cars and offer safe sex and HIV information, answer any questions and have condoms and lube available if they so wished. Most were very receptive to this material, but others drove away quickly. I would also hand out the small condom and lube packs to men in the sand dunes at Perth's Swanbourne Nude Beach. Packs were also left in toilets. My favourite was always the one at the University of Western Australia. Boy, was that a busy beat with students.

When the AIDS Council set up a support group for bisexual and married gay men in 1989, I just had to become involved, and helped to organise and facilitate social events. At one time, between 30 and 70 men would attend socials at private homes, but it gradually became more gay than bisexual, which was one reason why I stopped going for a while. On my return to group meetings, I found many of those attending were older married men. Seeing the need to reach younger bisexual men, we set up the new Perth Bisexual Guys' Group of the

WA Bisexual Network. Both groups serve a function and complement each other.

Decriminalisation of homosexual acts in private for consenting adult males has occurred at different times and rates in the different States and Territories of Australia, between the mid 1970s in South Australia and 1990 in Queensland. Tasmania remains the only state where it is still illegal.

My first 'gay' protest was at the Parliament House rally for decriminalisation of sodomy in Perth. Then in 1990 I helped re-establish the Curtin Stonewall Club and the Homosexual Information Office for gay, lesbian and bisexual students at Curtin University of Technology in Perth. In 1990 the HIO was renamed the Sexuality Information Department and restructured to thus encourage more lesbians and bisexuals. With Elaine Kemp and myself as the officers, and both out bisexuals, the Department flourished. We marched with a bisexual banner in our first Pride March in October 1990 and again at the Stonewall Day March in 1991.

In 1990 I attended the fourth National Conference on AIDS in Canberra, where ACT-UP Australia staged large protests against the Federal Health Minister over the availability of AIDS treatments, and delays in drug approvals. I was so inspired by ACT-UP that on my return to Perth I started organising to establish ACT-UP (Perth). In October, the group marched through the streets in the first Pride March in Perth.

ACT-UP (Perth) continued to be a watch-dog on the community, media and governments. In 1991 we participated in a national campaign to improve the drug approval systems and access to treatments. We received extensive media coverage when we occupied the foyer of the Health Department State Office. As a result of the national campaign and protests, the system was overhauled. Our next target was the Western Australian Health Minister, Keith Wilson. In July 1991, he axed a safe sex campaign, aimed at 16 to 25 year olds, to promote the use of condoms and safe sex practices, reputedly because of his recent conversion to Catholicism. In spite of demonstrations, and an occupation of Wilson's office, the Minister would not alter his decision.

In May 1992 ACT-UP (Perth) and three other groups launched their own Safe Sex Awareness Campaign for young people, with the distribution of small packs containing condom, lube, and safe sex information. These were first handed out at high schools to 16- and 17-year old students. The Education and Police Ministers called on schools to bring in the police if ACT-UP and the other groups, which included two student groups, arrived at schools to distribute material. There had been a constant barrage by the media, who are more concerned with controversy than the issues, and who are thus not prepared to cover stories about material distributed at Universities, etc, only schools. I was media spokesperson: we were committed to the campaign of making safe sex and HIV information freely available to young people, and providing easy access to condoms for those who choose to say 'Yes' to sex.

My new-found openness and confidence in public speaking has enabled me to speak to the media on bisexuality and on my own bisexuality. I have raised bisexual issues in the gay and lesbian communities where there has been a tendency to forget about bisexual people. Bi men are generally included as gay and bi women are generally excluded completely by many of the lesbian groups.

It was therefore a wonderful feeling to be part of the formation of the first Australian bisexual group for men and women. The Western Australian Bisexual Network (WABN) was formed in November 1991. There were four Perth groups in the Network, and we had a newsletter, *Biways*. We had contact with 55 other bisexuals or partners of bisexuals in WA and distributed 450 newsletters to individuals, adult book shops and groups in Australia and overseas. WABN hosted the first Australian Bisexual Conference in Perth in October 1992 as part of Pride WA.

Often, the biggest hurdle for bisexuals is not others, but ourselves. Far too many bisexuals deny their sexuality and have been socialised by the straight and gay communities into believing they cannot exist as bisexual people. The majority conceal their true identity from the world, even fooling themselves in the process. HIV poses a big risk to bisexual men who lack self-esteem because they cannot accept their sexuality, but continue to have unprotected sex because of their dual need to be with men and women.

A major effort is now being made here in Australia to reach bisexual men and their female partners. One of the key aims of the Australian Bisexual Network (ABN) is to provide information, education and support for bisexual people, their partners and others on HIV and AIDS issues. I hope that by our being open and speaking out on bisexual issues, others will take notice and consider bisexuals in any policy making.

On my return to Brisbane at the end of 1992 I set up the ABN, and National *Biways* magazine was born. In 1993, ABN established the first Bisexual Community Centre in Australia as a national resource and drop-in centre. I attended the conferences in New York in mid-1994, and the ABN banner was in the Stonewall 25 procession. Things are looking better for bisexuals in Australia now, but the battle for our rights, recognition and funding continues.

Conversations with a Bi Woman

Frances Murphy

For quite some time I've been politically active around many issues, including gay rights, but my bisexuality has always remained a personal thing, until now. The pain of being the naive Bi, the loneliness of being the only Bi, and the chiselling effect biphobia has had on my sexuality, have left me with no options but to 'get active'. As we increasingly challenge biphobia our enemies will become more apparent, but so will our allies. It is through solidarity with other Bis and other allies that we will become a force to be reckoned with.

What do you mean when you talk about the naive Bi?

I embarked on my 'active' gay life thinking that bisexuality was a real option. In many respects I'm glad I was naive. If I'd known the pain and embarrassment that I was about to endure, I'd have never opened my mouth. Of course, the pain and embarrassment would have still been there, it just wouldn't have been so damned public...

You mentioned the loneliness of being the only Bi ... didn't you know any other Bis?

No, I thought that I was the only one on the planet. Well, the only one north of the Watford Gap. The only Bis that I had known were back in the late 70s around the punk era and I guessed that they'd gone straight. I also had my own stereotypical views of bisexuals. I didn't seem to fit into those views. Biphobia had really affected me, and managed to keep me isolated from my brothers and sisters. I wasn't out and I wasn't proud.

What negative experiences of biphobia have you had?

I'm a NALGO [National Association of Local Government Officers] member and much to its credit Nalgo has a Gay section – 'Nalgay'. I was delighted when I found this out and I joined immediately. Not long after there was a local district meeting to which I was invited, in a city about thirty miles away. The meeting went well, until we got to 'membership' on the agenda. It wasn't about how to get more members, rather who could and who couldn't join. Exclusivity had never been mentioned on any of the literature I'd been sent but now, half way through the meeting, they were discussing who should and could be present. Bisexuals weren't allowed. I can't remember much after that as I left the room shouting something about double oppression. One very kind woman came out to see if I was okay. She did say that she didn't agree with the decision, but then she left to go back to the group, who were getting on with union business. I think that was one of the saddest and loneliest nights of my life. I left on my own and went home by train.

I hope I never belong to a group who would treat somebody the way they treated me. No one ever rang to see if I was okay. I had gone to that meeting to seek help and support. My management committee had just reported me for promoting Lesbianism at work; and my mum had recently guessed that I was gay and hadn't eaten since. I had been really hoping for some support.

That whole event really brought home to me how respectable biphobia was/is in the gay community and how sisterhood is a bit of a myth.

You referred to yourself as a gay woman

Yes, that's because I am gay. I also like to use the word 'Bi-Dyke' – a touch controversial, but it sums me up nicely. Being gay to me is very important – I am perceived as being gay, I experience homophobia, heterosexism is used to deny me my freedom of sexuality. I'm not gay because I fancy being gay ... I've enough oppression being a woman and being Irish without taking on another cross for the heck of it. I am gay, I feel gay ... my mum prays that I'm not. Of course that doesn't mean that every Bi will identify as being gay...

You talked about anti-lesbianism and anti-gay men prejudice?

Yes, not to be confused with homophobia ... I feel that reactive prejudice to biphobia from the lesbian and gay community could lead to hate for lesbians and gay men by the bi-movement or by individual bisexuals, and we cannot accept this as a basis on which to build our movement. We need to understand why biphobia has such a grip in the lesbian and gay communities. Of course understanding an oppression doesn't negate the effects of it. Nor should it stop us getting together to share the experiences we've encountered. I feel sure that the largest group of allies are in the lesbian and gay communities and in fact there are an increasing amount of bi-friendly lesbians and gay men coming forward. They need our support in return.

What have your partners/lovers felt about your bisexuality?

Over the last few years I have chosen only women partners and in the main they have been supportive around the issue. It's been difficult for them, because it so happens that they have all been lesbians. Fears have been around me having male friends; that people might assume they are Bis; that the lesbian community might disown them because they have a Bi partner, questions around their own sexuality and so on – but none of the relationships have ended because of the Bi issue. As for the fear of rejection because I'm a Bi – well that no longer exists. Personally I wouldn't want to sleep with a woman who wouldn't want to sleep with a Bi-woman, so the rejection remains with them, and not me.

Have you ever thought of not being Bi?

Oh yes … heterosexism makes me wish I was straight and biphobia makes me wish I was a lesbian – but remove those oppressions and that leaves me feeling glad to be Bi. It's really important that we are aware of the effects of heterosexism and biphobia on us – it isn't that they just hurt us and make us feel sad. They are an abrasive on our sexuality – and we can only combat them if we organise in a way that increases our own awareness, as well as others' awareness.

What's next then?

The continued building of a movement that addresses *all* oppression, racism, sexism, the lot – the debate about exclusivity and inclusivity needs to be had. I personally would not organise within a political movement that doesn't take on board the issues of racism and sexism – and in particular doesn't recognise the feminist perspective. We need to organise both separately and with our allies. We need to understand the threat that we make to the present status quo and not apologise for it. We need to get to grips with why biphobia has so much respectability within the gay community. We need to take responsibility to come out – to do that we need to create safe spaces.

What does Bi actually mean to you?

I really don't like answering this question until I've had a chance to discuss the political perspective, and it is only because of my experiences both politically and personally that I can have my own definition which has changed over the years and no doubt will again. I'm not sure if I chose my sexuality or if it chose me. Firstly Bi is how I identify politically. Personally I'm far more interested in woman/woman relationships on a sexual level, but I do have woman/man relationships on intimate friendship levels. I would not rule out sexual relationships with men. I am one of thousands and thousands of Bis in this country and my understanding of bisexuality is as different. The diversity of bisexuality is its strength, and I believe that the political fight for the right to be Bi could be amongst the most dynamic issues of this century.

Section III:
HIV, AIDS and Safer Sex

Introduction

Sue George

It seems almost too obvious to say that thirteen years of AIDS has had an enormous impact on how society and individuals see sexuality. It would now be impossible to write about sexuality without considering its effects, and the influence of AIDS on bisexual identity and behaviour has been particularly strong. Of course, at some level anyone who is sexually active has measured their likelihood of risk to HIV infection (whether or not they have written it off as remote) and may have altered their behaviour accordingly. Even for those people who are not sexually active, it affects what they might do, or what they think of the sexual behaviour of others. It has stimulated homophobia, and created an hysterical correlation between sex and death, which we had expected twentieth century medicine to have eliminated.

However, the effects of the epidemic on self-defined bisexuals, people who have sex with men and women however they identify, and the bisexual community in general, are more subtle and complex than this. For instance, the first bisexual group in the UK was established in 1981, the same year that the first cases of AIDS were reported in the US. So although the two events were not connected at that time, the bisexual community has expanded greatly since the late 1980s, at the same time as AIDS has really hit Britain. This expansion has come in tandem with a heightened awareness of bisexuality, as part of a seemingly non-stop media discussion about all forms of sexuality. Media awareness of bisexuality has been a mixed blessing: the subject has received much publicity, but in some places it has advanced the horror stories that bisexuals would 'spread AIDS'.

Like gay men, prostitutes, and injecting drug users, bisexuals have been considered as marginal, expendable people, whose behaviour made them intrinsically 'other'. It did not really matter whether *they* became sick or died, because they had brought it on themselves. However, as 'high risk sexual partners', bisexual men in particular have been seen as vectors of transmission between gay men and straight women, the guilty and the innocent.

Even in 1994, this view of HIV transmission remains widespread. David Blunkett, for instance, who at the time of writing is Shadow Health Minister, was quoted in the *Pink Paper* with the following:

> I don't seek to scapegoat anybody, but simply to draw logical conclusions. It is men who spread AIDS to women, it is bisexual men who spread AIDS from a high-risk group to a low-risk group – and it is not a judgemental statement but a simple fact of where AIDS developed, its incidence and the nature of its extension. I understand homosexuality and accept it. I cannot understand bisexuality which in my book is selfish libertarianism.[1]

Of course, this statement actually expresses the prejudice and lack of information described above. It describes a view of HIV risk which has no connection with safer sex behaviour, only sexual identity. Blunkett used the excuse of HIV transmission from men to women as the reason he did not vote to reduce the age of consent for gay male sex to 16. Clearly, he does not care whether gay men contract HIV.

This prejudice is reflected in the tabloid press, which has played on an already-existing suspicion of bisexuals by describing them as inherently risky sex-partners, lovers of orgies and multiple partners. For instance, according to the *News of the World*:

> experts warn that these perverts pose the biggest AIDS threat to the straight heterosexual population ... yesterday ... others were still contacting us with their own sordid experiences of this murky, dangerous world.[2]

The message seems to be that bisexuality is everywhere, that you can't spot a bisexual because they look just like you, and there may even be a chance that you could have sex with one if you have sex with a person whose sexual history you don't know.

This has a grain of truth in it – albeit very distorted. A number of projects in Britain, Australia and the US have found that many men who have casual sex with other men are not gay identified, and live ostensibly heterosexual lives.[3] (The article on bisexually active men in Sydney's 'beats' (see p188) looks at the behaviour of men in public sex environments.) At the same time Project Sigma, a University of Essex project looking at the sexual beahviour of men who have sex with men with reference to HIV/AIDS, found that 12 per cent of men who identified as gay had had sex with a woman in the previous year.[4]

These complexities are being increasingly acknowledged by those who work in the HIV/AIDS health education field, and have led to discussions about the connections between bisexual behaviour and bisexual identity. While people who identify with the bisexual community may not, as yet, be numerous, significant numbers are behaving bisexually. There is, however, no consensus about what – from an HIV perspective, rather than that of self-identity – counts as bisexual, or what connection there is or could be between bisexual sexual behaviour and identity.

Over the past few years, much of the work being done around gay men's issues has been directed towards 'men who have sex with men'. As part of the British government's policy outlined in the *Health of the Nation* document, gay and bisexual men have been targeted for HIV prevention work. This MSWM work was undertaken in the expectation that it would reach men who identified as gay, and men who did not, however they identified. Of course, their needs do overlap to some extent, but it is now becoming apparent that this approach is not necessarily meeting the needs of either group. Indeed, some reports indicate that non-gay identified men seeking gay sex would go out of their way to avoid identified gay men as sexual or social partners. They would also avoid AIDS agencies which they perceived to be part of the gay community.[5] In another case, a social and support group in a provincial area of Britain was set up for gay and bisexual men. At the first meeting, there were no bisexual men present, and the gay men there decided the group would be for gay men only.[6]

This confusion of gay and bisexual men is most noticeable in the *Communicable Diseases Surveillance Centre* (CDSC) statistics. These show 'gay and bisexual men' as the group of people who, in Britain, are most likely to be HIV+ or to have AIDS. However, they do not differentiate between gay and bisexual, give any indication of what they count as one or the other, or say how they would differentiate. As these are statistics reported to the CDSC by doctors, it is quite possible that bisexual men are included in another category, such as intravenous drug-users, when their method of transmission was men-men sex. The reverse may also be true. In other words, no-one actually knows how many bisexual men have AIDS or are HIV+.

This invisibility exists in other ways. For instance, although some people in the gay community still believe that people who are bisexual are confused, misguided, traitorous, etc, etc, many more of them simply ignore bisexuality. The vast majority of HIV prevention literature does not mention the fact that people may have sex with both genders; very few leaflets contain safer sex information involving sex with both men and women, and the word 'bisexual' is almost never mentioned in case it offends or alienates.

One organisation in England which has put bisexuality on its sexual health agenda has been the Health Education Authority. To date, they have produced several advertisements, commissioned a series of videos, published a 'working document' on bisexuality and HIV prevention, convened several meetings on defining bisexuality in the light of HIV, and commissioned issue papers on various aspects of the subject as a result. These measures have met with varying degrees of success. For instance, their first advertisement on bisexuality and safer sex was headed: 'If a married man has an affair, it may not be with a woman.' The picture showed the hands of two men clasped together, a wedding ring visible, with their smart jackets and tailored shirt sleeves prominent. This ad was certainly inoffensive, but it did not address the available evidence which shows that when secretly bisexual married men have sex with other men, it's likely to be furtive and purely genital.

The HEA produced a much sexier ad for young people's style magazines, showing two attractive torsos, one male and one female. It was captioned: 'Which do you find more attractive? If you're not certain, read on.' Interestingly, this ad was not supposed to be an ad for people who were bisexual, but instead for people who were 'confused and experimenting'! They had decided that men who were having 'affairs' with other men were bisexual, but young people who were experimenting with both sexes were not. This sounds pretty confused to me!

The story of the videos the HEA commissioned from Nicola Field

162

in 1991 is also shrouded in confusion. She was asked to make a series of short videos on bisexuality and HIV/AIDS which would be useful in provoking discussion. When she had made them, they were presented at several bisexual conferences for feedback, and given to groups convened by the HEA for comment. It seems that some gay men in these groups felt they should not go out because they were homophobic (although Nicola is a lesbian), and would bring up issues people could not handle. The videos remain unshown as a result.

Most of the bisexual-related work done by HIV prevention groups in the UK has been around men who have sex with men, with almost nothing for bisexual women. But although we are less at risk than the men, that does not mean we are not at risk at all. As with bisexual men, bisexual women have been perceived by some lesbians as 'spreading AIDS' into the lesbian community. This has been hinted at by women as diverse as historian Lillian Faderman (who uncritically speaks of lesbian HIV risk from bisexual women),[7] and comedian Lea Delaria (who does not sleep with women who sleep with men as part of a personal safer sex strategy).[8] But while lesbian identity is seen as protecting women from HIV/AIDS, many lesbians sleep with men. Available evidence would suggest that when they do, they are likely to sleep with gay/bisexual men.[9] Although woman to woman HIV transmission is as yet largely theoretical, transmission through penis-vagina or penis-anus sex with men is indisputable.

In the US, work around bisexuality and HIV/AIDS is more advanced than in the UK – sadly because it has hit much harder there. Bisexuality and HIV/AIDS activism has sought different solutions – one of them being the introduction of safer sex parties, as Zaidie Parr shows in her article. Although in the UK activists are working on bisexuality and HIV/AIDS in Edinburgh, and in England through the national Bisexuals' Action on Sexual Health, there still seems to be an air of complacency within the UK bisexual community. This is partly because the community is fairly new and small, but also, I think, because there is not perceived to be a problem.

According to the articles on safer sex in *Bifrost*, it would seem that safer sex is the norm for bisexual activists. This would reflect other work, such as the article in this section by Mary Boulton, which indicates that bisexually-identified men are more likely to have safer sex than men who behave bisexually but don't identify.

Perhaps this is the reason why, in the UK, bisexual men who are connected to the bisexual community have not died of AIDS, or become HIV+ in large numbers. It is those men who are not connected, who deny to themselves that they are taking part in risky sexual behaviour, who are most at risk. In some ways this would imply that strengthening the bisexual community and encouraging more people to identify openly as bisexual would help reduce HIV risk. Quite how this should be done, however, remains to be seen.

The articles which make up this section of the book take a look at some of the issues concerned with bisexuality and HIV/AIDS. They range from the research-based, such as the essay on men, women and safer sex by Mary Boulton, Ray Fitzpatrick and Graham Hart, to David Sands' personal and very painful story of watching a friend die from AIDS. Each piece adds to the complex picture that is starting to form of the highly complex inter-connection between identity, activism and sexual behaviour.

For myself, there are personal reasons to be involved in HIV/AIDS work, which I seem to be doing more and more these days. Anyone of my age (38) who came of age sexually before AIDS, looks back, past thirteen years of the epidemic, to a time which seems painfully innocent. The bottom line is that I feel I'm surrounded by death and I need to do something about it. In some ways I'm lucky: no-one who's really dear to me has died, despite the fact that many of my closest friends are gay or bisexual men. But people in the background of my life – close friends of close friends, people I'd chat to at parties, that I went clubbing with ten or fifteen years ago, or whose work I admired – are dying at an ever faster rate. They vanish, leaving more grief to be added on to the grief which never had a chance to be worked through, simply because there was too much of it. The choice for those left is that they either become numb/panic-stricken, or they do something.

Sometimes it seems strange to work on theoretical issues around bisexuality and HIV, at one remove from the realities of illness and death. That is partly because, in the UK at present, work around bisexuality and HIV/AIDS is more to do with prevention than care, while at the same time encouraging people, who are HIV+ or have AIDS and who behave bisexually (however they self-identify), to be open about it. In the UK, it is likely that at present they feel unable to do so and, given the amount of support they would be likely to receive, we can hardly blame them. But being open – about bisexuality, about HIV/AIDS, about our sexual needs and desires – is serious and important work. As the slogan says, *Silence = Death*. And if it hasn't done so far, if the crisis has passed you by, be very aware that it's far from over yet.

Notes

1 Quoted in *The Pink Paper*, 29.4.94.

2 *News of the World*, 22.3.92.

3 These include the San Francisco Men's Health Study, conducted by M.L. Ekstrand *et al*; outreach work done by Tigger and E.M. Thornton for Norwich health authority; and Mary Boulton *et al* and Mark Davis *et al*'s articles in this book.

4 Peter Weatherburn *et al*, *The Sexual Lifestyles of Gay and Bisexual Men in England and Wales*, HMSO, London 1992.

5 *The Meanings of Sex Between Men*, Australian Federation of AIDS Organisations, Victoria, Australia 1993.

6 Communication to author, January 1994.

7 Lillian Faderman, *Odd Girls and Twilight Lovers*, Penguin, Harmondsworth 1992, p297.

8 *Phase*, March 1994, p29.

9 The San Francisco Department of Public Health AIDS Office Prevention Services Branch, *Health Behaviors Among Lesbian and Bisexual Women: A Community-Based Women's Health Survey*, October 1993.

Bisexuals and AIDS

Liz A. Highleyman

The AIDS epidemic has had a profound effect on bisexuals. This influence can be thought of as threefold, involving the illness and death of bisexual individuals, the shift in focus of many bisexual organisers and activists towards AIDS-related work, and the effect of societal reactions to AIDS on attitudes toward bisexuals and bisexuality.

Bisexual communities and the bi movement have lost several of their leaders to AIDS. Such people include David Lourea, a founder of the San Francisco bi community who died of AIDS in 1992, and Cynthia Slater, a bisexual woman active in the leather-s/m community. Both were instrumental in bringing various communities (bisexual, gay, lesbian, leather, PWA) together. The San Francisco area bi community was especially hard hit; several of the founding members of BiPol (Bisexual Political Action Group) have died of the disease. The New York City bi community was also greatly affected. Bi communities in areas where the overall rate of AIDS has been lower, and bi communities that have historically had mostly women leaders (such as Boston) have been less visibly affected, but the emotional toll on those who have lost loved ones has been just as heavy. The effect of illness and death from AIDS has fallen particularly heavily on bi men. The bisexual movement to this day has a majority of women leaders, especially among older longer-term activists, in part due to the numbers of bi men that have been lost to the disease.

In addition to those who have died from AIDS, many other bisexuals, both men and women, have either curtailed their bisexual organizing and activism to care for the sick (either their own partners or through AIDS service agencies), or have shifted their activism to focus on HIV/AIDS-related issues. The bisexual movement as a whole has been slow to create bi-specific HIV/AIDS services and activist groups. BiNet USA has an HIV/AIDS task force that has been mostly inactive due to lack of personnel and resources. The Bisexual Resource Center in Boston has produced an educational brochure on safer sex for bisexuals, but in general bisexuals have been forced to obtain materials directed to homosexuals plus materials directed to heterosexuals in order to get a full complement of information. Even material that claims to be directed to 'gay and bisexual men' or 'lesbians and bisexual women' typically does not mention sexual activity with the other sex.

Bisexual AIDS activists have tended to work with the many groups that arose out of the gay/lesbian community, both service organisations and activist groups such as ACT UP. Unfortunately, bisexuals have sometimes not been welcomed in these groups. In part this has been due to the scapegoating of bisexuals in relation to AIDS transmission. In addition, many AIDS activist groups have tried to combine AIDS activism and gay-lesbian activism. Thus they rely on identity-based rather than behaviour-based conceptions of sexual orientation, and may feel that bisexuals are not really 'one of them' or are not committed to AIDS activism for the long term. Gay groups have had considerable success in educating their communities about HIV/AIDS, with the result that the rate of HIV transmission has decreased substantially among gay men as a whole. However the rates of infection continue to increase in several populations, including women, heterosexuals, injection drug users, people of color of all sexual orientations, and young gay men. Efforts are needed to target the populations who are most at risk, even when they do not correspond to neat identity-based categories.

One of the most profound effects of the AIDS epidemic on bisexuals has been the way bisexuals have been portrayed as 'vectors' of HIV transmission. The scapegoating of bi men began in the earliest years of the epidemic, as soon as sexual behaviour was recognised as a mode of transmission. It was claimed that bisexual men were spreading AIDS from the gay community to the (presumably straight) 'general population'. National blood banks included both gay and bisexual identity (regardless of behaviour) as exclusion criteria for blood donors.

Ironically, AIDS has perhaps contributed more than any other factor to increasing the visibility of bisexuals among the mainstream population. Unfortunately, though, this publicity has been mostly negative. A cursory search of a basic newspaper/journal database reveals that almost all references to bisexuals and bisexuality were in relation to HIV/AIDS. Particularly stereotypical articles in the mainstream US press scapegoating bisexual men have included: 'A Perilous Double Love Life' (D. Gelman, *Newsweek*, 13 July 1987), 'The Hidden Fear: Black Women, Bisexuals, and AIDS Risk' (L.B. Randolph, *Ebony*, January 1988), and 'The Risky Business of Bisexual

Love' (S. Gerrard and J. Halpin, *Cosmopolitan*, October 1989).

It has been speculated that AIDS has caused both bi men and bi women to increasingly prefer relationships and sexual liaisons with women rather than men. Because bisexual men have been so stigmatised, the organised bisexual movement has made attempts to distance itself from bisexual men who are not queer-identified. Bisexual organisers have had difficulty acknowledging the reality that there are many closeted married men who practise unsafe sex with men and then infect their wives, and have tried to claim that these men are 'not what real bisexuals are like'. This reluctance has hampered safer-sex outreach to one of the populations that needs it the most. Fear of AIDS has probably pushed many men and women, who had just begun to explore their bisexuality during the sexual revolution/ 'bisexual chic' era of the 1970s, back into the heterosexual closet or back into strictly gay or lesbian communities.

In the late 1980s, as awareness of AIDS among women increased, bisexual women began to be blamed for bringing HIV into lesbian communities. This has had the effect of exacerbating tensions between lesbians and bi women over issues of identity and fidelity to women and the women's community. Many lesbians deny or hide their sexual activity with men, which can prevent them from accessing relevant safer-sex information that is geared towards heterosexual women.

While AIDS was a major focus of the gay/lesbian and bisexual movements in the late 1980s and early 1990s, the emphasis on AIDS appears to be fading in the mid-1990s for several reasons. Many AIDS activists have become ill or died, and many others have burnt out. The tactics of the early AIDS activist movement are no longer effective, and the search for a cure has taken much longer and proved much more difficult than many expected. The gay/lesbian and bisexual movements are also experiencing the resurgence of other threats, such as the increase in right-wing anti-gay campaigns. While AIDS may lose centre-stage as a political issue, it cannot be denied that the profound effects of the epidemic on gay/lesbian and bisexual activism, and on our very conceptions of sex and sexual identity, will continue to be long-lasting and far-reaching.

Thanks to Christopher Alexander, Michael Beer, Melinda Brown, Wayne Bryant, Seth Gordon, Richard Handal, Michael Montgomery, Tim Pierce, Naomi Tucker, and members of the BIACT-L and BITHRY-L electronic mailing lists who provided material and references for this article.

It's About Numbers

Jackie Dutton

It's about numbers. Mathematics, statistics, people and where they belong – and death. Maybe it's not so strange that an AIDS activist trained as a mathematician.

Thirteen years ago I learned about vectors. A teacher told me that they were one way streets – you can go one way along a vector, as far as it goes, but you can't come back the other way. I think about vectors today and I don't believe in one way streets any more.

Women, and bisexual people, have often been described as 'vectors of transmission' in the AIDS crisis. So bisexual men take HIV infection, one way, to the heterosexual population; and bisexual women take HIV infection, one way, to lesbian women. These assumptions are naive, flawed and dangerous. Because people aren't vectors, and nobody is a one way street.

The idea of women as vectors of disease and corruption is repeated throughout history, by such disparate sources as the Torah and the 'racial experts' of Nazi Germany. Prostitute women have been held responsible for the spread of sexually transmitted diseases amongst troops ever since poverty and oppression have meant wars to troop to.

In Britain, women's bodies are policed by the state and many of its attendant structures such as the legal system, by the medical profession and by tolerated 'organised' religions. And in English, the very language of power can be gender specific. In the context of women's control over our own bodies, and in the context of AIDS, the language we use dictates that women don't fuck, we get fucked. Too many people, including some so-called educators, see sex as something that happens to women as a result of male choice, decision and control. This view of women as passive players in a game where men make the rules has led to an entrenched stereotyping, and often ultimate denial, of women's sexualities. If women are conditioned towards finding and expressing sexuality through men and not through ourselves, what does it matter if sex education in schools doesn't pin-point the clitoris?

After all, women don't masturbate and lesbian sex is foreplay waiting for a man.

Against this background, it is instructive to look at how some women who have obviously broken out of the popular stereotypes have fared in the AIDS crisis. There are many women who fall into this category, including women sex-workers, 'single' women, bisexual and celibate women. But I'd like to examine, in particular, some aspects of how HIV has affected lesbian women, and how this has affected their interaction with other women.

HIV and lesbians

HIV has affected all lesbians to some degree. As sexual deviants and sufferers from homophobia, as women and as people. Lesbians have been lied to, been told that they're not at risk of getting HIV through sex. This is partly as a result of a denial of lesbian sex. If women don't fuck, they can't fuck each other and therefore HIV cannot be transmitted. The truth is that lesbians do fuck – each other and other people. On the other hand, the myth that lesbians don't get HIV has not stopped AIDS being used as a tool in the further repression of a group of women already fighting for partnership rights and child custody rights, and against the discrimination visited upon all gay people.

Unfortunately, the simple and appealing idea that 'lesbians are safe' has not stopped lesbians getting HIV. But it has cut off diagnosed lesbians from vital peer support. The 'lesbian response' to HIV has come from the articulate, small, largely urban, groups of lesbians who are highly politicised and 'community' oriented. This response has helped shape how lesbians are perceived in the AIDS crisis.

In responding to state and media lies – and swallowing some of them – many lesbian 'communities' found that AIDS helped to separate them from other women; and to drive further underground the truths that some dykes fuck men and some dykes shoot drugs. And this even before the debate about woman to woman transmission came to the fore amongst lesbians. Some of the information produced stated vaguely that 'SM practices' were the only routes of transmission relevant to lesbians. This added further fuel to an already bloody SM/vanilla 'debate' that raged for more than a decade.

Like every other section of the population, the lesbian 'communities' have been divided along battle lines over issues raised by HIV transmission. Some of these issues are general and have been

addressed by other sections of the population. There are questions like:
are we safe?

if we are, why are we safe and how do we stay safe?

if we're not, what do we do about it?

if we're safe, do we feel relieved, glad, indifferent or jealous, or angry or confused?

which of these emotions is it wrong for us to feel?

In 1989 ACT UP London were ridiculed for providing dental dams at a women's event. Some years later, dental dams have been sold as safer sex materials by chemists, dental suppliers, sex shops and stalls at Lesbian and Gay Pride. Lesbian women, amongst others, have bought them because debate has been provoked within their communities. It was certainly an achievement of AIDS activism that issues around woman to woman transmission began to be discussed beyond the coffee tables of academic researchers. More disturbing is the fact that six years on, information on transmission through oral sex is still sparse. Whilst heterosexual men continue to go down on women, this lack of published research cannot be treated simply as a consequence of lesbian invisibility or of sexism. It does however add to apathy and a widespread denial of risk which also ignores the prevalence of drug use and non-same sex among women who define themselves as lesbians.

And where does this leave relations between lesbians and bisexual women? And heterosexual women?

The vilifying statement that 'bisexual women spread HIV to lesbians', which is certainly not always pronounced by lesbians, has produced shifts in the inter-relationship on both emotional and political levels. Bisexual women, as 'vectors of transmission' are seen to present the same deadly threat to lesbians that bisexual men, in the same role, are seen to present to the heterosexual population as a whole. Heterosexual women are also viewed as vectors in this context. Once upon a time, the question, 'why can't you just stick to women?' was a plea for political correctness. Now it's a plea for an illusion of safety.

Inequality and AIDS

Nothing about the AIDS crisis is new. As one New York activist wrote, 'AIDS turns on the light' to inequalities that existed before. Sex has never been safe for women, any women.

Rape, unwanted pregnancy and fertility-damaging sexually transmitted diseases have all long affected women's sexual choices. In spite of the feminist health lobby of the 1970s and 1980s, access to adequate contraceptive facilities and to safe, legal abortion on demand is still not available to many women. For diagnosed women, reproductive choices are further curtailed. If a woman is HIV positive and pregnant the situation is complicated by several factors. One of these is the imperfectly understood probability of transmission of HIV from a woman to her foetus during pregnancy, birth and possible breast-feeding, and the questions this raises for the woman. In these circumstances many doctors recommend termination. Even if termination is her choice, a diagnosed woman may still face difficulties in finding a clinic, especially outside major cities, willing to carry out a termination on a woman with HIV.

A woman's reproductive potential may be used to deny her access to drug trials for treatments for any disease. In the case of drugs that work on HIV itself, anti-viral drugs, the fact that few are yet licensed means that most treatments of this type are carried out on trial and 'named patient' (formerly known as 'compassionate access') bases. Similarly, although there are licensed drugs used in prophylaxis and treatment of HIV-related and opportunistic infections, many more are still on trial and coming up for trial. The consequences in terms of treatment options for women, and other groups of people who have less access to experimental treatments, are far more marked where so many of the treatments are experimental. For women, as well as black people, children and drug users, even licensed drugs may be less effective and their actions more unpredictable because the demographics of the original trials may not lead to a full understanding of how a given drug works in the bodies of people other than white men.

Research into illnesses that affect exclusively women is under-resourced and under-publicised. It is not unique to HIV and AIDS related conditions that women are treated symptomatically rather than for the root causes of their ill-health. In the case of HIV infection, women are frequently diagnosed far into the course of HIV disease, when doctors have few other options left to explore. This has obvious implications for treatment choices. The current clinical definition of AIDS does not include conditions that affect exclusively women. Raging cervical cancer and pelvic inflammatory disease are not listed as AIDS defining illnesses for a woman who is HIV positive. It's not a question of semantics when an AIDS diagnosis can lead to an increase in healthcare and welfare benefits.

Restricted reproductive rights and choices, restricted access to treatment drugs, and poor access to general healthcare apply to all women, be they heterosexual, bisexual, lesbian or celibate. But it's also vital to any analysis of the AIDS crisis to realise that being marginalised isn't something that happens only to women, or only to bisexuals. When Puerto Rican women were sterilised under Operation Bootstrap in 1950s North America, it wasn't just because they were women. It was primarily because they were Puerto Rican.

Issues of race and power have always influenced healthcare. The colonisers of North America distributed smallpox-infested blankets to the Native American population. And racism has proved intrinsic to the path of the AIDS crisis. Black Africans have been dying of AIDS-related illnesses for more than two decades. But when AIDS first impinged upon most white westerners it wasn't as a syndrome that was killing black Africans, or as the 'junkie 'flu' that was causing the deaths of injecting drug users in large North American cities. AIDS hit the headlines when its effect upon a small number of white men were documented. AIDS hit the headlines because these men were part of a group with some political will, some sense of organised community, and, more importantly, some power as white men. In spite of political differences and initial squabbling, community leaders organised in the same way as they'd organised to fight for sexual liberation in the 1960s and 1970s; and they fought because they were scared. But AIDS retained coverage because other groups with power were scared. Perhaps they found white gay men in the bars of New York City easier to identify with than either black Africans in Uganda or junkies in the ghettos of the same New York City.

It is an over-simplification to say that a virus can't choose; it can't, but people can. And the choices that we make are based largely on the information to which we have access. Our ability to fight HIV in our bodies and in our communities depends upon how much information we have; our access to resources; our access to public attention through the media; and our power.

In societies where power is taken away from whole groups of people, the impact of the AIDS crisis, like that of TB, is drastically different in different communities. HIV infection presents a radically different reality depending on factors such as ability to pay. AIDS worsens all those deep and existing inequalities based on age, gender, race and ethnicity, class, sexuality, disability and poverty. The demographics of AIDS is not a pretty picture.

The need to act together

As long as the effects of AIDS are unevenly distributed throughout the population, there are consequences; both in terms of how 'highly affected' groups view themselves, and how they are viewed by other people. Fear and blame are never far apart. Some sections of the population have traditionally been held responsible for such social evils as crime and disease – drug users, prostitutes and immigrants. In Britain and Northern Europe, AIDS has helped another group of people to be perceived in a similar way. The identification and resultant fear of gay men in the AIDS crisis brought a new wave of queer bashers screaming out of their closets and into the media and on to the streets.

Popular myth and popular ignorance dictate that black people brought AIDS from Africa; gay men became affected through being 'cosmopolitan', well-travelled and promiscuous, and the safety of white heterosexuals is put at risk by bisexual men, injecting drug users and prostitutes. This betrays a hierarchy of power, and a hierarchy of how importantly people's lives are regarded. We step outside our own demographic groups to interact socially, politically and sexually with others. We become 'vectors of transmission' when we interact with those whose lives are more worthy, and therefore more precious than ours.

For a set of people which is, or becomes, isolated from others, the tendency is to insulate itself. The term 'voluntary ghettoisation' is usually inappropriate and is loaded with historical meaning, but it is certainly true that there can be an illusion of safety in 'sameness' and numbers. This has happened within the AIDS crisis, but internal divisions within affected communities weaken our power. So it is dangerous when, for example, non-injecting drug users reject those who inject, or younger gay men reject the experiences of the 'clone generation'. These divisions, both within and between affected groups, are not solely because of AIDS. This is a pattern typical of embattled groups fighting for self-determination, respect, resources and healthcare. But it's not helping the fight against AIDS. Gay men fighting drug users fighting women fighting people of colour for the same small portion of the same pathetic healthcare budget is not going to save any lives, or even any lifestyles. If the way that this pandemic has been portrayed has succeeded in isolating us from 'normal mainstream society', we can't afford to stay divided from each other.

It is unusual to see coalitions of stigmatised and affected groups fighting for both our common and our different needs. But where this has happened, advances have been made. AIDS activists and drug users of different backgrounds and sexualities have fought together to gain and maintain needle/syringe exchanges with greater freedom from police harassment. Treatment activists with widely different access have shared information to make it available to people living with HIV/AIDS. Widespread pressure and the formation of AIDS Clinical Trials Groups (ACTGs), which include trial participants, has led to more 'fast tracking' and improved access to new drugs. There is a base on which to build, and a way forward.

Division, and its effects, is one of the many tragic aspects of the AIDS pandemic. But the main tragedy is that some people are contracting HIV whilst the knowledge, resources and power to avoid transmission remain in the hands and minds of others; and that people are dying of opportunistic infections that are often both treatable and curable. It is these factors, and the fundamental inequalities that give rise to them, that have allowed AIDS to become a crisis in every continent.

The AIDS crisis is about contradictions, where perceived risk and educational funding don't necessarily correlate. It's about greed, where new treatments are developed and patented in an aura of stock market secrecy, and drugs are trialled and data collected on the groups of people who may not be the most affected but are the most affluent. It's about politics and priorities, power and information. It's about silence from governments, organisations and individuals.

But the AIDS crisis is fundamentally, and eventually, about fighting for our lives, and the lives of our lovers, our families, our friends and our children.

Men, Women and Safer Sex: Bisexual Men in England and Scotland

Mary Boulton, Ray Fitzpatrick and Graham Hart

HIV infection and AIDS are perhaps the most serious threats to health that we have faced this century. At the time of writing this article (1992), the World Health Organisation estimate is that 9-11 million adults worldwide have already been infected with HIV, the cause of AIDS. Of these, nearly 1.5 million have progressed to AIDS and nearly 90 per cent of those with AIDS have died.[1] In the United States alone, more than 179,000 people have suffered from AIDS and almost two thirds of them have died. By the end of 1991, AIDS was the second leading cause of death among men 25-44 years of age.[2] The figures for Europe are lower but no less worrying: an estimated 85,000 people have developed AIDS and 500,000 have been infected with HIV.[3]

In the UK, as in most Western industrialised countries, gay and bisexual men have particular reason to be concerned about HIV and AIDS. Since the epidemic was first recognised, homosexual and bisexual men have constituted the largest group with HIV infection and AIDS in these countries. By 1991 two thirds of the 15,500 adults in the UK identified as HIV antibody positive were gay or bisexual men, as were over 80 per cent of the 5000 who had developed AIDS[4] although the incidence of infection amongst other groups is now rising more rapidly.

Relatively little is known, however, about how bisexual men (or bisexual women) in the UK or other Western industrialised countries have responded to the threat of HIV and AIDS or how far they have adopted safer sex guidelines. This is surprising given the initial interest in bisexual men as a potential 'bridging group' between the gay community and the heterosexual population. Despite concern that men who have sex with both men and women could provide a route for the virus to spread to the 'general' (heterosexual) population, little effort has been put into establishing the knowledge, attitudes and behaviour of bisexual men in relation to safer sex or HIV/AIDS.

Bisexual men have participated in research on changes in sexual behaviour amongst homosexually active men in response to HIV and AIDS, but bisexual men have rarely been distinguished from exclusively homosexual men in the analysis and reporting of such research. Thus, while evidence from a number of sources suggests that only a minority of homosexually active men *in general* now engage in unprotected anal intercourse, especially with casual partners, it is difficult to establish whether or not bisexual men *in particular* follow the same pattern of behaviour. Moreover, research on homosexually active men generally ignores female partners and heterosexual sexual behaviour. As a result, almost nothing is known about bisexual men's perceptions of risk of HIV infection in relation to women or the extent to which they had adopted safer sex practices with their female partners.

This chapter describes the findings of a study designed to cast some light on these neglected areas. Sixty behaviourally bisexual men in major cities in England and Scotland were recruited from a variety of sources including genito-urinary medicine clinics (15), an advertisement in a bisexual magazine (11), Bisexual Groups (9), the gay community (10), a prior study of homosexually active men (9), and through 'snowballing' to contacts of respondents themselves (6). While the numbers are too small for the study to be 'representative' of bisexual men in the UK, the findings provide some indication of the range of responses amongst bisexual men to the threat of HIV and AIDS.

Characteristics of the sample

The social characteristics of the sample are given in Appendix 1. It is on the whole young, white, middle class and predominantly single, as is generally the case with studies of homosexually active men. However, the sample is distinctive in that a quarter are married and a third live with a woman.

All the men had had sexual contact with both men and women at some time in the five years prior to interview, and most had a history of contact with both men and women over a considerably longer period. The median number of partners over the course of their lives was 24 for male partners (range 1 to 850) and 8 for female partners (range 1 to 203). A very high proportion of the men also indicated a degree of bisexuality when asked to describe their current fantasies and attractions. Using the Kinsey Scale,[6] which was designed to measure sexual attraction on a *continuum* from exclusively heterosexual to exclusively homosexual, 93 per cent indicated some degree of both homosexual and heterosexual attraction. Sixty-five per cent described equal or almost equal degrees of homosexual and heterosexual attraction.

Not all of the men, however, described themselves as bisexual. Fifty-six per cent described their *private* sexual identity as bisexual but almost as many described themselves in other terms: 22 per cent identified as gay, 7 per cent as straight and the rest used other terms including 'transvestite', 'unrestrained', 'normal' and 'various'. Over half the men (54 per cent) were not open about their sexuality and allowed a *public* identity of 'heterosexual' to prevail. These are the covert or 'closeted' bisexual men. Only 18 per cent maintained a public identity as bisexual while 13 per cent had a public identity as gay.

There were also marked differences amongst the men in the social worlds which they inhabited. About half the men lived in an apparently *heterosexual* context, that is, married or living with a female partner. An example is John, a 44 year old administrative officer in the civil service, married, with 8 male partners and 1 female partner in the last year. He lives with his wife and three children in the home counties but stays in a flat in London during the week. He has little contact with the gay or bisexual community except for meeting partners, and spends most of his social life with other married couples and their families.

A quarter of the sample lived in a *gay* context, that is, substantially involved in the organised gay community, belonging to gay organisations and regularly using gay pubs and clubs. Typical of these men is Michael, a 23 year old librarian with 5 male partners and no female partners in the last year. He identifies as gay and most of his friends are gay. He is a member of a gay sports centre where he works out twice a week, and regularly goes to a particular gay pub and several gay clubs at weekends.

Finally, about a quarter (22 per cent) of the men lived in a *bisexual* context, that is, they were involved in the organised bisexual community. These men can be illustrated by Paul, a 28 year old research scientist with no male partners and one female partner in the last year. He knows a number of bisexual men and women through the Bisexual Group of which he has been an active member for many years, attending meetings and conferences which he helps to organise. Three men could not be classified in this way: all were socially marginal to these main groupings.

Sexual Behaviour

(i) Activities with Partners in the last year

All but 4 of the men had at least one partner in the previous year: 80 per cent had male partners and 73 per cent had female partners. Sixty percent had at least one male *and* one female partner. Numbers of male partners greatly exceeded numbers of female partners: for those with male partners, the median number of partners in the last year was 6 (mean 20, range 1 to 100); for those with female partners, the median number in the last year was 1 (mean 2, range 1 to 24).

Thirty per cent of the men had had unprotected penetrative sex with male partners during the previous year, while twice as many (57 per cent) had unprotected penetrative (vaginal or anal) sex with female partners. Sixty-five per cent of the men had had unprotected penetrative sex with at least one male *or* one female partner in the previous year and 22 per cent had had unprotected penetrative sex with *both* a male *and* a female partner.

(ii) Activities with Current Partners

At the time of interview, 93 per cent had at least one current partner. In total, 77 per cent had at least one current male partner and 57 per cent at least one current female partner: 58 per cent had *regular* male partners, the same number *casual* male partners, 47 per cent had *regular* female partners and 23 per cent *casual* female partners. Forty per cent had both male *and* female partners.

A high proportion had no penetrative sex of any kind with their male partners or always used condoms: only 35 per cent of the men with current male partners engaged in unprotected penetrative sex. 20 per cent of those had unprotected insertive anal sex with *regular* partners and 14 per cent of these with *casual* partners. Men were less likely, however, to have unprotected receptive anal sex with casual male partners (11 per cent than with regular male partners, 29 per cent).

A very different pattern is found with female partners, where a considerably higher proportion of men engaged in high risk sex. Of the

179

34 men who had female partners, all but four engaged in penetrative sex. Sixty-eight per cent engaged in unprotected vaginal sex. It appears that more men (36 per cent) always used condoms with casual partners than with regular partners (14 per cent), although the number of men with casual female partners is small (14). Thirty-five per cent of the 34 practised anal intercourse with their female partners, a quarter of those with regular partners and a fifth of those with casual partners having unprotected anal sex.

Considering sexual behaviour with all partners, 55 per cent had had unprotected penetrative sex with at least one male *or* one female partner and 10 per cent with *both* male *and* female partners.

The differences amongst bisexual men who inhabit different social worlds can be seen in relation to these figures. While numbers are small, there appear to be different patterns of sexual behaviour amongst men in different contexts. Amongst men who live in a *bisexual* context, the single most common pattern is to have no unprotected sex with either male or female partners. Amongst men who live in a *heterosexual* context, the most common pattern is to continue to have unprotected intercourse with women and to have no male partners or no unprotected sex with male partners. Men who live in a *gay* context are more evenly divided between those who have unprotected sex with men and those who do not; they are less likely to have a female partner but virtually all who have, have unprotected sex with them.

Knowledge of safer sex and perceptions of risk of HIV infection

(i) Knowledge of and attitudes towards safer sex

Almost all the men regarded themselves as very (24 per cent) or reasonably (63 per cent) well informed about HIV and AIDS, and this was reflected in their knowledge of what constituted unsafe sex. Virtually all recognised that unprotected passive anal intercourse was unsafe, although there was some confusion about oral sex, vaginal intercourse and active anal intercourse. Vaginal intercourse without a condom was considered *safe* by 9 men and vaginal intercourse withdrawing before orgasm by 15. Unprotected active anal intercourse with men was considered *safe* by 5 men and with women by 7. Most confusion was in relation to oral sex, with about half the sample considering it *safe* and half considering it *unsafe*: 42 per cent considered oral sex with women unsafe and 40 per cent considered it unsafe with men.

Attitudes towards safer sex were remarkably positive: 45 per cent indicated that it was 'better' or 'no different' from their sexual activities generally, and the same percentage that it was 'acceptable', though a sacrifice. Somewhat less favourable attitudes were attributed to sexual partners: 27 per cent indicated that their partners felt it was 'better' or 'no different' and 45 per cent that it was 'acceptable', though a sacrifice.

(ii) Perceptions of risk of acquiring HIV
Forty-eight men (80 per cent) had considered having the HIV antibody test and 27 (45 per cent) had had a test. Of these, 4 were found to be HIV antibody positive. The men who were not known to be HIV antibody positive were then asked what they thought the likelihood was that they were infected at the time of the interview and what they thought the chances were that they would become infected in the future.

Only 4 men thought there was any significant possibility that they might be HIV antibody positive at the time of interview. All of these men had considered having the test but had decided not to. A third of the men who replied recognised a small possibility that they might be positive, most notably those who had been tested in the past and found to be negative. Fifty-nine per cent thought that there was virtually no chance that they would be HIV antibody positive. Almost all of those who had not considered having the test fell into this group.

Similar results were found when the men were asked to estimate their own chances of becoming infected compared with other sexually active men who were gay or bisexual. Sixty-nine per cent (of 51 who replied) felt that they personally were at *lower* risk of infection than other gay or bisexual men. Risk was discussed almost entirely in relation to sexual contact with men.

Finally, the men were asked about what they thought their chances were of becoming infected with HIV by a female partner in particular. Only 3 men (of 54) felt there was any 'real' possibility of infection from a woman. One of these was Liam, a 41 year old company director, married, with 100 male and 4 female partners in the last year. He said, 'I'm as likely to get it from a woman as a man because the type of sex I'm liable to have with women, with the exception of my wife, is 'fantasy' sex with women who are part of that scene. And they are more likely than most women to have HIV.' A further 7 men acknowledged the 'theoretical' possibility of infection but felt it was remote in real terms. The comments from Michael, a 59 year old surveyor with 60 male and 2 female partners, are typical of their views: 'It's less likely than from a man as there are fewer women who are HIV positive, but it's still a physical possibility.'

Eighty-one per cent, however, felt the chances of infection from a female partner were negligible. Most (32 per cent) said it was because very few women were HIV positive; others indicated that whatever the prevalence of HIV amongst women in the area, *their* partners were not the sort to be positive. For example, Gregory, a 32 year old computer programmer with 1 male and 2 female partners said 'Even in Edinburgh, the kind of women I would sleep with, I wouldn't expect to sleep with any drug addicted women. I suppose there's the assumption on my part that I'm sleeping with low risk women compared with some women in Edinburgh.' Thirteen per cent added that female to male transmission was less efficient than male to female transmission. A surprisingly large number (17 per cent) based their assessment on the assumption that their female partners were monogamous.

(iii) Perceptions of risk of transmitting HIV to female partners
Few of the men in the sample felt that they put their female partners at risk of HIV infection. Some were aware that the issues surrounding risks were different in relation to female and male partners, and made comments such as, 'With men, the risks are equal. With women, the risks are very one-sided.' However, what they generally saw as significant in this was *not* that their female partners were at risk from them but that they were not at risk from their female partners.

The main reasons offered for this view concerned the men's perceptions of their own risks of having HIV infection. Only two of the men who *currently* had female partners (3 of those who had female partners in the previous year) thought that there was a significant possibility that they were HIV positive. One, George, a 31 year old carpenter with 4 male and 2 female partners, routinely used condoms with both male and female partners. The other, a 58 year old accountant with 60 male and 2 female partners, always intended to use condoms with women but sometimes did not. He was aware that this put the women at risk should he be infected with the virus himself, and regretted his 'lapses'. The other 32 men who had current female partners felt that the likelihood of their being HIV positive was negligible. Of these, 22 had unprotected sex with women but felt that, since they were very unlikely to be HIV positive themselves, the question of risk to their partners was simply not relevant. They justified continuing to have vaginal sex without a condom by reference to their efforts to protect themselves from becoming infected by avoiding unprotected penetrative sex with their male partners. So long as they were not putting *themselves* at risk with their male partners, they did not feel they were putting their *female partners* at risk by having unprotected intercourse with them.

Conclusion

Perhaps the most striking finding of the study is the marked difference that was found in sexual behaviour with men and women. On the one hand, only a minority of men now engage in unprotected intercourse with *male* partners, particularly with casual male partners. This is consistent with studies of homosexually active men in general, which repeatedly show significant changes in behaviour towards safer sex, although the trend is even stronger amongst this sample of bisexual men. A high proportion do not have penetrative sex of any kind with male partners – a third, compared to a quarter of the sample in studies of gay men. Similarly, the proportion who always use condoms was high – about twice that reported amongst gay men.[8] This extensive practice of safer sex is consistent with the findings of a number of studies which have shown that the prevalence of HIV infection is lower amongst bisexual men than amongst exclusively homosexual men.[9]

On the other hand, the study also shows that bisexual men continue to have unprotected intercourse with women. In an early study of 58 bisexual men in the San Francisco Men's Health Study, Ekstrand *et al* found that only a very small proportion (5 per cent) engaged in unprotected vaginal sex.[10] However, two more recent studies carried out in the UK and Australia found that unprotected vaginal sex was the common practice amongst bisexual men.[11] This study provides further evidence that the shift to safer sex which has occurred with male partners has not occurred to the same extent with female partners. Virtually all the men who had female partners had penetrative sex with them and two thirds had unprotected penetrative sex. Nevertheless, the proportion of men always using condoms with their female partners was higher in this study than in a study of men attending an STD clinic, where less than 10 per cent did.[12]

The differences in sexual behaviour with men and women partners appear to be related to different levels of perceived risk of becoming infected with HIV. Levels of knowledge of safer sex were high amongst the men in this study and attitudes generally positive. However, few men perceived themselves to be at significant risk of infection and this perception was particularly marked in relation to women. The men did not feel that they were at risk of infection from their female partners and the majority continued to engage in high risk sexual activities with women. This contrasts with their behaviour with their male partners, where the majority recognised the potential risk to themselves.

A fundamental concern amongst those who are trying to predict the HIV/AIDS epidemic, and alter its course, is the extent to which bisexual men constitute a distinct and identifiable 'bridging group' which may act as a conduit of infection from the gay to the heterosexual populations. The findings of this study suggest that this is not likely to be the case, to any large extent. About half the men in this study had had unprotected penetrative sex with *either* male *or* female partners in the previous year and a similar proportion with current partners. However, less than a quarter had had unprotected penetrative sex with *both* male *and* female partners in the previous year and only one in ten with current male and female partners. In general, the men had adopted 'risk reduction strategies' which entailed being very careful in some partnerships – particularly with casual male partners – in order to feel free to have unprotected sex in other partnerships – particularly with women. While this entails greater potential risk than the adoption of safer sex with everyone, it may nevertheless contribute to reducing HIV transmission.

The concept of a distinct and identifiable 'bridging group' is also challenged by the findings of this study which show marked differences in sexual behaviour amongst the men in the sample: behaviourally bisexual men do not constitute a single 'group' in the sense of sharing common attitudes and behaviour. Men who lived in a bisexual context were more likely than any of the other men to have had *only* safer sex with both male and female partners. This may reflect the influence of the bisexual community both in facilitating the men's openness to women about their homosexual activities and in making them aware of the importance of safer sex with both homosexual and heterosexual partners. Amongst these men and their partners, safer sex appears to have become the normative practice in all sexual encounters.

Again men who live in a heterosexual context were less likely than men in a gay context to have unprotected penetrative sex with their male partners. This may be simply because the former were less likely to have a 'regular' male partner, which is the context in which most

184

unprotected penetrative sex occurs. Alternatively, it may be because men in a heterosexual context were particularly careful in their relationships with men as a way of keeping their homosexual activities 'private' or 'secret' from their female partners. Men in a heterosexual context were also more likely than men in a gay context to have unprotected penetrative sex with women. Many had quite consciously adopted the strategy of restricting themselves to safer sex with their male partners in order to continue unrestricted sexual activities with their female partners, amongst whom condom use was not expected and might require 'explanation'.

This diversity amongst bisexual men, and the social contexts in which they live and manage their sexual relationships, is a major finding of this research. While bisexual men in general are well-informed about HIV, have positive attitudes towards safer sex and have reduced their risk behaviour, particularly with male partners, men in different situations inevitably respond to the threat of HIV infection in different ways. A minority of men continue to engage in high risk activities. Those concerned to prevent the spread of HIV amongst behaviourally bisexual men must take account of these differences in devising and conducting health education activities.

We would like to thank the Economic and Social Research Council for funding the research and Zoe Schramm-Evans for conducting the interviews.

Notes

[1] J. Chin, 'Global estimates of HIV infections and AIDS cases: 1991', *AIDS*, 5 (suppl 2) 1991, ss57-61.
[2] CDC, 'The HIV/AIDS Epidemic: The first 10 years', *Morbidity and Mortality Weekly Report*, 40 (22) 1991, p357.
[3] Chin, *op.cit.*
[4] CDSC, 'AIDS and HIV-1 infection in the United Kingdom: monthly report', *Communicable Diseases Reports*, 24.1.92, 2 (4), pp17-18.
[5] For example, P. Davies, A. Hunt, M. Macourt and P. Weatherburn, *Longitudinal Study of Sexual Behaviour of Homosexual Males under the Impact of AIDS*, Final Report to the Department of Health, 1990.
[6] A. Kinsey, W. Pomeroy, and C. Martin, *Sexual Behaviour in the Human Male*, Saunders, London 1948.
[7] Davies *et al*, *op.cit.*; and R. Fitzpatrick, J. McLean, M. Boulton, G. Hart and J. Dawson, 'Variation in sexual behaviour in gay men', in, P. Aggleton, P. Davies and G. Hart (eds), *AIDS: Individual, Cultural and Policy Dimensions*, Falmer Press, London 1990.

[8] Fitzpatrick *et al, op.cit.*

[9] M. Boulton and P. Weatherburn, *Literature Review on Bisexuality and HIV Transmission*, Report commissioned by the Social and Behavioural Research Unit, Global Programme on AIDS, World Health Organisation, 1990.

[10] M. Ekstrand, T. Coates, S. Lang and J. Guydish, 'Prevalence and change of AIDS high risk sexual behaviour among bisexual men in San Francisco: The San Francisco Men's Health Study, Abstract MDP31', *5th International Conference on AIDS*, Montreal, Canada, June 1989.

[11] R. Fitzpatrick, G. Hart, M. Boulton, *et al*, 'Heterosexual sexual behaviour in a sample of homosexually active men', *Genito-Urinary Medicine*, 65, 1989, pp259-262; and G. Bennett, S. Chapman and F. Bray, 'A potential source for the transmission of the human immunodeficiency virus into the heterosexual population: bisexual men who frequent "beats"', *Medical Journal of Australia*, 151, 1989, pp314-318.

[12] C. Sonnex, G. Hart, P. Williams and M. Adler, 'Condom use by heterosexuals attending a department of genito-urinary medicine: attitudes and behaviour in the light of HIV infection', *Genito-Urinary Medicine*, 65, 1989, pp248-251.

Appendix:
Sample Characteristics

Age:	Mean 34 years		
	Range 19 to 71 years		
Marital	Single	45	(75%)
Status:	Divorced	2	(3%)
	Married	13	(22%)
Living	With female partner	19	(32%)
Arrangements:	With male partner	3	(5%)
	Other	38	(63%)
Social	Middle class	39	(65%)
Class:	Working class	6	(10%)
	Students	7	(12%)
	Unemployed	8	(13%)
Ethnic	White	57	(95%)
Group:	Afro-Caribbean	3	(5%)

On the Beat: A Report on the Bisexually Active Men's Outreach Project

Mark Davis, Gary Dowsett and Ulo Klemmer

There is still little useful data on men who have sex with men and women in Australia. Crawford et al,[1] using data from the Social Aspects of the Prevention of AIDS investigation (SAPA)[2] argue that there are many men with a bisexual practice who were sufficiently attached to gay communities through their social and sexual practices to be receiving the educational message about safe sex and HIV transmission. Consequently, levels of unsafe sex among these men were low. However, the sample on which Crawford et al report is different from that studied by Bennett et al in their work on men who frequent beats, because of different strategies of sample recruitment. This latter project reported worrying amounts of unsafe heterosexual and homosexual sex.[3]

What is clear from these studies and the reports of Frazer et al in Queensland[4] and Campbell et al in Melbourne[5] is that we ought to desist from classifying a group of men as bisexual at all. Rather than assuming there exists a bisexual identity waiting to be discovered, we should concentrate on discovering the patterns and nature of the bisexual practice.

The addition of the word *bisexual* in the phrase so common in HIV/AIDS work – *gay and bisexual men* masks a diversity of sexual interests among these men. The use of the category bisexual also masks our ignorance of this diversity. It could be that we are talking of, at any given moment, up to 38 per cent of the adult male population, according to Kinsey et al.[6] It is for this reason that we conducted this exploratory intervention/research project to help clarify some of the outstanding questions about men who have sex with women and men.

188

Analysis of the difference between men who were having sex with men only and those who had sex with men and women during the period covered by the SAPA survey highlighted a major distinction that has implications for the sort of education research that needs to be done. These bisexually active men showed lower levels of involvement in gay community social events and activism compared with gay men but higher levels of sexual involvement, meaning more use of beats, sex cinemas, saunas and the like. This implies that education built on gay community social events and activism is not going to reach bisexually active men equally well. It also points out the importance of education in sites of sexual interaction, the most prominent of these being beats.

Beats are public environments where certain men meet for sexual interaction. These places include toilets in public parks; shopping centre car-park toilets and environs; and parks, bush tracks, scenic areas in nature reserves. A great variety of men are known to use these settings for sex, including bisexually active men. We intended to develop an approach to outreach and education in the beats setting, letting the beat worker directly pursue a relationship of trust over time, which might be extended to a small number of men such as known sexual partners or other men recognised from the same beats. We wanted to explore the possibility of developing in the men an interest in a social connection with others like them. We aimed to find out what it is that obstructs such possibilities and what will foster such interest. If small clusters were accessible, we intended to try out safe sex education strategies which addressed the needs of these men and which could be used by the AIDS Council of NSW (ACON) for further development.

We extended the relationship between the beat worker and the client beyond the exchange of information on the beat. We wished to investigate the possibility of a more dense and detailed exchange, one which allowed the beat worker, and researchers, access to the dynamics of sexual encounters between these men and other such men. Such exploratory connections have been made by one or two of the ACON beat workers in the past; hence we sought to develop it systematically. The project therefore sought to explore the educational possibilities growing out of that more dense relationship.

The project lasted for four and a half months and included 65 separate sessions in the field. More than 20 different beats were investigated. Most were located in Blacktown, an older traditionally working-class suburb with the problems which accompany high unemployment. Others were in Castle Hill, a newer residential

189

development of housing estates and up-market shopping centres in the north west of Sydney. These two areas were chosen because the size and structure of the beats were similar, and non-gay and married men were known to use beats there; the social class characteristics of the areas chosen were different from each other.

Interactions with bisexually active men on the beat

Interactions with men in the beat setting are shaped by three broad influences: the physical layout of the beat; the patterns of use that are determined partly by the site; and the familiarity of the beat worker with the setting and the beat users with him. For example, beats where men can walk around, meet and talk with some privacy, facilitate contact between workers and men, whereas toilets without any easy way of men talking inhibit verbal interaction. Another important aspect of the interactions is the self-selection by beat users and *target* selection by the beat worker. Some men choose to talk with beat workers and others do not. This means that suppositions based on discussions with these men are not typical or readily generalisable to all beat users, or more specifically to all bisexually active men. Additionally, beat workers approach the beat users and initiate conversations with some pre-conceptions in mind. Often a worker's supposition about the *type* of man he is approaching is wrong. For example, the worker initially decided to approach men with wedding rings and who looked *straight*, in an effort to talk to bisexually active men. However, many of these men said they were gay and had no sexual relationships with women. At other times a man assumed to be gay and with very typical patterns of social interaction in the gay community was also having sex with women. These apparent contradictions are reflected in other research findings[7] and alerted us to the non-fixed nature of sexual identity and the difficulties of conducting outreach to bisexually active men.

Beat outreach activity can be broadly divided into two forms of communication – non-verbal and verbal. For some bisexually active men, non-verbal interaction proved to be the most common form of communication. Non-verbal interactions involved eye contact and exchanging pamphlets like *Safe Sex and AIDS*. This happened when the beat situation did not facilitate discussion, when the man was not prepared to talk or when some interruption occurred. Wherever possible the non-verbal interaction was conducted to facilitate verbal interaction but this was not always successful. During the fieldwork bisexually active men seemed to avoid verbal interaction more than gay-identified men, although this is a subjective observation and should be cautiously interpreted. Printed material, such as *Safe Sex and AIDS* are therefore essential, and more sophisticated versions could be developed, particularly for non gay-identifying men who hold misconceptions about HIV/AIDS. The material could be developed to avoid triggering denial of sexuality, and reflect some of the major social and interpersonal problems faced by bisexually active men.

When the beat worker and user were able to find an appropriate situation verbal interaction ensued. The worker talked to 26 bisexually active men, contributing the body of the data on interactions in the field. During these interactions the field worker would explain that he was an educator from ACON; ask if a discussion about safe sex and HIV/AIDS could proceed; question and probe for knowledge of HIV/AIDS and safe sex practices; and perhaps provide printed information. As the worker became familiar with the local beat circuit he found it easier to make contact with men. He made repeat contacts with a number of men who became well known to him; and interactions that had been non-verbal become increasingly friendly and verbal. Broadly, however, bisexually active men spoke of sex in the beats and very little else, while gay men were more interested in social activity and talking about their personal lives, relationships, etc. Unfortunately the majority of bisexually active men were not inclined to discuss their sexual practices with women. This could reflect experiences of being rejected by gay male sexual partners once bisexual practice is disclosed, fears of emotional turmoil and losing partnerships with females if exposure is risked, or a motivation to protect the privacy of female sexual partners. However, discussion with some bisexually active men suggested a deeper dynamic based on denial of sexual practices.

Some bisexually active men were prepared to talk at some length with the field worker. These successful interactions seemed to be based in certain facilitating aspects of the interaction, for example: a fairly private and uninterrupted situation; denial and avoidance not having been triggered; the emergence of some basis for discussion, like a common experience or focusing on practices of beat use *per se*; familiarity with sight of the field worker; being introduced by a third party; or a request of some kind. Once this type of contact was established the interaction was fruitful and the field worker was able to build good rapport on future occasions.

It was not easy to find out if social networks among bisexually active men exist around and away from the beat. The suggestion is that they do not exist – especially since most of the bisexually active men talked to had intact and desirable hetero-social networks. Alternatively, some men would employ gay community venues like bars or interact with gays in the beat setting. This meant that a *bisexual logic* of social networking was not available to education work, an important finding from the project. The finding also suggested that group-based activity or any form of clustering on the basis of *bisexuality* would be a novel and threatening experience for most men.

Individual experiences

TIM[9]

Tim is 16 years old. When the beat worker met him he was wearing shorts, t-shirt and running shoes that were all quite worn. He has a girlfriend, who was shopping while he was doing the beat. He was very comfortable talking with the outreach worker about sex and was not ashamed of what he was doing and did not have any other strongly negative emotions attached to his homosexual practice. He spoke of his sexual practices and interests quite openly. Tim has heard of AIDS but has no safe sex knowledge. He does not read newspapers and AIDS was not discussed at school. Although he has wide experience of male-to-male sex including receptive anal sex, he has never used a condom for anal penetration.

Tim presents a number of dilemmas. He has no knowledge of safe sex and does not engage in activity that would improve his awareness and knowledge about HIV/AIDS. Additionally, the sex he has with other men is on-the-run. He participates in all manner of sex including risky practices and perhaps not always of his own choosing. The worker gave Tim the number for the Fun and Esteem Project[10] and also his own number but there has been no further contact. It seems group-based peer education with young gay men would not be appropriate for this young man (cultural differences, difficulties explaining his involvement to his partner, etc).

JONATHAN

Jonathan is 79 and has been having sex with men since his wife died.[11] He found out about beats from the first man he had sex with – a man from work. Jonathan does not care at all about the possibility of AIDS.

He enjoys receptive anal sex but does not use condoms for various reasons: he cannot put them on; he is too embarrassed to ask the other person to put one on; he says he believes old people cannot get HIV, only young people do; he washes himself out when home with antiseptic cream. Jonathan believes that he is too old to be worth worrying about for HIV transmission. A contrasting example of a myth about HIV transmission documented from the beat setting was that someone who is young and not in the leather scene will not come in contact with HIV. These misconceptions seem to relate back to ideas of health, illness and related perceptions of the generational aspects of the HIV epidemic more generally.

MIKE

Mike is in this thirties and has a non-English speaking background. He approached the worker in a beat and asked for oral sex and then somewhere to go for sex. This was a completely unambiguous sexual initiation. Yet when the worker explained that he was from ACON and that he would like to talk about safe sex, Mike swore and asked the outreach worker to talk to the 'fuckin' poofters' instead, and promptly left.

This non gay-identifying man is subject to the wider community beliefs that AIDS is a gay problem and does not associate it with his own sexual practices. His response may also be denial of the import of his sexual behaviour, or a fear-driven response to authority and resentment at having been *trapped* in the beat setting, and through his sexual initiation. He exemplifies perhaps in an extreme way the problems for the AIDS educator trying to work across the boundaries of sexual identity and meanings.

DOUG

Doug is an Aboriginal man in his mid thirties. On the beat he was open about his sexuality – almost brazen. Doug was unique among the informants in his great openness about his sexual lifestyle and also his willingness to discuss with the beat worker sexual practices with his wife. He has sex with both men and women, including anal sex with men, where he prefers to insert but does occasionally receive. His HIV knowledge was comprehensive and accurate except for failure to use water-based lubricant with condoms. This suggests a failure of either knowledge – not knowing about water-based lubricant – or a failure of practice, where proper lubricant use is omitted despite the appropriate knowledge. In Doug's case though there is a suggestion that he is putting forward a socially desirable response regarding condom use and he may not ever, or frequently, use condoms.

He is not married but lives with his partner. They also have children. He thoroughly enjoys his sexual lifestyle; both heterosexual and homosexual. His partner does not know of his current sexual practices with men.

Doug was passionate about his partner and children and was strongly motivated to maintain his family unit – something he felt was not possible in a gay relationship. For him sex with men was an added sexual thrill which did not obscure the importance of heterosexuality. Doug's example points out that for some bisexually active men, family relationships and sex with women exceed the importance placed on beat sex and sex with men.

Bisexual practices

The beat setting is an arena of sex play open to more than just gay men, and for many men may be an opportunity for physical and pleasurable release. This eroticisation then forms part of the background against which sex in the beat and safe sex education is conducted. Some gay men preferred to have sex with straight men from the beat setting and participated in generating the meanings of bisexuality or of straight-acting men. Others adopted masculine demeanour as a basis for operating sexually in the environment. The investigation of bisexuality can therefore not be separated from the derivation of meaning and desire built on wider ideas about masculinity and sexuality.

The social relationships between men in other settings also pose possibilities for sexual interaction. Based on the small group consultations conducted as part of the CHAP fieldwork, gay men offered some insights into sex on the beats and elsewhere with non gay-identifying men.[12] Men mentioned being able to obtain sex from men picked up at mainstream nightclubs. Body language, well-judged ambiguity, possessing masculinity but being able to recognise opportunities for sex: all were part of the skills needed. Others spoke of the widespread adolescent sexual networks of their youth leading them to suppose that a large proportion of men were interested in sex irrespective of their sexual identity. Many options for sexual contact existed if the situation was managed correctly, e.g. the gym, football clubs, phone lines for social support, straight friends, etc.

From this perspective, the construction of identity of the men using the beat who also have sex with women is problematic for us. The field notes are full of examples of contradictions of identity and behaviour.

For example, men who described themselves as gay had girlfriends; married men adopted the label bisexual in a way that signalled the diversity of their sexual interest not a lifestyle; non-gay men disregarded advice about safe sex since they were not 'faggots', 'queens', or 'poofters'. This contradiction of practice and identity is widely documented and must be viewed as central to understanding bisexual practice.[13]

Most striking was the observation that male-to-male sex among ostensibly non-gay men relied more on the situation than on social identification of sexual preference. For example, the outreach worker worked with two prisoners who were lovers while incarcerated, yet married in the outside world – they spoke of themselves as straight and as mates. From their point of view, sex between men in the prison setting happens if the situation is right, usually when guys are 'out-of-it' on drugs.

Other young gay-identified men were shown to be occasionally or frequently having sex with women, yet they had adopted mainly gay sexual and emotional attachments. One man in particular called himself gay to the gay beat worker and other gay men, described himself as bisexual to his brother who knew of his sexual activity with men and women, and apparently is heterosexual in the eyes of his parents, girlfriend and school mates.

The sexual situation of men having sex with men is far more complex than *bisexual* or *homosexual* can encompass. Sexual identity, particularly in the case of bisexuality, seemed to be contingent on the situation. Unlike gay identity with its many variations and diverse cultural practices, bisexual identity, investigated through the beats setting, is limited and has little cultural support.

One stereotype of bisexuality is that it is a half-way label between homosexuality and heterosexuality.[14] These stereotypes seem to work against bisexually active men. This investigation uncovered disparaging attitudes to bisexually active men among some gay men who had been bisexually active, many who had themselves been married.[15] These gay men more recently found themselves providing support to bisexually active men. Their previous experiences led some of the gay men to use a stereotype which viewed bisexually active men as not well-adjusted and conning their male and female partners. This stereotype places pressure on bisexually active men to change their sexual practice and conform to other men's notions of sexual identity. This raises concerns about the extent to which gay men would be willing to educate these men unconditionally.

One bisexually active man spoke of the conundrum of emotional and physical satisfaction related to bisexuality. His wife was not prepared to have sex with him any more, yet he found the sex in beats and saunas impersonal. His dilemma was how to find physical and emotional satisfaction at the same time. Another bisexually active man described his life as a constant struggle, leading him to want to opt out, although he did not speak of suicide. This reflected not so much problems with sexual satisfaction or identity but his domestic arrangement, where his wife's knowledge of his bisexual practices led to much emotional turmoil.

Relations in marriage once bisexuality is found out can be emotionally difficult.[16] This could be part of the reason that bisexually active men do not disclose their sexual relationships with women to beat outreach workers, are covert on the beat, and tend not to become involved in social networks. From their perspective breaking down heterosexual associations and entering something unknown or what at best seems flimsy and alien, would be daunting. These men's commitment to heterosexuality, with beats-derived sexual contact limited to sex, seems logical from this point of view. Most men preferred not to discuss the sex they were having on the beat and there were definite barriers to discussing sex with women. The men in the beats setting were committed to keeping their two sexual lives separate, and therefore believed they were not at risk of infection.

A notable aspect of beat use is the constant presence of surveillance instigated by local government and the police. The beat worker observed police entering beats and acting threateningly, kicking in doors and verbally harassing users. Through networking, the worker became aware that contact with the police is a normal part of beat life and something that all users deal with, if not themselves directly, by association with those who have.

Other men who perform surveillance roles include council workers, cleaners, shopping centre security guards. Bashers even tend to see themselves in a sanctimonious light – *cleansing* and ridding the beat or park of 'poofters'. Other forms of surveillance are signs saying the areas are patrolled and that loiterers will be prosecuted. The education that can be done in the beats is contingent on decisions of local government authorities, supermarket chain management, and the police.

Beat users resent this activity. There is a suggestion from the field notes that men less able to deal with men in authority – younger, working-class, and non-English speaking men – are more vulnerable to the consequences of surveillance. One young Asian man had been harassed by police and called 'you little Asian poofter'. This man had no idea of his legal standing in the beat and asked the beat worker about these aspects. In general, the beat worker's role is conducted in response to surveillance harassment – giving information about legal rights, supporting men, and managing relationships with councils and police directly.

The structure of all social interaction on the beat is partly the result of the need to be wary about beat using. Checking out the beat is a necessary preliminary phase in all beat use to guard against bashers and police. Managing this threat collectively through information exchange contributes to the development of social life on the beat. Unfortunately, because many bisexually active men seem less able to participate in this collective action, they are potentially more vulnerable. They do not interact so readily with each other and with gay men, and therefore do not develop a supportive network that feeds them information about police, bashers, HIV/AIDS, etc. Bisexually active men are therefore more isolated than most beat users, possibly because of increased fears of exposure, and less support, which is directly related to the pervasive surveillance of the beat setting. Moreover, surveillance of beat sex is actually part of the surveillance of all men's sexuality – it signals to all men that such possibilities exist, and that they are being watched as they contemplate them.

Some bisexually active men denied that they were at risk of infection on the basis that they were not gay as such. Denial of risk for HIV transmission and the difficulties of opening up discussion meant that there is much we do not know. Bisexual practice is formed in complex ways and in other social settings that have not been investigated. Future research needs to be linked with other strategies for outreach – sex cinemas, classified ads, work with heterosexual men, masculinity, etc, to comprehend the diversity of bisexual practices. Wider cultural notions about bisexuality and HIV transmission will need to be understood to communicate more effectively about bisexual practice and HIV/AIDS. More may be achieved by investigating heterosexuality, gender relations and safe sex education for bisexually active men, in parallel with beat work, gay-community education activity, and the diversification of outreach to sex cinemas, classified ads, etc.[17]

SECTION III: HIV, AIDS AND SAFER SEX

Opportunities for Extending Outreach to Bisexually Active Men

There are a number of opportunities for education outreach in the beats setting and other forms of outreach built on better insight into the structure of bisexual practice. Men, whether or not they are also having sex with women, obtain male to male sex in ways limited only by imagination, and built on frameworks of male association, the commercial aspects of sex and communication patterns. Future programmes dealing with bisexuality will need to consider this complexity.

In the beat setting the existence of social networks among men was documented and these are probably the basis for increased outreach and educational activity. Future work could be modelled on the action-research method employed in this project. Even though these strategies were succesful with a range of men, some bisexually active men are largely absent from these social activities – preferring to restrict their interactions to sex. This is consistent with other research showing bisexually active men are less inclined to participate in gay identified social, cultural and political activities.[18] Investigation of the social networks among bisexually active men in the beat setting proved difficult. Most bisexually active men apparently resisted lengthy interaction with the field worker, or avoided verbal contact altogether.

However, a number of bisexually active men and many gay identified men were willing to talk to the field worker and participate in the education process. These successful contacts and discussions were achieved when certain facilitating aspects of interactions were in operation. This activity can be termed social attachment. Work in the beat has to be structured so as not to trigger defensive reactions on the part of bisexually active men in the early part of the interaction: and it needs to happen over longer periods of time, and be focused in particular beats to increase opportunities for contact. Social attachment, combined with traditional outreach and HIV/AIDS education strategies, increases the opportunities for successful work with bisexually active men in the beat setting.

The project was funded by the Australian Federation of AIDS Organisations. All correspondence should be directed to Dr G.W. Dowsett, Sociology Department, School of Behavioural Sciences, Macquarie University, Sydney NSW 2109, Australia.

Notes

[1] J. Crawford, G.W. Dowsett, S. Kippax, D. Baxter, D. Berg, R.W. Connell, P. Rodden, and L. Watson, *Social Aspects of the Prevention of AIDS Study A, Report No. 8. Men who have sex with both men and women*, Macquarie University, School of Behavioural Sciences, Sydney 1991.

[2] The Social Aspects of the Prevention of AIDS (SAPA) Study was based on a questionnaire administered to 535 gay and bisexually active men in metropolitan and regional New South Wales and the Australian Capital Territory. The findings of this research have been reported elsewhere and relevant articles are cited in the references for this chapter.

[3] G. Bennett, S. Chapman and F. Bray, 'Potential source of transmission of AIDS into the heterosexual population: bisexual men who frequent "beats" ', *Medical Journal of Australia*, 161, 1989, pp314-8.

[4] I.H. Frazer, M. McCamish, I. Hay and P. North, 'Influence of human immunodeficiency virus antibody testing on sexual behaviour in a "high-risk" population from a "low-risk" city', *Medical Journal of Australia*, 149, 1988, pp365-68.

[5] I.M. Campbell, P.M. Burgess, I.E. Goller, and R. Lucas, *A Prospective Study of Factors Influencing HIV Infection in Homosexual and Bisexual Men – report of findings, Stage 1*, University of Melbourne, Department of Psychology, Melbourne 1988.

[6] A.C. Kinsey, W.B. Pomeroy, and C.E. Martin, *Sexual Behavior in the Human Male*, W.B. Saunders, Philadelphia 1948.

[7] Bennett *et al*, 1989; and Crawford *et al*, *op.cit.*

[8] *Safe Sex and AIDS*, AIDS Council of NSW, safe sex education pamphlet. Lists a comprehensive range of sexual practices and describes their relative risk, in a convenient pocket size.

[9] Names and social situations have been changed.

[10] Fun and Esteem Project, ACON peer education project with men under 25 years of age.

[11] For this pattern of sexual behaviour see R.W. Connell, M.D. Davis, and G.W. Dowsett, 'A bastard of a life: homosexual desire and practice among men in working-class milieux', *Australian and New Zealand Journal of Sociology*, 29 (1), 1993, pp112-135.

[12] Mark Davis, Gary Dowsett, Bob Connell, Robert Ariss, Tim Carrigan, and Murray Chapple (eds), Class, Homosexuality and AIDS Prevention: Resource material for use in HIV/AIDS education, National Centre for HIV Social Research, Macquarie University, Sydney.

[13] J.H. Gagnon, 'Disease and desire', in S.R. Granbard (ed), *Living with AIDS*, The MIT Press, Cambridge, Mass., 1990, p181-211.

[14] Gagnon, *op.cit.*

[15] Connell, *et al*, *op.cit.*

[16] ACON support groups for women partners of bisexual men, key informant interview with project worker, 1991.

[17] Crawford *et al*, *op.cit.*

[18] *Ibid.*

Safer sex parties in the US bisexual community

Zaidie Parr

It was not until several years after the initial spread of the HIV virus among gay and bisexual men and other disadvantaged groups in the USA that its transmission could be clearly linked to particular types of sexual activity. Once 'safe' and 'unsafe' sexual behaviour were, to a certain extent, identifiable, the lesbian gay and bisexual communities started working to inform people of the need to practise safer sex, using group presentations and videos. Safer sex is commonly defined as sexual activity that is currently deemed to be safe with regard to HIV transmission – in particular all sexual activity that does not involve the exchange of blood or bodily fluids.

The AIDS epidemic requires us to face the need for healthier sexual conduct and a sense of ethical and personal responsibility in sex. However, despite the urgency of the situation, the silencing and oppression of gay and bisexual men in America has rendered any change in sexual lifestyle problematic. For some, having promiscuous sex is a way to constantly affirm their identity as gay men, which society tries so hard to suppress. Even as I write, Huw Jones, in a recent article (*Pink Paper*, 17.3.95.) has described how, in New York, the epicentre of the AIDS epidemic in the West, seroconversion among young gay men is rising despite the city's access to some of the most experienced HIV prevention groups in the world. One solution that is now to be tried by HIV prevention activists in New York is the monitoring of commercial sex venues in order to prevent the spread of HIV in the city's sex clubs – the bathhouses and backrooms which one New York newspaper recently referred to as the 'killing fields'. This may be problematic however; although studies estimate a 35-45 per cent HIV prevalence rate among gay men in New York, many gays and lesbians fear that introducing 'gay sex police' to monitor sex in clubs is the first step to tougher restrictions on gays.

For this reason I believe that the radical step taken by some bisexual activists in the USA some years ago, of assisting the development of safer sex practice amongst bisexual men and women by hosting safer sex parties, is important. Bisexuals in some cities in the USA can now attend Jack and Jill Off Parties with their peers, where safer sex is the norm, and those unwilling to comply with this rule are asked to leave. Some may find the idea of this type of outreach to the bisexual population disturbing and even distasteful. But, although an unusual idea, safer sex parties are about saving lives – an opportunity for educational outreach which fits the needs of some bisexuals. The organised bisexual community in the USA seems to have accepted the introduction of safer sex parties quite happily, which suggests that, for those who choose it, this 'hands on' approach to safer sex may be a success.

For bisexuals, our ability to practise safer sex and prevent the spread of HIV is influenced by our oppression as 'invisible', excluded, and marginalised people, our lack of peer contact, and factors such as isolation and low self esteem, as well as our variable access to safer sex information and safer sex resources. It seems that these parties may go some way towards combatting problems of social isolation and build confidence in learning and practising safer sex. It must be emphasised that no one need have sex at these parties if they do not wish it, and that the parties are not intended to be exploitative in any way. In fact, safer sex parties are governed by extremely stringent rules of behaviour, as you will see from the rest of this article, which consists of some well thought-out suggestions from US activists on how to organise them. When reading the *Party Rules* which follow it may come as a shock to realise the degree of responsibility required to practise safer sex. You may also consider public acts of sex not to your taste. But if this is your reaction, remember that studies still show that unsafe sex often takes place within a relationship in order to express love and intimacy; although cultural differences may prevent safer sex parties initiatives in countries other than the USA, nonetheless it is vital that we reconsider how to express these loving emotions.

In 1991, one of the first organisers of safer sex parties described some useful groundrules for anyone wanting to organise a safer sex party of their own:

> There can never be too many safe sex products around. Boxes of latex gloves, lots of rubbers (both lubed and unlubed, flavored ones if you like), saran wrap (it comes in colors at Christmas time), WATER-BASED (oil-based eats the rubbers) lube (especially good in dispenser

bottles), and paper towels are together in a number of convenient spots around the room. There are perhaps 10 or 13 safe sex product stations at a party for 75 people. As you can imagine, you will not want to stop doing what you are doing at your sex party to look for a new rubber. Put plenty of safe sex product stations all around where the action will be.

There can never be too many places for people to have sex. I suggest air beds, futons, couches, foam pads, big pillows, as many soft places as you can fit into your sex space.

Music is important. Occasionally the person controlling the music at the Jack and Jill Offs has put on something so absurd (*The 1812 Overture* for example) that it killed the ambience of the party for half an hour. I like music that is not too imposing or too much in the foreground. The volume should encourage conversation, not discourage it.

Food: light snacks are best. *People will congregate around the food and talk and eat. Put the food in a place where it will not interfere with the flow of traffic or the flow of the sex.* Make certain to have some non-alcoholic drinks. There is usually some beer and wine at the Jack and Jill Off Parties, but I have never seen anyone there drunk.

I find that about one out of every ten persons with whom I discuss these parties wants to go to one. I take new people if they are bi, gay or lesbian. I rarely introduce heterosexual men to these parties. A free anonymous hot line called San Francisco Sex Information gives people information about the Jack and Jill Parties if they ask. The caller is given an address and told to write about why they want to go to the Jack and Jill Off. Perhaps similar information services such as the Amsterdam Gay and Lesbian hot line would be willing to tell people about your party. If your local bi organisation has a newsletter or magazine, they may be willing to publicise your party. Be certain to give an address which will allow you to screen your letters. Personal ads in alternative newspapers may attract the kind of people you want.

Sex police: certain people at the Jack and Jill Off Parties have to be sex police. They keep their eyes open to assure that everyone is abiding by the rules. Usually the crew takes turns so that some of them can play while the others work. Likewise someone has to watch the door. The door person has a great deal of responsibility. They must decide if the person seeking admission is drunk, crazy, stupid, or probably a lot of fun.

In order to organize your own sex party, you will have to put together a group of people to do these tasks as well as finding a space for the party, making up invitations, promoting the party (however discreetly), buying snacks and safe sex products, decorating the space, providing music, and cleaning up afterwards.

SAFER SEX PARTIES

The invitation to John and Beth's 'Sex Party VII' outlined the Party Rules:

Every party must have rules. Read 'em, learn 'em, live 'em.

- *No oral, vaginal or anal penetration without condoms or latex gloves.* Some latex and latex-compatible spermicide will be provided and everyone is asked to bring their own. (Spermicide use is not mandatory. However, placing a small amount on the inside of a condom increases sensitivity for the wearer and reduces the risk of transmitting STDs). Gloves and condoms must be replaced before each interaction with a new partner.
- Dental dams (latex gloves cut apart) are required for oral/vaginal or oral/anal contact. Any 'sex toys' that come in contact with bodily fluids must be covered with latex before use. They must be washed and covered with fresh latex before use on another person.
- Your hosts are Beth and John. On first violation of a rule you may be asked to leave by a host. A host will ask you to leave on a second violation. You must leave at a host's request.
- You are here at your own will and may leave if you wish. You will not suffer stigma for leaving. However, if you must leave early, please do so quietly and respectfully.
- *The party will end* at midnight. The hosts have to be out early the next morning.
- If you feel someone is not following a rule, please inform a host.
- If someone's activity makes you feel uncomfortable, but is following the rules, leave the room. Contact a host if you feel you should. Accept other people's sexual practices as you would hope they accept yours. Celebrate diversity!
- A section of the space will be designated as 'no sex' space. It will be as 'separate' as the accommodations allow.
- There will be, no doubt, kinky sex (s/m, bondage, etc). If this makes you uncomfortable remember that you were warned.
- Consentuality is important. In fact, consentuality is required! Do not touch someone without asking them and receiving verbal permission. Never feel bad about saying 'no' to any activity. You control your body. Don't be upset if someone says 'no' to you, it is their right and it isn't an insult. 'No' means 'no' unless you have negotiated a safe-word. The default party safe-word is 'oatmeal'.
- No smoking, except on the outside balcony. Please don't scare the neighbours.
- No alcohol or illegal drugs to be consumed at the party. Don't arrive drunk or intoxicated either. Safe sex is sober sex.
- Confidentiality: Names of people attending this party are not to be revealed in public (this includes electronic networks) unless those specific people agree to have their names revealed.

- 'Just watching' is O.K. Asking someone to not watch is also O.K.
- Taking pictures and/or making audio or video recordings is prohibited.
- Please exercise all possible caution not to damage any property. You will be held responsible for any damage you may cause.
- The hosts are not responsible for pregnancies, diseases, emotional trauma, relationship trauma, or new relationships or other problems resulting from attending or not attending this party.
- You must be at least 18 years old to attend.
- Everyone will be required to sign that they agree to abide by these rules before entering the party.

The invitation 'Sex Party VII' also included the Party Un-Rules:

O.K. So you have (supposedly) read what this party is *not* all about in the rules and consent form. So what *is* this party about?

This party is about: kissing ... hugging ... cuddling ... friendships ... fucking ... sucking ... loving ... lusting ... snuggling ... eating ... drinking ... blissing out ... massaging ... rubbing ... watching ... spanking ... masturbating ... licking ... chewing ... decadence ... celebrating ... dancing ... dreaming ... talking ... holding ... fantasizing ... caressing ... moaning ... and much, much more!

This party is for *you*. You are not obligated to do anything you do not want to do. You don't even have to give out your phone number to anyone afterwards! You can be completely selfish, as long as you continue to treat others with respect. You can keep your clothes on, or take them all off, wear sexy lingerie – whatever you feel comfortable in.

It's O.K. to attend the party and not be sexual at all. Please feel free to come and hang out in the non-sexual space that we provide. This will be an area where people can sit down, relax, watch movies, listen to music, eat or just talk. This space will be separate from the 'play' space.

People may be engaging in bondage, whipping, spanking, dominance play, etc. If you are uncomfortable with these activities you do not have to be in the room. However, it is O.K. to be in the room and not engage in such activities.

This party is not a meat market. Being invited does not mean that the host(s) want to sleep with you. People will not be sizing you up as to your attractiveness or worthiness. There are going to be people of all ages, sizes, ethnicities, and sexual/sensual desires. The atmosphere at these parties is warm and respectful. Long-lasting friendships are often formed. You need to bring several things with you to this party. First, bring food. People will be expected to leave at midnight, which is after the Metro closes – so be prepared to walk, drive, or take a taxi home. Also, bring your favorite sex toys as well. Dildos, vibrators, whips, restraints, whatever. Finally, if you have any safer sex supplies, please bring them along. The more supplies that are around, the more warm and spontaneous things will be.

Everyone is asked to arrive by 8.30 p.m. Since the party is so short, it's in your best interest to show up early. There will be time for a group discussion on safer sex, the party rules, and whatever is on people's minds. This will be a time where people can ask questions about and discuss the rules. Any questions, problems, or reservations you may have can be raised at this time and discussed with the whole group. Remember – there are no stupid questions except the ones that remain unasked!

Allow yourself to come to the party without expectations on all levels. Expecting to find your 'soul mate', or the hottest sex of your life, only leads to tension and disappointment. It is against the spirit of our parties to expect and/or demand that other people at the party fulfil your desires.

If you are feeling some discomfort about anything, please call us. We try to be flexible on everything – except the rules for safer sex!

Lustfully yours,
Beth and John.

A woman organiser defined a safe sex party as creating an environment where negotiation about safe sex is not necessary because safer sex is the rule: 'People can experience safe sex and try out new things without becoming a social outcast', she said. 'A safer-sex party is about having a social space where it's okay to be sexual. It's about breaking some of the conventions we usually live by in a way that's controlled enough to be safe. It's about explicitly talking and negotiating about things we often leave to custom and nonverbal cues. It's about setting boundaries, and possibly choosing to set them in other places than where you usually do. And it's about proving that safe sex can be hot sex. It's also about all the things any other party is about – having a good time with friends, talking and socialising.'

I would like to thank all the men and women at the International Conferences to Celebrate Bisexuality, who ran workshops or supplied other details on how to organise safer sex parties, particularly those at Amsterdam in 1991, and at New York City in 1994. Very special thanks to: Bill Powell, Tom Limoncelli, Cappy Harrison, and Jay Sekora, without whose help and information this article could never have been written.

Sado-Masochism
and Bisexuality

Gyan Mathur

This article discusses sado-masochism (SM) and is being written from the point of view of an individual bisexual sado-masochist (SMer). First, we need to be sure that we are talking about the same thing when we say 'SM', so here are a few definitions. SM has had a bad press in some quarters, and this is due to a misunderstanding of what we are all about.

The first thing to be clear about is that SM has nothing to do with abuse. SM is about people sharing pleasures by consent. It has got nothing to do with injuring and killing people for 'amusement' – that is criminal violence. At the time of writing the Law Commission is consulting the public on precisely this question of how much 'injury', if any, can be legally consented to, in recognition of the fact that SM involves consent whereas crime, such as domestic violence, does not.

The particular pleasures that are involved in SM include what most people would call pain. You might well ask how anyone can enjoy such things; well, let's just say that some people do. A Martian might easily think that this isn't any stranger than the idea that a person can enjoy having a hard object thrust into her vagina or his/her anus; the only difference is that, if the hard object is an erect penis, this is generally accepted as 'real sex' whereas many people don't accept SM as such.

Exactly what do SMers enjoy doing? There are almost as many answers as there are individual SMers, and in any SM erotic act (or 'scene' as we call it) there are both dominant ('dom' or 'top') roles and submissive ('sub' or 'bottom') ones, which give opposite pleasures, respectively the pleasure of doing things and of having them done. Broadly, our pleasures can include things that cause physical pain, such as beating and spanking; things that restrict movement or cause sensory deprivation, such as tying up, blindfolding, or suspending the sub from the ceiling in a safety harness; and things that cause humiliation, for example where the dom leads the sub around on a lead and addresses her/him as 'slave'. There are many subtle variations on these themes, limited only by the individuals' creative imagination.

Some SMers like to take the role of the 'top' all the time, while others always prefer to be the 'bottom', but many of us take both roles, either with different partners or at different times with the same person. This is known as 'switching'.

A common image of an SMer is of someone wearing leather or rubber, or a military-style uniform. Many of us do indeed get sexual pleasure from dressing up in these ways and from seeing other people dressed as such. This is known as fetishism. There are many different forms of fetish clothing, including high heels, thigh-length boots, restrictive corsets, wet-look plastic and cross-dressing. Part of the pleasure for some fetishists is that the style of the clothes can indicate a role, and in particular military uniforms and some styles of leather wear can suggest a dominant role which some of us find highly erotic. However, not all fetishists practise SM and many SMers do not dress in fetish clothing.

Of course, not everything that an SMer does counts as SM. Many SMers also engage in conventional sex (known as 'vanilla sex' to imply no added flavours). Equally, not all non-vanilla sex is SM; many people would say that heterosexual anal intercourse was unconventional sex (indeed at the time of writing it is technically illegal in the UK), but few would say that it was SM. Some people would say that water sports (where one partner urinates on the other) counts as SM because it can be humiliating; others would disagree and say, for example, that because it involves the exchange of body fluids, it is not SM as such, even though SMers are among the people who practise it. Some people who use a narrow definition of SM have reclaimed the word 'pervery' to mean a broader range of non-vanilla sex, including SM, fetishism and many other things. This word makes fun of the conventional horror of 'perverts' in the same way as some bisexual, lesbian and gay people use the word 'queer' with pride.

It might seem that SM activities concern imbalances of power but they are actually games between people who see each other as equals. Often the role-playing is an important part of the pleasure. In a way, SM games are similar to role-play games such as 'Dungeons and Dragons', where one might take on the persona of a wizard or a goblin for the duration of the game; in SM one can take on a role such as 'mistress', 'slave', 'naughty school child', or whatever – although the major difference is that SM games are intended to be erotic.

Having explained SM sexual practice, I shall say more about consent, as this is a very important point. Spanking someone without consent is assault; tying someone up without consent is kidnapping or unlawful imprisonment. In the same way, penetrating someone's genitals without consent is rape or indecent assault. Done by mutual consent, between people who understand each other, all these things can be a source of immense pleasure. Because the objective is pleasure, long-term injuries, such as breaking someone's leg, are not part of SM.

It could be said that SMers are more concerned about consent than many people who engage in more conventional sexual practices. How many people would accept the withdrawal of consent in the middle of a sexual act? This is what we do as SMers; we have got what we call 'safe-words' which we agree before a scene, and if the 'bottom' uses the safe-word, then the 'top' stops immediately. If the bottom is gagged, then a visible or audible signal is used, such as dropping a handkerchief or ringing a hand-bell. Of course we need to trust each other for this to work, but then, most sexual activities involve a lot of trust; if you are lying under a man twice your weight and enjoying being penetrated by him, there is not much you can do if he accidentally hurts you, except to trust that he will stop when you ask.

Often it is the bottom who asks the top to stimulate her/him, and equally the top can use the safe-word to stop a scene with which she/he feels uncomfortable. It should also be stressed that just because someone has played SM games before, or is at a party with other SMers, it does not mean that they automatically consent to anything; consent always needs to be negotiated. Even outside SM, a non-consensual kiss or touch can be construed by the courts as assault.

You may be asking, how safe is SM in other ways? As far as the risk of spreading HIV, hepatitis, and other infections goes, the activities that I have described do not involve the exchange of body fluids and so are extremely safe. Indeed, it is said that some people first started exploring SM as a response to the spread of HIV. It is however true that a severe beating can in some circumstances draw blood, for example if the skin was already damaged. Within the SM community there is an absolute rule that any implement (cane, whip, etc) which becomes contaminated with blood is either destroyed or else dedicated for use in future only on the person whose blood is on it. Some implements can also be sterilised but this is not always possible; for example, a leather whip is difficult to wash properly and will be damaged by hot water.

Another aspect of safety is the possible risk of serious injury. The

usual implements SMers use, used in good faith, cannot do this. SMers learn such things as which parts of the body can safely be hit, and the correct way to tie someone up without restricting their circulation, in much the same way as people exploring 'vanilla' sex learn how to stimulate a partner's genitals without hurting them. Of course there are always risks associated with people who act in bad faith and do things without consent (ie not SMers). There have been cases where people consented to be tied up by someone who then murdered them (the Colin Ireland case). These involved strangers who had picked each other up in bars and gone home together – this is potentially a risky thing to do regardless of the activities one enjoys; there have been equally notorious murder cases which did not involve SM.

So, where does SM fit in with bisexuality? For one thing, SM activities are in a way gender-free – they needn't involve close physical contact, so differences in people's genitals, body hair, body smell even, needn't make any difference. If you are tied face down so that you can't even see the person who is whipping you, communicating only by body-language (and if necessary the safe-word), it makes little difference whether that person is a woman or a man; what counts is the emotional and sensual rapport between the bottom and the top. Thus, some bisexual people find SM a particularly gender-free way to express ourselves sexually with the people we love or lust after. My own experience has been that there are a greater proportion of overtly bisexual people in SM circles than I am aware of in society at large.

Many bisexual people also wish to alter the gender-based differences in power that are found in society. This is similar to the way in which some SM role-play games subvert the participants' conventional roles and allow us to explore facets of our personalities that are hidden in everyday life. People who 'switch' between 'top' and 'bottom' roles have much in common with those bisexual people who adopt different roles in relationships with women and men.

As is obvious from what I have said about consent, no SMer worthy of the name would try to coerce an unwilling person into 'trying it out'. None of the SMers whom I know believe, either, that our way is 'better' than anyone else's. Here is another relationship between SM and bisexuality: bisexuals do not, in general, believe that our way is better than other people's, nor would we try to persuade a gay person to 'give it a try' with a member of the opposite sex, or a heterosexual person with the same sex, if they were not interested in doing so. Of course we, bisexuals and SMers, might be supportive to a friend who wished to explore their sexuality. Yet too often, other people assume that we are trying to 'recruit followers', and oppress us for that reason; this is true for bisexuals and for SMers. We share similar oppressions; and no matter how frightening some of us SMers might look, with our whips, chains, leather or rubber when you see us playing our SM games, underneath it all, we are as diverse a range of people as any other group in society.

I said 'SM games', and I would like to emphasise that point. We really do talk about 'play' and 'games', and some SMers even call their erotic partners 'playmates'. Like many other bisexual people, SM bisexuals (and SMers who don't consider themselves to be bisexual) see our sexuality as *fun*, something to be enjoyed, to allow us to share pleasure. As bisexuals and as SMers, we can explore aspects of sexuality that are commonly excluded from more conventional relationships, and these are two facets of the same ideal of sexual liberation for everyone.

Tony

David Sands

As I begin to write this piece it is June and within two days of Gay Pride 1994. Inside I am buzzing with excitement. It will be a day of celebration and, as they say, gay abandon; when I can wander around a large London park holding hands with another man if I want to; kiss him if I want to; be completely myself in public.

But I know that the festival atmosphere will be punctuated throughout the day with some tough memories. I will bump into people I haven't seen for months and perhaps years. People I knew when I was younger mainly. Those that I don't see that often, simply because we move on to other things, different attitudes.

And there will be ghosts milling around in the crowds. Friends that aren't alive any more but who are with me, and with their other friends, in spirit. Tony will be one of them. I met him when we were about twenty years old, and I said goodbye to him in a south London crematorium two Januarys ago.

He was HIV positive and had known that for about ten years. During 1993 I watched him struggle for a few months. Then I watched him decide that his life was so lacking in quality it wasn't worth living any more, and watched him give up to die.

After we became friends through working at the same restaurant we lost contact for several years. Then I bumped into him in a local club. He had moved close to where I was living and had been allocated a flat by the Terrence Higgins Trust, he said. That's how he informed me of his HIV status. No fuss, no embellishment, it was just fact.

I started to visit him about once a week and we would go out to the local club and get drunk or just have a good time on a Friday night. It was good to see him regularly again. It reminded me of our youth, how he had educated me into the London gay scene, and had been a great support to me when my first gay relationship foundered after about six months. I was devastated by the break-up but his calm advice was soothing and stood me in good stead in later years.

211

I didn't tell him that in the intervening years of our friendship I had had the odd fling, and even relationships, with women. It didn't seem important or relevant. What was important was that he was available to me as a friend and I could help him do stuff like shopping when he got tired.

Tony's world was extremely gay-oriented. Because I can appreciate both sexes, and since many of my close friends have a straight life style, I sometimes felt a sense of claustrophobia around his world. This did not bother me much – I merely had a vague feeling that something was missing.

This sensitivity receded somewhat when I discovered that Tony's cousin, John, was being cared for by a buddy who was a heterosexual man. He came to Tony's funeral, and meeting him made me realise that Aids can be a focus not just for the solely gay community, but also a concern of straight and bisexual people.

In 1992 Tony had been forced to stop work when it became too much for him. Deprived of a work structure, his spirits went down, and he caught pneumonia and was hospitalised.

When he returned to his flat, he began to lose confidence in approaching activities that before he had taken for granted; he gave up driving, for example, since he felt he was a danger on the road, and used public transport instead.

'The weekend starts here,' I would shout most Fridays, and we would have a few drinks before going out to a local gay club. This routine went on for some months, until one night, shortly after arriving at the club somewhat the worse for drink, Tony asked if I minded him going home as he was feeling ill. Fine, I said, offering to leave with him. No, he replied, you stay and have a good time.

As he queued for his coat, I went over and asked if he could leave me some cigarettes as I had run out. Tony opened his cigarette case containing several hand-rolled cigarettes and I helped myself. It was the last time we did that Friday night run.

In the weeks that followed I would do some shopping for him along with mine. He normally asked for ready meals; I advised him that they weren't that nutritious, but as his appetite was poor, he just wanted what tasted good.

His heavy smoking worried his friends and family in case the pneumonia returned. But he carried on regardless. I believe his social isolation, imposed by his inability to travel that far, and the death of many friends through Aids, made it difficult for him to quit. It was no surprise then, that he wound up back in hospital just before Christmas 1992 with TB.

Tony hated the hospital. He lost weight and his good looks faded a little. Spending Christmas with his parents, he rallied, and returned to his flat soon afterwards. One evening I called round after work. I pressed the buzzer, entered the block, and walked along the corridor to his flat. Oddly, the door was open. Tony had rushed from the intercom back to his bedroom.

The room was stifling hot, with a fan heater blasting insistently. Tony lay under the duvet, his body wracked with the shakes. I looked on, stunned, as the whole bed shuddered.

I pretended to be unfazed, and offered to sit in the front room while the episode faded in case he wanted to be alone. But he said just stay, the shakes would pass soon. They did, and I went to the bathroom, and began crying. It was grotesque to me: that he was suffering so much and all I could do was weep. I dried my face and went back to the bedroom concealing my wretchedness. Tony hated people to cry for him, or feel any pity.

Sometimes we did talk about his illness and possible death, but mainly he wanted his mind taken off the whole thing and we carried on with the business of having as good a time as possible. Once he asked if I would still go and see him when he was close to death and in hospital. I replied yes, of course.

About a fortnight later his long-standing friend Stafford and I went round. It was Saturday afternoon and Tony was in the middle of selling his Chesterfield sofa to family friends. Although he was very businesslike and buzzing with activity, he looked like a concentration camp inmate. He was evidently extremely sick, and I felt helpless and angry.

The friends left with their purchase and Tony put the £300 in a drawer, saying he would spend it on a holiday. Stafford and I left. As we got in the car we agreed that he was unlikely ever to see another holiday; and we concluded that he'd given up and was just going through the motions of living for the benefit of family and friends.

A week later Tony was back in hospital. He couldn't even keep food down. A nurse cheerily said that they were hoping he would pick up soon. I felt very angry with them, and believed they were just glossing over the harsh fact that he would not last much longer.

A couple of days later his cousin John died. Once a highly-influential figure in gay activism, he had been suffering from Aids for some time. The doctors advised us to tell Tony, as it would be worse if he found out for himself later. His mother Betty broke the news to him. John's death was hard for her too, as she had been his 'mother', since his own had died when he was a teenager.

Betty told me Tony just nodded when she told him about John. Tony was unable to react much outwardly, but I guessed he was devastated. Anyway, it was hardly encouraging news for someone fighting for his own life.

John was buried the following Saturday. I was at the hospital that afternoon visiting Tony, who seemed to be sedated. He didn't know if it was five am or five pm, and by the single, dim, ultra-violet light in the room, I gazed forlornly at his skinny supine body, and watched his chest wafting gently up and down. I could barely find any conversation, and he was too weak to be that interested anyhow. After about fifteen minutes he said, 'Would you leave now please, David.' I slipped the *Capital Gay* I had brought for him to read into the waste bin and squeezed his hand as I left, merely saying 'Bye, Tony'.

I sat in the waiting room, waiting for his parents to arrive. About thirty minutes later they turned up – straight from John's funeral. Dressed in a black coat adorned with a red ribbon, Betty clipped smartly into the ward, her face bleak, signalling anger, grief, a hint of panic.

She had obviously demanded some straight talking from the doctor, who had told her that there was little hope and that when the time came, they would 'make him comfortable'. As she relayed this to us, she broke down and I seized her hand. We sat for a short time huddled over the sickening prognosis, and I left shortly after.

Two days later a message on my answer-machine from a hollow-voiced Betty droned a call-me message. I paced the room, then picked up the phone.

The funeral was permeated with a sense of relief that Tony's suffering was over. Death from Aids is mostly an appallingly drawn-out affair. The question is always will the person survive this bout, or die this time. There's never any surety.

A massive stigma still surrounds an Aids sufferer, even among a large section of the gay community. Patients often experience isolation; friends can be too scared or embarrassed to visit them. It is this element which is most damaging to the sufferer, who often approaches the end of his or her life in a state of terror, loneliness and isolation.

This makes me furious, but having gone through my experience with Tony, I can understand why some people find it impossible to continue friendships with people who start showing Aids symptoms. It's a very hard ride for family and friends.

Betty gave me Tony's cigarette case and lighter. I used them for a week or so, then couldn't face the painful memories they provoked. I keep them in a drawer.

Section IV:
Bisexual Politics

Introduction: What are Bisexual Politics?

Sharon Rose

If, like most people who have been influenced by the sexual politics movements, you accept 'the personal is political' as a fundamental part of your belief system, you may be surprised that we have a separate section of this book labelled 'politics'. And, indeed, having to think about why we needed such a section and which articles to put in it, has made us consider what we mean by bisexual politics, and the ways in which political expression among bisexuals is similar to and different from politics in, for example, the women's and lesbian and gay movements. Gathering pieces for this book and talking to people who have been involved with organising bisexual activity over many years has revealed that, to a much greater extent than with other sexual politics groups, people who are attracted to a bisexual organisation are most likely to be looking mainly for support, and much more likely to move on once they have received the personal support and solidarity they needed. This is probably just as true for most people who are already politically active elsewhere when they get involved with the bisexual community.

It is also clear that a substantial number of the groups and individuals within the bisexual community do not consider themselves to be political, which leaves the rest of us with something of a dilemma.

SECTION IV: BISEXUAL POLITICS

Although everyone would hopefully acknowledge that a bisexual community could never have developed outside the context of strong and effective sexual politics movements, this does not make the bisexual community inherently political. Those people who do want to work on bisexuality within a political framework may find they have to do as much persuading inside the bisexual community of the validity of their position as they do outside it. Some of the openness and tolerance which can be observed among many bisexuals in the community almost certainly comes from this unwillingness to impose a collective dogma, but if progress is to be made in developing an autonomous bisexual political analysis, some of the peaceful co-existence may have to be sacrificed in favour of more open debate. It is up to the bisexual community to decide if this is what it wants.

As things stand now, at least in Britain, it does not seem appropriate to talk of the bisexual *movement*, as this suggests a body of people united in their desire to take political action to transform society. A community can certainly contain individuals and groups for whom this is true, as the bisexual community undoubtedly does, but so far it seems to lack any agreement on goals that all bisexuals in the community might wish to work towards, or any clear idea of how to achieve the goals it does have. Several articles in this section cover the activities of organised bisexuals in various industrialised countries. Despite the fact that many of these other communities are larger and/or more organised than in Britain, they still seem to focus primarily on support and solidarity functions. It would be interesting to know if a higher proportion of the active members of these communities regard themselves as political than do in Britain.

Because there has been a large organised bisexual movement in the US for much longer than anywhere else, we are aware of more groups and individuals there who put an emphasis on political activity, and there, as well, such groups have developed from support networks. BiNet USA is the national coalition of bisexual activists, 'committed to building bridges, breaking stereotypes, bringing equal rights and liberation to all'. They do excellent work in a number of areas, including media education for bisexuals, but reading their literature, there still seemed a certain lack of focus on specifically bisexual political goals, and in common with bisexual political activists everywhere, BiNet's stated intention is to 'eradicate all forms of oppression'. While this could be interpreted as being incredibly vague, it is true that challenging the monosexual values of this society does hold the potential for bringing about a fundamental change in many existing values and assumptions.

WHAT ARE BISEXUAL POLITICS?

Articles such as Dave Berry's in this section, on the history of the Edinburgh bisexual group, or Wayne Roberts' in section I, on becoming bisexual in Australia, show that much excellent work has been done by bisexual activists to build politically from a base of providing and receiving personal support. And it is a crucial part of the liberation process for any oppressed group that such support (what radical feminists would call consciousness-raising) is available. But what the bisexual community as a whole has to face is that, at present, what is discernible is the potential for a political movement, rather than that movement itself. For example, some of the political men in the British bisexual community point to the presence of strong women leaders as evidence of a successful fight against sexism, but not all these women define themselves as feminists, while some men and women in the bisexual community still question the right of women to meet separately from men at times. Thus we are some distance from our potential political movement where women and men can work harmoniously together with an agreed political agenda.

Another difficulty with trying to organise the bisexual community politically is the problem of whether people who might be expected to join, given their sexual behaviour, are actually prepared not only to define themselves as bisexual, but then make organising with other bisexuals one of their political priorities. It is easy to be critical of the bisexual community, and because it is so diverse, there are any number of ways to feel alienated from it. It is impossible for 'the movement', this book, any aspect of bisexual politics, to be everything to every person. It is unrealistic to expect that, but, because bisexuals are so used to feeling like outsiders, they tend to get disappointed in advance if the one place they might hope to feel completely at home is not absolutely perfect.

Despite these difficulties, there is plenty of organising going on, both in terms of political action and support networks, as a glance at the resources section of this book reveals, and the number of groups seems to be growing. Two sizable groups within the bisexual community are pagans and Quakers; we also have Marxists and anarchists, trade unionists and keep-fit enthusiasts, and many others. Unfortunately, most of the self-consciously political groups in Britain, such as BiOnic, have been short-lived. However, the very act of coming together as bisexuals has served to raise our profile, which has in turn encouraged more people to identify as bisexual, which has in its turn helped to change attitudes, for example, in making parts of the lesbian and gay movement more inclusive of bisexuals in recent times.

217

SECTION IV: BISEXUAL POLITICS

There is a strong element among bisexual political activists of people who work hard within lesbian and gay campaigns and actively identify with the lesbian and gay movement, even though lesbians and gays may not always realise that there are bisexuals in their midst. But as Kevin Lano points out in his article, it was antipathy to how they had been treated by the lesbian and gay movement that turned some other members of the bisexual community away from political activity. Throughout this troubled relationship, there have been various attempts at reconciliation, such as the conference organised in Boston in 1985 between the two communities, and the group, LeBiDo, for discussion between lesbians and bisexual women, which ran in London in 1993.

Politically active bisexuals, as the articles in this section show, divide into two main, though obviously overlapping, groups: those concerned with the politics of bisexuality itself, and those who aim to bring insights gained from the bisexual community into their other political activity. Whether the lesbian and gay movement counts as 'other' depends on your political outlook. In this context, it is interesting to note that many of our contributors mentioned the 'Lesbians and Gays Support the Miners' group as a significant political reference point in the 1980s, as it demonstrated to them the possibility of working productively to break down society's artificially created boundaries. This seems to be what all our contributors are striving for in their diverse political activities, deriving no doubt from our sense, as bisexuals, of the importance of bridging all those divides which we have been told by society must stay in place.

Personal communications with Sue George, Zaidie Parr and Beth Reba Weise have been invaluable in helping me write this piece, but they bear no responsibility for what I have made from their contribution.

Bisexual History:
Fighting Invisibility

Kevin Lano

The first wave of gay liberation movements, in the late 1960s and early 1970s, were often quite open and accepting of bisexuals, as part of their aim to change consciousness and validate homosexuality. Writers like Dennis Altman, immersed in the movement, could promote the 'withering away of the difference between gay and straight' as the ultimate aim of gay liberation. He reported the acceptance of transvestites and transexuals, and the genuine efforts made to understand differing experiences, as part of the enthusiasm and optimism of these early groups. Bisexuals such as Kate Millet, author of the landmark feminist text, *Sexual Politics*, were often significant in these movements. She was supported by much of the women's movement, in the face of great hostility, after she came out as bisexual. Ironically, in later years, the women's movement began to replace the anti-lesbian prejudice of the early movement with an exclusionist and hurtful ideology against heterosexual collaboration. Similarly, by the time the gay liberation movement lost its initial impetus in the mid 1970s, the links between the lesbian and gay movement and the radical left had been severed, and bisexuality became more of a marginal issue, even seen as a threat to lesbian and gay culture.

The Growth of the Bisexual Movement

The UK

In the UK, the current wave of the bisexual movement came partly from the men's antisexist movement and the women's movement, with a strong input from the lesbian and gay movement. The antisexist men's conference of February 1980 held a workshop on bisexuality, which inspired a special issue of the *Antisexist Men's Newsletter* in 1981, and also led to the initial meeting of the London Bisexual Group

(LBG), at Heaven, which attracted 80 people. In the summer of 1982, about 40 people were attending weekly meetings, and the group had about 2000 telephone enquiries per year. In January 1984 the magazine *Bi-Monthly* was published by the LBG, becoming the only magazine specifically aimed at bisexuals in Europe. 1984 also saw the beginning of the London Bisexual Women's group, which grew out of the often hostile attitude of lesbians in the women's movement towards bisexual women. The NUS (National Union of Students) held a workshop on bisexuality that year at its lesbian and gay conference, but soon bisexuals were to be explicitly excluded from these conferences, a situation which did not change until 1992. The lesbian and gay conference of NALGO adopted a similar position. The pages of *Bi-Monthly* in 1984 were often taken up with the conflicts between the bisexual movement and the lesbian and gay movement, and the prejudice against bisexuals in the latter.

1984 ended with the first national bisexual conference, held in London, which attracted 40 people, including sympathetic gay men, and the inauguration of the energetic bisexual group in Edinburgh. The conference produced three manifestos (two of which were reprinted in *Bisexual Lives*), and the formation of the 'Radical Lesbian and Gay Identified Bisexual Network', which reflected the tension between those people who felt they were lesbian and gay first and bisexual second, and those who reacted against politics altogether, because of the sceptical attitude of the lesbian and gay movement.

1985 saw significant gains for the bisexual movement, but sharper conflicts with the lesbian and gay movement. The second bisexual conference was held at the London Lesbian and Gay Centre (LLGC), starting on 13 April, the date the centre opened. But it was held there despite the hostility to bisexual groups at the centre, and the decision of the management committee to accept no further bookings from them. Bisexuals were heavily involved in fundraising for Pride '85, and the Pride committee supported the efforts of bisexuals to be re-admitted to the centre. Also in 1985 the Brighton bisexual group started, and a group of bisexuals marched with the 'Lesbians and Gays Support the Miners' contingent at a miners' rally in London. Off Pink Publishing was also born. Finally, at a second meeting of LLGC members, the ban on bisexual individuals was lifted, after a promise that bisexuals would not behave in a heterosexual manner in the centre.

In January 1986 *Bi-Monthly* reported that 'the number of bisexual groups has reached double figures', and in July the fourth national bisexual conference was organised by the London bisexual women's group. Towards the end of the year, an attempt was made to form a political organisation of bisexuals, Bi-Action, which however did not survive very long.

By 1987 the hostility to lesbians, gays and bisexuals engendered by the AIDS panic was in full force, and bisexuals marched with others in a protest against the remarks of the Tory council leader in Wombourne, Northampton, who said that the cure for AIDS was to 'gas 90% of the ruddy queers'. The fifth national bisexual conference in Edinburgh attracted 120 people, and Ken Livingstone became the first (partially) out bisexual MP. In 1988 the campaign against clause 28 was producing the largest demonstrations ever on lesbian and gay rights in the UK, with 20,000 people marching in Manchester and 30,000 in London. Efforts to create a bisexual caucus within the Organisation for Lesbian and Gay Action (OLGA) were rejected in 1987, but eventually accepted after much campaigning in 1988. As the Campaign for Homosexual Equality (CHE) passed a motion that year stating that the word 'bisexual' should be used in campaigning work, it seemed that bisexuals had finally received recognition from the lesbian and gay movement. The book, *Bisexual Lives*, published by the Off Pink Collective, was launched in April 1988, and quickly became an alternative best seller.

In 1989, the seventh national bisexual conference was held in Stoke on Trent, but *Bi-Monthly* magazine unfortunately folded after reaching its twenty-first issue, due to exhaustion on the part of the editorial group. The magazine had consistently produced a high level of analysis and debate, covering issues such as SM, transsexuality and child sexuality, which the mainstream gay press ignored or treated in a facile way, and in addition it provided contacts and information on the growth of the bisexual movement. Until 1991, when *Bifrost* started, there was no regular bisexual publication. The eighth bisexual conference was held in Edinburgh and was considered to be one of the most enjoyable conferences so far, in addition to being the largest, with 150 people.

However, little coherent happened on a national level until the ninth conference in London in September 1991. This attracted over 200 people and provided a starting point for several national initiatives, such as the politically bi group, BiOnic, and the bisexual centre collective. The relationship with the lesbian and gay movement was still a strong preoccupation, with all the invited speakers being prominent and sympathetic figures in the lesbian and gay movement. The bisexual movement itself grew more strongly once the monthly

221

newsletter, *Bifrost*, began, and groups became active in Brighton, Bristol and Norwich. Conferences specifically on politics were held in London and Sheffield (where it attracted the attention of the *News of the World*, who infiltrated it). 1992 saw a large bisexual contingent on the Pride march, and a visible presence at the Pride festival. The NUS lesbian and gay campaign voted to re-admit bisexuals, and the NUS sponsored a conference on bisexuality.

Direct action flourished, such as stickering posters on the London Underground, and leafletting outside showings of the biphobic film *Basic Instinct*. The movement continued to grow, with the tenth conference being held in Norwich, and over 25 groups being listed in *Bifrost*. The second international bisexual conference was held in London at the end of 1991, and attracted participants from all over Europe, the US and even Australia. A successful bisexual women's dayschool was held in Sheffield, and a group of SM bisexuals began to organise, becoming involved in the 'Operation Spanner' campaign against the prosecution of a group of gay men who took part in consenting SM. One of the first TV programmes produced by bisexuals about bisexuals was also shown, on BBC2's *Open Space* programme in July 1992.

Expansion continued in 1993, when 250 people attended the eleventh conference in Nottingham, the largest yet. Two further women's dayschools were held, and a group, LeBiDo, started meeting in London to bring together lesbians and bisexual women for discussions. Scarlet Press published *Women and Bisexuality* by Sue George, the first book on bisexuality to be published in the UK since 1988.

In 1994 the movement grew further, both politically and socially, with the setting up of a group on bisexuality and AIDS, called Bisexuals Action on Sexual Health (BASH), and campaigning for more research in the area and more effective outreach. The first meeting of an academic network, Bi-Academic Intervention, also took place, indicating that perhaps 'bisexual studies' are not too far away. The twelfth national conference returned to Edinburgh in August for the tenth anniversary of the Edinburgh bisexual group.

In 1995 BASH was particularly active, obtaining a substantial grant for national safer sex education from the Red Hot AIDS trust, carrying out bisexuality awareness workshops for local health authorities, and initiating safer sex workshops for students in higher education. The thirteenth national conference was held in Birmingham.

222

Europe
Bisexual groups have existed in West Germany and The Netherlands since the early 80s, when the *Initiative Bisexueller Frauen Und Männer* had local groups in five regions of West Germany. National conferences were organised in West Germany in June and November 1985, and a further national conference took place in West Germany in 1986, but there were few contacts or groups. In 1990 bisexual men and women from the former GDR were able to participate in national German meetings and groups have been formed in Magdeburg and Potsdam. In 1992 a legally registered, non-profit-making society, BINE, was founded, following a long and controversial debate about whether it was desirable to have an official organisation to legally sanction the existing bisexual network. Because national meetings have been held in Germany from the beginning of the movement, there is a strong emphasis on personal contacts at a national level, linking local groups.

In Holland, a national network of the several regional groups, *Landelijk Network Biseksualiteit* (LNB), was set up in 1986, which produced the magazine *Bi-Nieuws* for several years. Bisexuals have participated strongly in the Dutch National Gay Pride day. Amsterdam was the venue for the first International Bisexual conference, in 1991. At that stage there were 11 local groups in the Netherlands, loosely linked in the LNB, which provided speakers and support to local groups. In Amsterdam the group met in the lesbian and gay centre, and organised a phone line. As with the UK, however, the lesbian and gay organisations had an ambiguous attitude towards bisexuality, sometimes limiting the use of the word to their youth groups.

One notable difference between the movements in mainland Europe and the UK is the ability of groups in the Netherlands and Germany to obtain some government funding, a situation which has only rarely occurred in the UK, and only in the context of AIDS/HIV and safer sex education.

In 1992 two bisexual groups started in Finland, briefly in Turku/Abo, and a more established group in Helsinki, meeting in the Helsinki gay centre. Tentative organisation of bisexuals also occurred in Belgium in 1992 and Paris, France in 1994.

The USA
The bisexual movement in the USA is, perhaps unsurprisingly, the largest and longest established in the world. In San Francisco there was

a Bisexual Center in the Castro from 1976 to 1984, closely linked with the gay community, and doing counselling and social events. In 1983 the BiPol organisation was founded, and did much work to combat media prejudice. Its conference in 1990 led to an outburst of activity in the Bay area, so that in 1991 there were 52 bisexual groups organised into the Bay Area Bisexual Network, including a Bisexual People of Color Caucus. In San Diego there were groups for bisexuals such as Bi-Forum, and California produced the first glossy bisexual magazine, *Anything that Moves*, and the book, *Bi Any Other Name*, edited by Loraine Hutchins and Lani Kaahumanu, featuring 70 contributions from bisexual men and women. The bisexual contingent was the largest on the 1991 Pride march in San Francisco. More recently bisexuals have initiated the safe sex 'Jack and Jill Off' parties as a sex-positive response to the AIDS crisis, as discussed by Zaidie Parr in her article in Section III of this book.

On the East Coast, the Boston Bisexual Women's Network was perhaps the largest organisation for many years, with 850 members in 1987, and forming the core of the East Coast Bisexual Network, which now has 2000 members. When they first participated in the local gay pride march, in 1984, there was some muted hostility from lesbian and gay organisations, but by the following year their participation was welcomed, and a conference was held in October 1985 to try to bring together lesbian and gay groups and bisexual groups. By 1989, the Boston networks were still gender segregated, with the men's network producing a magazine, *Bi-Monthly*, and having a membership of about 250, and the women's network producing the magazine, *Bi-Women*, and having a membership of 1000. The East Coast Bi Network was set up as a non-profit corporation campaigning for the benefit of bisexuals, and a new gender-inclusive network, 'Biversity', was set up in 1991. Acceptance by lesbian and gay organisations has now reached the point where the local lesbian and gay centre has changed its name to the 'lesbian, gay and bisexual' centre.

At a local level, many groups are active. New York and Washington groups, for example, started in 1986. At a national level there is one main group, following the demise of the Multicultural Bi Network in 1993. This is BiNet, which links a large number of regional and local bisexual groups, and has an activist politics. An alternative but much smaller network, the Bicentrist Alliance, was also set up in 1993, and is more restrictive in its definition of bisexuality and more conservative in its politics. National organisation by bisexuals reached a peak in the lesbian and gay march on Washington in 1993, in which leading bisexuals played a key part. In the celebrations around Stonewall 1994, however, bisexuals were still incorporated in only a token manner, with their designated speaker being left until late in the programme and finally omitted completely.

New Zealand and Australia

The situation in New Zealand and Australia for bisexuals has been somewhat different than in the rest of the industrialised world for a number of reasons. Lesbian separatism has been a dominant strand of feminism in these countries, so that bisexual women have often been strongly motivated to organise as bisexuals, to a greater extent than men. In addition, in New Zealand there was a strong and successful campaign in 1985-86 to equalise the age of consent for straights and gays at 16. This campaign involved many supportive heterosexuals via groups such as HUG – Heterosexuals Unafraid of Gays – so the involvement of heterosexuals and bisexuals alongside gays and lesbians in campaigns for sexual liberation has been more accepted than elsewhere. The first national bisexual conference in New Zealand happened in Wellington in 1990, and these have been held annually since then. The Wellington women's bisexual group was set up in July 1988, and published a newsletter and held regular meetings. A bisexual group was also initiated by women in Christchurch in 1989, which has been involved with lesbian and gay groups. A new glossy lesbian and gay magazine, GLO, has now made explicit the need for alliance between bisexuals, straights and lesbians and gays, and features a regular column on bisexuality.

In Australia a network of bisexual groups in West Australia was formed in November 1991, comprising a mixed group, a men-only group and a women-only group. A magazine, Biways, was produced, and bisexuals became involved in AIDS campaign work. The network became national in 1993, including groups in Sydney, Adelaide, Brisbane and Melbourne, with Biways as their newsletter. There was a bisexual contingent on the 1993 and 1994 Mardi Gras, including a float with a symbolic broken white fence, and there is a continuing debate with lesbian and gay groups on the acceptance and validity of bisexuality. A bisexual centre was established in Brisbane in October 1993, and has been the focus of successful safer sex projects which have received external funding.

Non-Western Cultures

The definition of bisexuality, and the concept of a bisexual identity, used in this article is specific to industrialised countries. In industrial countries, similarities of culture and politics have led to similar developments in sexual politics and movements. Such movements do not exist widely outside these countries. Of course there are people we would describe as bisexual all over the world – sexual diversity exists everywhere. For example, in South Asian and North African cultures, there is significant bisexual behaviour by men, with varying degrees of social stigmatisation, but this is not usually perceived by the men themselves as making them 'bisexual'. In Brazil there are transgender (originally male) prostitutes whose clients want both a feminine body shape and a penis. And in some third world countries, there are self help organisations for sexual minority groups. The new *Bisexual Resources Guide*, edited by Robyn Ochis (see Resources Section), contains a comprehensive listing of more than 1400 bisexual and les-bi-gay groups in over twenty countries, though they are predominantly in industrialised countries.

Coming in From the Cold: Bisexuality and the Politics of Diversity

Paul Chandler

Why do you look so sad and forsaken
When one door is closed
Don't you know another is open

Bob Marley[1]

It was about five years ago that I first met 'out', politically active lesbians and gay men, and began to develop a political awareness around my own sexuality. For years before then I'd kept my homosexual feelings secret. As well as being attracted to some men I'd also always found some women attractive.

I valued women's friendship and could never understand why most of my male friends only viewed women as potential sexual partners with whom any conversation was a 'chat up'. In fact my 'difficulty', as I saw it then, was not being able to develop closer relationships with women because of my inability and unwillingness to engage in male gender behaviour. At the same time I continued to fantasise about beautiful, loving relationships with men. However, all my male friends were straight (as far as I knew) and I had no idea how to meet others who felt like me; if indeed there were any. The upshot of all this was that I became terrified of sexual relationships in general, and sadly became resigned to the idea that I would never have any.

When I finally met positively 'out' lesbians and gay men in a college students' union, my perspective began to change. During the next few months, as my political awareness began to develop, I started to re-examine my own sexuality, and came to the conclusion that I must have been gay all along. Just as I was getting comfortable with this idea and started building up the courage to 'come out', an impossible thing happened – I started having a relationship with a woman! The effect was traumatic and turned me upside-down. Unfortunately I soon discovered that my own excitement wasn't shared by our lesbian and gay friends. Just as I had been tentatively opening the door out of the closet I found it slammed shut again in my face. When I first cautiously used the term bisexual, it felt like having my knuckles rapped. It was explained to me that, if such a thing as bisexuality did indeed exist, then under the current political climate it could not be discussed in a way that was not threatening to lesbians and gay men; to try to do so would be undermining twenty years of struggle for lesbian and gay rights. I was also subjected to many of the common myths about bisexuals. Both of us felt trapped and isolated. We neither identified as straight, nor felt accepted as ourselves by the lesbian and gay community. I tried to resolve this situation in my mind by saying that politically I was gay whilst personally being heterosexual. Although never feeling entirely happy with this, I tried to live with it over the next four years.

A few months ago I came across a book in which people who positively identified as bisexuals spoke out about their experiences and set them in a clear political context.[2] I could immediately identify with these experiences and avidly read cover to cover with a mixture of elation, rage and tears. I realised that the label 'bisexual' could act as a vehicle to transport me out of my sense of exclusion and powerlessness. It could allow me to come out of the closet and assert that I was definitely *not* straight whilst at the same time providing a strategic position from which to challenge the hetero/homo orthodoxy and allow my experiences to enter the discourse of sexual politics. Additionally, identification with the term bisexual could allow me to begin making contact with a network of people with whom experiences could be shared and mutual support given. I decided to phone the National Bisexual Support Line.

At last I felt that I could continue the process of coming out started those five years ago, this time as a bisexual gay man. It is as part of that process that I felt compelled to start writing this article. In particular I wanted to explore my experience of exclusion, within a political context.

Exclusion and division

The question of the politics of inclusion and exclusion is one of vital importance to any movement. It is essential about recognising the existence of various oppressive tendencies within the movement itself; then looking at ways in which these other 'strands' of oppression can be struggled against both *within* and *without* the movement. I believe that the process of resolving these issues can lead a movement in one of two directions: either to expand its consciousness, bringing new growth and radicalisation, or to a 'fragmentation' where a reformist element comes to dominate, winning valuable civil rights victories, but narrowing the radical vision of the original movement.

The emerging bisexual movement seems to be as a result of the latter outcome within the lesbian and gay movement. Bisexuals and other 'sexual minorities' (cross-dressers, transsexuals, hermaphrodites, etc) directly experience the exclusivist tendencies in the lesbian and gay communities. As bisexuals we have come to name our combined experience of the heterosexism of straight society and exclusivism of the lesbian and gay communities as *biphobia*.

The radical, inclusive concept of gay, as it was first used in the late 1960s and early 1960s/70s has narrowed to become virtually indistinguishable from what has been termed 'The Myth of the Homosexual'. We must remember that the term 'homosexual' is a relatively recent invention, first coined in 1869. The early gay liberation movement recognised this term to be a construction of hetero-male thought and a tool of oppression. This false concept was called 'The Myth of the Homosexual' and many asserted 'we are *not* homosexuals, we are gay'. Within the bisexual movement we have called this dualistic hetero/homo myth *the monosexual framework*.

The necessary claiming of the political label 'Lesbian', by women facing sexism in the gay liberation movement and heterosexism in the women's movement, has had the effect of reducing the term gay further, so that it is now generally only associated with men. A recognition of the reduction in the meaning of gay has led some to either question its continuing political usefulness or strive towards new definitions.[4]

We can learn much by examining the history of the lesbian and gay movement in this country. Let's take as an example the rise and fall of the Gay Liberation Front (GLF) in the 1970s, a detailed account of which is given by Jeffrey Weeks.[5] In essence, the GLF seemed unable to sustain its original radical ideas and practices. White, middle-class men greatly outnumbered women and black people who found an unwillingness to address issues of sexism and racism *within* the GLF, whilst the experience of disabled people seems to be invisible in the accounts I have read. A tension was also growing between the reformers, or 'activists' as they were called, who advocated civil rights issues, and those wanting to continue the momentum of the 'counter-culture'. The assumption underpinning the activists' arguments seemed to be 'we're no different from anyone else except for what we do in bed'. The activists were working to create a *positive* myth of the homosexual which, whilst paving the way for many to 'come out', and leading to valuable civil rights victories benefiting all lesbians and gay men, was nevertheless still within the monosexual framework; ie, the existence of bisexuals and other sexual minorities was not included within their arguments. The various tensions within the GLF were not resolved and led to splits, fragmentation and its eventual demise.

The lesbian and gay movement, of course, has not been the only one to experience such processes. Within the women's movement questions of heterosexism, racism and class have caused pain and bitterness. Within black struggles tensions have occurred around questions of cultural identity, sexism and sexuality.

All too commonly those of us who raise our voices are silenced; we are told that 'now is not the time to raise such issues', and accused of 'diverting' or 'undermining' the struggle. It is easy, tempting perhaps, to get so caught up in the struggle against one form of oppression that we ignore the diversity within our own communities, failing to recognise the links between our own experiences of exclusion and those of others; the ways in which different forms of oppression feed off each other. Black gay activist Essex Hemphill states:

> Coming out of the closet to confront sexual oppression has not necessarily given white males the motivation or insight to transcend their racist conditioning. This failure (or reluctance) is costing the gay and lesbian community the opportunity to become a powerful force for creating *real* social changes that reach beyond issues of sexuality.[6]

The general pattern that seems to emerge in liberation struggles is one of a constant battle between radicalising tendencies and reformist or assimilationist tendencies. A newly emergent liberation movement bursts onto the scene with creativity and radical energies, the joy and pride of self-realisation acting as a powerful unifying force amongst its diverse members. After the initial euphoria the diversity within the movement becomes more apparent. Reformist or assimilationist tendencies trigger traditional divisive forces leading to fragmentation. The organisation might dissolve altogether or change into a single issue lobbying or rights group gaining wider recognition with its new found 'respectability'.

Who gains from these processes? It is the dominant minority: these processes have always served as tools to disempower any movement which threatens the status quo. The disintegration processes link into a strategy of 'divide and rule', and the desire for respectability enables 'co-opting', or 'assimilation' strategies.

The shared experience of our oppression is what unites us; the assimilated/internalised values of our society are what divide us. The realisation of *internalised oppression* is common to all oppressed groups. It was feminism in particular which demonstrated the importance of 'consciousness raising' groups in developing personal empowerment through overcoming internalised oppression. Black liberation groups have called this process 'decolonising the mind'.

All our minds are indeed colonised from the moment of birth, by the dominant ideology of the culture or society into which we are born. We are socialised into many constructed identities around gender, class, race, sexuality, physical condition and so on, which are set within a hierarchical framework of domination and submission. The socialising process works through oppressing us where we don't fit into the prescribed roles and rewarding us with power over others where we do. Our very language sets up oppressive structures within the mind.

This theme of internalised oppression was taken up by Monica Sjöö and Barbara Mor in their discussion of Wilhelm Reich's work: 'Left-wing males who see no connection between labour exploitation and sexual exploitation have failed to make a total analysis – or, in Reich's terms, they have failed to undergo a total revolution; on the neuron level they are still wired for oppression'.[7] (They go on to note, however, that Reich was a strict heterosexual who 'missed the connections between bisexuality and psychic wholeness'.)

Identity Politics and the Development of Subcultures

The processes of organising around positive identities have come to be called 'identity politics'. Over the last two decades identity politics have changed the political landscape, with the principle of 'autonomy' or 'self-determination'; the right of any oppressed group to define its own oppression and to organise and lead the struggle against that oppression. There are, however, dangers inherent in identity politics. We have already seen how its liberationary language can be used to mask diversity and deny certain experiences, through allowing the possibility of competing liberation claims ('who's more oppressed than whom?') and a hierarchy of oppressions ('which form of oppression is more important?').

231

The second danger is the potential for identities to become assimilated into the dominant ideology, losing their political, liberationary meaning. Having been through a process of consciousness raising and developing a positive identity around a particular oppression, a community or subculture begins forming around this identity. There is a powerful force from the dominant host culture to categorise and create new stereotypes around this emerging subculture. Also, the greater sense of 'safety' and 'freedom' experienced by individuals within this subculture reduces the drive to further consciousness raising. Energies are instead devoted to the development and strengthening of the subculture against oppressive, external forces. As the subculture evolves, the original *political* meaning of the label, as a term uniting a diverse people experiencing one form of oppression, can become gradually replaced by a more fixed, 'social' definition with its own codes, dress sense, rules, etc. This new social identity becomes increasingly exclusivist and open to assimilation into the mainstream. The processes of assimilation are most clearly seen in the fashion and music industries where new and creative ideas always seem to originate from within a subculture.

For people within the subculture the social identity becomes part of their personal identity. They therefore begin to feel threatened when those who have been excluded begin to articulate their experience politically. Bisexuals and other sexual minorities, by asserting our existence, challenge the monosexual framework of the lesbian and gay subcultures, causing insecurity in the social identity and hence come to be perceived as threatening. This is the source of biphobia in the lesbian and gay communities.

Developing a Politics of Diversity and Freedom

The crucial question arising for a bisexual movement then is how to avoid the patterns of the past, which have led to the political necessity of our movement in the present. It is around this question that there is an urgent need for debate. I would like to suggest a few possible strategies as a contribution to this discussion.

Striving to include diverse perspectives: This could be done by respecting autonomy both *within* and *without* the movement. Ensuring that any group has the opportunity to create its own safe spaces within all of our gatherings, groups and socials. Ensuring that members of such self-defining groups are present in all decision-making processes, and that their perspectives are seen as equally valid.

Diverse perspectives could also be included by inviting representatives of other movements to our events. For example, when there are discussions or workshops on HIV/AIDS, representatives could be invited from organisations such as BHAN, SHARE, Positively Women, etc.

Building alliances across the barriers of difference: 'To reconnect across the lines of our common differences of race, gender, class, religion, sexual orientation, physical condition, or appearance is the creative act that founds a new world'.[8] This could be achieved through affiliations, contingents at political actions, participating in social and cultural events, providing speakers and running workshops at events, etc. Solidarity is important, both in expanding our own awareness and in developing greater support for ourselves. For example, the 'Lesbian and Gays Support the Miners' campaign is cited by Jeffrey Weeks, who quotes from a Welsh miners' leader: 'You have worn our badge, "Coal not Dole", and you know what harassment means, as we do. Now we will pin your badge on us, we will support you'.[9]

Developing non-hierarchical structures of organisation: We must not allow ourselves to fall into the trap of old-style organisational structures with leaders, committees and representatives, but rather look towards 'self-assembling' groups and networks, consensus decision-making processes and so on. Valuable ideas for group processes and community development are found, for example, in the writings of Starhawk.[10]

Acknowledging the gifts and gains of other movements: Often ideas, processes and strategies arising from one movement are taken up and found useful by another. It is always important to acknowledge our sources and heritage: As Kobena Mercer and Isaac Julien point out, quoting Audre Lorde in support, 'the black struggle became the prototype for all the liberation struggles of the late 1960s: gays, women, peace, ecology and anti-establishment. But, although gays derived inspiration from the symbols of black liberation, they failed to return the symbolic debt, as it were, by proceeding to ignore racism.'[11]

Continuous Consciousness Raising: Consciousness raising is an ongoing process; 'coming out' never stops. Two questions we need to be constantly addressing are 'What is bisexuality?', and 'What does it mean to be bisexual?'. As part of this process an exploration of our 'innate' spirituality is vital. The term 'coming out inside'[12] has been used to describe such a process of 'exploring and developing gay-self inside' and 'reclaiming a gay-centred spiritual tradition'.[13]

To quote the editors of *Bi Any Other Name*: 'the bisexual

community and movement is a strong, growing, viable force for coalition between groups. Bisexuals are a part of many different struggles. This diversity is certainly our challenge. It is also our unifying strength.'[14] Loraine Hutchins and Lani Kaahumanu go on to argue for 'an inclusionary, multicultural feminist politics' which 'recognises the complexity of sex, race and class oppression, and how each affects and depends upon the others to survive'. My hope for a bisexual movement is that it would not become a struggle for an identity, but rather, part of a wider movement towards a new level of consciousness that moves *beyond* the politics of identity, beyond the ghettoisation of the subculture, into a politics of diversity and an exploration of our innate spirituality.

> In this oh sweet life
> We're coming in from the cold
> We're coming in, coming in, coming in
> Coming in from the cold
>
> Bob Marley

Notes

[1] Bob Marley, 'Coming in from the Cold', *Uprising*, Island Records, 1980.

[2] Loraine Hutchins and Lani Kaahumanu (ed), *Bi Any Other Name: Bisexual People Speak Out*, Alyson Publications, Boston 1991.

[3] Don Kilhefner, 'Affirmation or Assimilation', in Mark Thompson (ed), *Gay Spirit: Myth and Meaning*, St Martin's Press, New York 1987.

[4] Mark Thompson, 'The Evolution of a Fairie: Notes Toward a New Definition of Gay', in *Gay Spirit: Myth and Meaning, op.cit.*

[5] Jeffrey Weeks, *Coming Out: Homosexual Politics in Britain from the Nineteenth Century to the Present*, Quartet Books, London 1977, 1990.

[6] Essex Hemphill, Introduction, *Brother to Brother: New Writings by Black Gay Men*, Alyson Publications, Boston 1991.

[7] Monica Sjöö and Barbara Mor, *The Great Cosmic Mother: Rediscovering the Religion of the Earth*, Harper & Row, San Francisco 1987.

[8] Starhawk, *Truth or Dare: Encounters with Power, Authority and Mystery*, Harper & Row, San Francisco 1987.

[9] Jeffrey Weeks, *op.cit.*

[10] Starhawk, *op.cit.*, and *Dreaming the Dark: Magic, Sex and Politics*, Unwin, London 1982, 1988, 1990.

[11] Isaac Julien and Kobena Mercer, 'True confessions: A discourse on images of black male sexuality', in *Brother to Brother, op.cit.*

[12] A term used by Don Kilhefner, Mitch Walker and others in *Gay Spirit, op.cit.*

[13] For the beginnings of a reclaiming of a gay-centred spiritual tradition see for example: Judy Grahn, *Another Mother Country*, Boston Press, Boston 1984;

and Arthur Evans, *Witchcraft and the Gay Counter-Culture*, Fag Rag Books, Boston 1978.
[14] Loraine Hutchins and Lani Kaahumanu, *op.cit.*

Politically Bi

Simon Scott

In the radical early years of the gay liberation movement of the 1970s, one of the rallying cries was *'Every straight man is a target of gay liberation'*. The development of this movement has made such a position anachronistic today. This is a great shame. The point was not any desire to harass people – an appropriation of 'gay plague' ideology – but to recognise that all of us are capable, whether or not we are psychologically prepared for it, of having erotic relationships with people of the same sex. The self-censorship and partial ghettoisation of the gay 'community' has created an insularity, however politically justified, which can no longer articulate such sentiments.

This is in no way to dismiss gay liberation. It exploded in activism in the early 1970s, mobilising many people around ideas of revolutionary erotic and emotional possibilities. Its fight against homophobia and compulsory heterosexuality, still being waged, provided a political focus and activism which let people see the possibilities of grassroots activism. Like the women's liberation movement from which it took much inspiration, new forms and structures of sexual and political relationship were proposed, and to some extent achieved.

But both these movements, like most other radical impulses, came up against the problem of power. In order to achieve tangible results, a strong tendency arose to homogenise different positions. No longer allowed to simply co-exist in mutual recognition of validity, factions arose which insisted on the exclusive correctness of their particular perspective. This caused major divisions which continue today. They are a major waste of resources: ideas have been replaced by dogma in the struggle to control the infrastructure and institutions built up by the grassroots movement.

How, why, and to what effect this happened are complex historical questions. For me what is important is to recapture the perspective of the movement's radical origins. Today I think the best chance of achieving this is through an articulation of political bisexuality.

Explicitly bisexual activism is still very muted in Britain, but my encounters with similarly motivated people at the National Bisexual Conference in London have given me confidence in its potential emergence as a dynamic force.

For me, being bisexual means recognising that my erotic and emotional attachments with men are just as enriching as those with women. This does not mean that I am forced into a lifestyle of multiple sexual partnerships or liaisons – that issue is open. My current lover is a woman, and we are both monogamous. Yet we both see ourselves as bisexual people. This is because, although my most rewarding and exciting relationship is with her, this does not negate the strong emotional and erotic attachments I have with other women and men.

Although the term 'bisexual' is misleading in this sense – we need to invent new words – the political goal is the recognition that there is no inherent hierarchy of importance or intensity in the relationships you have: you make those evaluations according to the criteria which suit you. In our degraded and unhealthy society this must remain a long term goal. Relationships are so suffused with objectification, fear and hidden agendas, that it is very difficult to create egalitarian relationships. For example, my present 'Relationship' has to work against strong ideological forces: the assumption that we are promoting and living compulsory heterosexuality and monogamy; the wider social power imbalance between men and women which inevitably enters our own interactions; and so on. Practices should reflect the constant attempt to achieve this egalitarian goal, thereby creating a freer environment, and we should be fully satisfied with nothing else. By 'practices' I mean everything from interpersonal relationships to the structures of our organisations and the networks we facilitate.

A partial attempt to operate this way has been made by the ACT-UP campaign in the United States. The urgency of the AIDS crisis drew together people of widely different backgrounds and experiences. But the structure of organising they took was to be open to any idea about how to promote and develop the campaign. Those who were interested would then undertake the action, supported by the rest. Everybody had an equal say in how the political agenda was set, with no deference to presumed expertise, and no positions of authority. Rigid structures, holding back more radical options, have been resisted. The pay-off in terms of interpersonal relationships seems to have been relaxation and greater fun – lesbians and gay men started sleeping with each other! It is up to us to learn from such practical examples, to improve on them, to forge open alliances and democratic ways of organising.

We have learnt from feminism the systematic and brutal way in which men, as a group, have oppressed women. We have learnt from gay liberation the systematic and brutal way in which straight men and women, as a group, have oppressed lesbians, gay men and bisexual people. Similarly, we have to learn from bisexuals how lesbians and gay men have suppressed our voices and identities. Of course the parallel is far from exact. Lesbians and gay men have far less institutional power to oppress bisexuals, compared to the unavoidable and persistent physical and ideological presence of homophobia. The point is not to see them as the enemy, but as similarly oppressed people who have not followed through a basic maxim, that *all* oppression is unacceptable. More importantly, it should be recognised that exclusions and bigotry within radical movements are the counterproductive effect of vanguardist politics.

So, to return to the notion that 'Everyone is a target of bisexual liberation'; in practice this would work in varying ways according to who you were aligning yourself with or against. Since it is straight-identified society which has the real economic and political power, straights remain the primary target of a more confrontational, militant activism. And though we cannot afford to ignore the real and pressing problems in the relations between some lesbians and gay men, on the one hand, and many bisexuals on the other, the approach should be more conciliatory and sympathetic, based on the fact that in many ways our enemy is the same.

Perhaps I can draw on my more 'traditional left' experiences to make this clear. In the Anti-Poll Tax Campaign we witnessed a highly productive coalition of anarchists, Trotskyists, Labour Party and Union activists, as well as ordinary people with no previous activist experience. Far from being a politics of the lowest common denominator – so tame nobody could complain – we got on with a strong campaign against the common enemy: the Poll Tax and those who were implementing it. It was often an unstable and acrimonious alliance, because different political theories entailed different ideas about how to organise. But if we were to avoid wasting our energies on faction-fighting, we had to criticise constructively, and ensure we always remembered who, materially, were our enemies. And we left the sectarianism to our autonomous group meetings, and the pub afterwards!

The visibility of a politically bisexual movement works on many fronts. First, for both society in general and for lesbians and gay men, it will promote positive images of bisexuality, opposing the widely held stereotypes of bisexuals as people who cannot make up their minds, closets who have the best of both worlds without having to live with homophobia, and so on. Such stereotypes, of course, are accurate descriptions of some people, but these are a minority of those who identify as bisexual rather than the norm. This first step in demystification will open up bisexual history, discovering those people in the lesbian and gay movements who were secretly bisexual, or whose open bisexuality has been suppressed. Then there is the necessity to work alongside other oppressed groups, such as people who choose to practice SM, in order to forego common ground out of parallel experiences of ostracism. It seems to me that we need an active bisexual community, which is a source of emotional support and also recognises the different priorities we may have – without invalidating the priorities of other movements.

The point is to recognise that bisexuality is a politics of diversity. Not, however, one with a laissez-faire agenda. It must be actively opposed to homophobia and biphobia, and consistently sensitive to institutionalised power imbalances and their psychological consequences. That is why the issue of informed consent must be integral to any examination of the validity of sexual practices. I am proposing, for those who are politically bi, a *libertarian* agenda: one which sees the persistent vigilance against all exclusions and forms of oppression and exploitation as a necessary precondition for a truly revolutionary project.

This article previously appeared in *Beyond Sexuality*, Kevin Lano (ed), Phoenix Press, 1992.

Breaking the Barriers to Desire

Peter Tatchell

Everyone is potentially bisexual. The struggle for lesbian and gay equality is about the right of *all* people to share the joy of same-sex relationships without guilt or anxiety, and without the fear of prejudice and discrimination. To reject out of hand the idea of falling in love with someone of the same sex is irrational and illogical. It just doesn't make sense to me to exclude automatically the possibility of emotional and sexual relationships with half the population.

Yet that's exactly what a majority of people do, and lesbians and gay men pay the price for this type of sexual phobia and repression. We have to suffer the devaluation and denigration of our lives, in order that those heterosexuals who are anxious about their own sexual identity can feel secure and superior in their exclusively opposite-sex relationships.

Fortunately, most lesbian and gay people are more generous than these heterosexual supremacists. Our suffering has taught many of us the virtue of compassion and understanding. We are thus fighting for homosexual equality not only for our own sakes, but *also* for the sake of heterosexual men and women. For they, too, are diminished by the system of sexual apartheid which preaches the supposed superiority of heterosexuality, which is justified as 'normality' and 'human nature'. Exclusive and compulsory heterosexuality is neither of these things. Nor is it humane or civilised: it requires the suppression of all sexual feelings towards people of the same sex.

The struggle for sexual liberation is ultimately about the right of *all* people to express the full range of emotional and erotic desires – both heterosexual and homosexual – which are intrinsic to the human condition.

The radical wing of the lesbian and gay movement has always had a vision of a sexually emancipated society in which the bisexual potential of all people is recognised and accepted. It's a vision of a future where individuals no longer feel the need to repress their attraction to people of the same sex, and where everyone feels free to express their homosexual desires without being racked by guilt and humiliated by discrimination.

Is that really such a shocking idea? If not, why is society so hung-up about people 'promoting' and 'flaunting' their homosexuality.

Perhaps it's because, deep down, even arch homophobes recognise that the human capacity for emotional tenderness and sexual fulfilment is not limited to male-female relationships. Indeed, the hysteria against homosexuality is an implicit acknowledgement of the fragile and tenuous nature of exclusive heterosexuality. After all, if same sex relations really are so unnatural and loathsome, why do they have to be negated and repressed by the combined forces of parliament, police, press, and pulpit? And why does heterosexuality have to be so vigorously promoted, with special privileges, such as the monopoly of moral validity, and financial and legal advantages?

The anti-gay bigots are right. A positive affirmation and acceptance of lesbian and gay sexuality is likely to lead to an increase in the proportion of the population having same-sex relationships – not necessarily for their entire lives, but certainly for significant periods. The number of people who are exclusively heterosexual and exclusively homosexual would probably decline. For the majority, bisexuality would become the norm.

Where's the evidence for this suggestion? Despite heterosexual proselytising, and the vilification of homosexuality, same-sex relations are *already* incredibly common. This is borne out in research by Kinsey, Masters and Johnson, Pomeroy and others. Their findings suggest that in western societies about:

- 10 per cent of the population is exclusively or predominantly homosexual
- 15 per cent are bisexual for all or part of their lives
- 25-35 per cent have at least one homosexual experience leading to orgasm during their lifetime
- 50 per cent have had some emotional attraction and/or sexual arousal towards people of the same sex.

If homosexual desire is widespread in a homophobic society, imagine how much more common it would be in a gay-positive culture. Nearly everyone would be in on the act.

And why not? Shouldn't people be free to choose their sexual partners? Shouldn't their choice be respected? After all, there's no rational reason why exclusive heterosexuality should be the majority sexual practice. With artificial insemination by donor, even the argument that we need heterosexuality to reproduce the human species is no longer tenable. Even if there was never again a single act of man-woman intercourse anywhere in the world, the perpetuation of new generations could readily be assured by the technique of self-insemination.

The liberation of heterosexuality from the function of human reproduction, together with the equal validation of homosexuality, would mean that sexual free will could at last triumph over biological necessity and social repression. As a result, male-female relationships would become more of a conscious choice and a rational pleasure, rather than a traditional expectation and moral obligation. Same-sex love would cease to be a minority desire and instead find expression in most people's lives.

The creation of a society which celebrates sexual fluidity, ambiguity and diversity is in everyone's interest. Without it, prejudice and repression will continue to thwart enlightenment and emancipation, to the detriment of human happiness. With it, free-ranging desires can transcend the exclusivity of the hetero-homo divide to the erotic and emotional enrichment of us all.

The Transgender Identity as a Political Challenge

Rachel O'Connor

I have been an out political bisexual for twenty years. I started life as male, having heterosexual relationships. After many unsatisfactory liaisons with what seemed stereotypical women who wanted me to conform to the male stereotype, I met a lesbian. At the time she did not realise her sexual orientation, but through our short relationship we talked about our dislike of having to play male and female roles. I gradually developed my female persona and she moved into lesbian circles. For a time I was accepted within women-only groups as a male lesbian – an exciting time when gender definitions within the lesbian feminist community were open to interpretation. I seemed to fit in and enjoyed what was for me a non-oppressive, role-free community. Everyone I met was female, but the gender spanned from diesel dykes to hyper femmes.

Eventually I was rejected (or felt rejected). By then, however, I had fully developed a female identity. I contacted the London Transvestite-Transsexual community and started to socialise mainly with males. I looked very androgynous and was attracted to both women and men, to whom I related as a woman. Suddenly I realised I was bisexual.

I attended the first London Bisexual Group meeting in Heaven disco on 1 September 1981. The group would meet in the cave-like surroundings of Heaven just before the evening's dance session. The atmosphere was exciting and fun, since there was always some kind of preparation going on for the coming night's entertainment. Initially about 30 people attended, but gradually this increased to nearly a hundred each week. The main reason for this number – apart from the stimulating discussion groups – was that Bi-group members gained free access to Heaven after the meetings.

I gradually became involved in the organisation of the group and

243

helped to plan the topics for discussion. I found the people more open-minded than either gay or straight people when discussing issues of sexual and personal identity. A lot of people were just entering the alternative sexuality scene and were unaware of concepts of political correctness. They seemed to be prepared to form views on things from their own experience rather than from what they read in the gay or straight press. For me, the strength of Bi-group was its diversity and willingness to experiment. I made a lot of friends and lovers through the group and I know I could not have met people like that anywhere else.

With the peak of Thatcherism, my identity became more feminine. With this new femininity I found I could manipulate more easily. By now the term 'post-feminist' had arrived and the politics of female representation had shifted. There was now no defined liberated appearance for feminists. Male and female stereotypes were back in the mainstream with a vengeance. Even being gay seemed to mean conforming to a new set of rules, different from straight life, but just as restrictive of individual freedom.

Thatcher's Britain was oppressive, enforcing a return to division in straight society: male-female, gay-straight, black-white, rich-poor. But an undercurrent of liberation existed in the London club scene, especially at Beyond (from 'beyond the pale') and Kinki Gerlinky. Transvestism, sadomasochism, homoeroticism or simply addiction to fashion were the forces which brought people to Kinki Gerlinky.

The TV/TS community is primarily male and heterosexual, well organised but non-political. It seems to me that it is made up of four main categories.

Transvestites: 80 per cent of the TV/TS population, heterosexual, dressing for sexual excitement. The sight and texture of female clothing are used as instruments of fetishism in masturbation. Occasional dressing, approximately once per month, having no desire to have hormone therapy involving the growing of breasts or sex-change surgery.

Transgenderists: 10 per cent of the TV/TS population, mainly heterosexual with some bisexuals, dressing for the experience of enjoying the female gender role. Regular dressing 20 times per month or more, with sometimes a permanent identity change to the female role. Fetishism is less important, it is more a case of choosing to live in the female gender role. May take female hormones to grow breasts, but still no desire to have sex-change surgery. In the US the word 'transgenderist' is used to define transvestites and transsexuals.

Transsexual: 2 per cent of the TV/TS population. Initially heterosexual, but with a long-term desire to move into complete female mode and a clinically defined homosexual relationship perceived as heterosexual by the transsexual and male partner. Some transsexuals become lesbians, continuing to have relationships with women after the operation. Transsexuals undergo a complete identity change and experience an urgent desire for hormone therapy and the sex-change operation. They are different from transvestites in that there is no fetishistic element: the motive is to be a woman. Transsexuals can originate from transgenderists.

Drag queens: 1 per cent of the TV/TS population. Mainly gay or bisexual, dressing for exhibitionist reasons or simply for entertainment. Much more political than mainstream TV/TS culture, seen in some circles as spearheading gay politics. Drag queens usually have no intention of appearing as convincing women and sometimes use imagery and comments that are misogynist.

The issue of whether TV/TS (male-female) people should be allowed to attend women-only groups has been a problem at bisexual conferences I have attended. But each year the attitude has loosened. Initially only post-operative TS's were allowed, then people who had lived in their chosen role for six months. The London Bisexual Group constitution used to include a Transsexual seat on the committee of five women and five men, though recently this position has been removed. The future of bisexual TV/TS people is still unresolved and more tolerance is required before TV/TS-identified people can feel comfortable in the bisexual community. Obviously, there is no problem for very convincing TS's provided they stay in the closet. For female-male TV/TS's, things seem easier and I have yet to hear any debate about whether they should be excluded from men-only meetings.

The transgender identity is an inevitable consequence of the free human spirit. Transgenderism is all around us; playing out exclusively male or female identities limits personal expression. It has always been thought that maintaining the difference between male and female gender stereotypes was necessary for the continued reproduction of the human race. But in my opinion, different behavioural standards for men and women are simply a convenient means of organising labour and the marketing of products. In organisations dependent on hierarchy, the male/female division is just one more way to keep us in our places. Today, the post-industrial, post-feminist urban wasteland needs new sex roles for men and women.

SECTION IV: BISEXUAL POLITICS

Ten years ago, on Prestel (a minute version of the Internet operating only in the UK), I started an organisation called the Neutron Society. The society's aim was to prevent the old gender rules from getting on to computer networks. I wrote a downloadable program called 'Gendertest' which I distributed throughout the UK via my computer and modem. The program asked 80 personality questions and the person doing the test had to award him/herself points for agreeing or disagreeing with comments. At the end of the questionnaire, a gender identity number would flash up indicating whether the person was masculine or feminine. Most of the contacts were men, yet a sizeable percentage scored as feminine, which caused them to think about themselves. As a result, the Neutron Society gained many active members.

Soon more and more work will be decentralised and organisations will have to change. Already on the Internet people can relate to one another in different ways – some men choose not to be known as men and use neutral names while others become Net transgenderists and are known as women. At last, gender is relegated to a secondary consideration.

Dwelling in the House of Tomorrow: Children, Young People and Their Bisexual Parents

Karen Arden

The issue of bisexual parents and their children doesn't seem to attract much attention in the bi movement. Earlier this year I found myself assuming I'd have to organise my own childcare at a bi event, instead of expecting it to be provided. And it wasn't realised until *after* the deadline for this book that the subject of children had not been covered. These attitudes reflect a wider society that marginalises not only children but also parenting issues – even as it pressurises us to reproduce. (Thus we are penalised if we do have children *and* if we won't, or can't.) Perhaps bi people are also influenced by our connections and shared history with the lesbian and gay community, in which coming out as a parent has at times been harder than coming out as lesbian or gay.[1] There are still people in these communities who see parenting as something done only by 'breeders'.[2] I would argue that thinking about kids is something *all* adults need to do, on a political as well as a personal level.

I want to concentrate here mainly on my own concerns as a bi parent with a three-year-old. My child, Sam, is imaginative, assertive and can be very affectionate.[3] Sam loves television, books and a tribe of sisters, brothers, friends and animals that no-one else can see. At the moment I feel very positive about being a bi parent. I haven't always, and perhaps doubts will arise again as Sam grows older. Things will certainly be different in the future. I'd like to describe how some of my thinking as a parent, and as a woman in a primary relationship with Sam's father, has already changed, as I've had to confront various issues connected

247

with bisexuality.

We live in a culture that assumes that parenting comes naturally, without the need for much support, exploration of the subject, prior experience of childcare, or a great deal of extra resources. The work of parents or childcare providers in our society has low status (despite the lip service paid to it by some men), and this reflects the generally lower status of those who do most of this work, day in, day out: women.

The difficulties for women in female-male relationships can sometimes be glossed over by lesbian and gay men when they talk about bisexuals enjoying 'heterosexual privilege'. The fate of even women-oriented, feminist bi women in apparently right-on female-male relationships doesn't always feel very privileged when a child becomes involved! Not only did I experience this myself when Sam was a baby, but I have also seen it occur in too many other similar couples. There seems to be a tendency to adopt (resentfully and not so resentfully!) more traditional gender roles at this particular time.

The already stressful first year of Sam's life was complicated, soon after the birth, by my becoming quite ill with ME, from which I'm still recovering. Although my male partner enjoyed, and was good at, caring for and playing with Sam on a daily basis, I was left to anticipate any of Sam's future needs (eg, larger clothes) and do a lot of the housework (apart from more 'glamorous' tasks like cooking). I also lost a lot of emotional security from my partner just when I needed it most. However, I had to put up with this and even justified it to myself (for example, 'We'll swop roles next year as we agreed before Sam was born', ignoring the difficulties I was having at the time). The choices available to me were now dramatically limited and, in sharp contrast to our life together before Sam, I was very dependent on my partner, financially, physically, and emotionally. Leaving was never an option, because it would have meant leaving Sam, who I could not care for on my own.

After a time, I felt safe enough to issue some ultimatums to my partner, demanding more practical and emotional support, including not just giving it, but also anticipating it. He agreed to knuckle down. We then discovered that he didn't know *how* to do much of what I was asking of him. My partner had not been expected or taught to acquire many traditionally 'female' skills. He did end up learning most of them (and now I have to remember this when I find myself leaving traditionally male jobs/roles to him!)

Looking back, I now realise what a terribly difficult situation we were both in as new parents. For a long time after I began to challenge

248

my partner on his sexism, I blamed him heavily for his earlier lack of emotional and practical support. I now feel that this was only partially justified, and it did result in resentment from him later on, which also had to be dealt with. The double stress of my constant exhaustion and our 24 hour responsibility for a baby brought out, at times, our worst characteristics and conditioning. Developing new – ie, anti-sexist – behaviour is difficult at the best of times, and can be next to impossible when under this much pressure. Unable to give each other much support, and not getting a lot outside the relationship, my partner and I ended up taking things out on each other. Although there was a lot of pressure on us to cope on our own (especially being middle-class!), we gradually learnt to ask for support from elsewhere (and it then became so much easier to support each other).

Sometimes I think that having a baby with a woman would have been easier, although I know that in reality, there would have been a whole set of different problems. Through our experiences, my partner and I grew enormously as people and in our understandng of gender, and have been brought closer together.[5] However, sexism (external and internalised) never goes away, and it continues in subtle ways to rear its ugly head in our relationship. I believe that as bi women and men in relationships we all struggle under patriarchy, especially when we have kids – but never forget, you men out there, who usually struggles the hardest!

As bi people most of us have had to do some thinking to get to where we are, and thus we may be in a better position to question society's norms, including those concerning parenting. This is true especially for those of us who have the resources and leisure to do so.[6] We may be able to make parenting what Sandra Pollack and Jeanne Vaughan call a 'revolutionary experience'.[7] For, as Tom Kalin says, 'A gay [or bi, or lesbian, or queer] identity transcends given categories of what it means to *be* in the world.'[8] As bi people we don't really have established patterns or models for many aspects of our relationships, even our supposedly 'normal', 'heterosexual' ones. In the same way as we often have to be radical in our approach to relationships, so we can be radical in our approach to parenting. Hopefully we can answer *yes* to Pollack and Vaughan's question about the possibility of offering children an 'alternative to traditional socialisation',[9] a socialisation which is not particularly child-centered or liberating at present.

In Britain, children and young people desperately need more respect, care, commitment, and responsibility. They lack adequate rights, resources, and support. There is widespread public acceptance of the intimidation, manipulation and 'punishment' of children, physically and mentally – all of which passes for normal. Many adults wouldn't behave in this way towards their friends, yet feel it's acceptable to treat children like this. I don't always behave towards Sam as I would wish, and don't always find it easy to apologise afterwards.

Children are discriminated against in a variety of ways by adults. For instance, they cannot vote, and are legally required to spend a substantial part of their lives in the education system. Our culture has little tradition of really listening to children and young people, or acknowledging that their feelings and opinions are important.

Children and young people are an oppressed group scarcely recognised as such. Bisexual people must examine the links between bi oppression and the oppression of children and young people. There is a similar lack of power, choice, resources. This similarity may be hard to appreciate, because we aren't often encouraged to draw parallels between different oppressed groups, for instance, between a society which is homo/biphobic, and a society which is, to use Lucia Valeska's word, 'childhating'.[10] And how come it's OK to say 'I don't like children', but not to say 'I don't like disabled people'?

Early on I used to worry about how Sam would cope at school with the 'burden' of having two out bi parents, whilst feeling relieved we were of opposite genders. I also felt vaguely uncomfortable with the few American children's books Sam's father found about lesbian and gay families – because, I think, they featured such families. I was worried by the idea of Sam seeing my partner or myself with other lovers (of whatever gender), fearing that Sam might see this as a betrayal of the other parent.

Now I think that probably these reactions resulted from two very different sources. Firstly, from my own homophobia: homosexuality and non-monogamy may be good enough for me, but they aren't for Sam. And secondly, they resulted from a desire, at whatever cost, to spare Sam any kind of pain – pain *I*'d endured at home as a young person. Children suffering at the hands of parents who could have done a better job was especially resonant for me. However, when I read *Different Mothers*[11] (in which 'sons and daughters of lesbians talk about their lives'), I was struck by the fact that their parents' lesbianism was just *one* of the many issues that these young people had to deal with. For me what shone through as the crucial issue was the *quality* of parenting each child received. None of the children in the book who grew up feeling bitter about their parent/s put it down to lesbianism specifically. They felt rather that it resulted from a lack of parenting skills or concern – like neglecting children for new lovers. (I want to point out that such behaviour – in any parent – occurs in the context of a culture which, as I said earlier, denies support and status to parents. This doesn't mean however that I'm condoning the damaging or abusive actions of some parents.)

I began to see the danger of dwelling excessively on Sam's potential suffering without *also* acknowledging the gains of having bi parents, especially supportive ones. The problem is, of course, not my bisexuality, but society's attitude to it. I realised that children equipped with lots of support and self-esteem, and (probably) more information than their peers, might even *benefit* from a more unconventional home environment. As Dorothy Riddle says, such children 'become exposed to the concept of cultural and individual diversity as positive rather than threatening'.[12] For young people to have more choices in a society where they have so few can only be a good thing. (Although greater choice is obviously hollow unless it is accompanied by support and resources to follow choices through.)

As Sam grows older, some aspects of home life may well be hard to accept and talk about to others. I don't think I want to hide anything significant about myself from Sam as time goes on, and if I did, I suspect Sam wouldn't thank me for it later. I want to talk to Sam about homo/biphobia as early as possible – to let Sam know both what difficulties there may be to face, *and* how much there might be to gain from the different lifestyle of my partner and myself. I also think it's crucial to give Sam lots of information on sexuality. We adults don't generally give young people much information about subjects which can have a big impact on their lives: child abuse within families, war, child sexuality, what HIV is and how to protect against it, environmental pollution and damage, honest information about family relationships, the fact that biological sex is not fixed ... We have this crazy notion that if we keep quiet about certain 'difficult' issues, somehow children will be 'protected' from them. Instead, of course, children tend to absorb and perpetuate damaging mainstream beliefs about these issues.

I want to be sensitive to how Sam is feeling about my sexuality at any time. I'm prepared to compromise and negotiate on the issue of badge-wearing, posters around the house, behaviour in front of Sam's friends, etc. My partner is prepared to do this, too, although we sometimes differ in the extent to which we think we will be able to compromise. I also want Sam to mix with children from other alternative families, especially those with bi parents. I hope this will give reassurance that Sam's not the 'only one', and will provide a potential source of support and security. Although Sam obviously needs support from immediate family and friends, it's crucial that it is also provided by all of you out there – Sam's wider family in the bi community.

At present Sam comes home from nursery talking of girlfriends and boyfriends. Sam seems to want to marry a different person every week. This openness to the possibilities of love is inspiring, and I want to encourage that. Yet I hate sometimes having to vaguely allude to the restraints of our backward culture. Perhaps Sam needs to know, rather than finding out the hard way, that most people think that you can only have girl/boyfriends of 'the opposite sex' (and then just one at a time), that not everybody gets married (although Sam is aware that my partner and myself aren't), and that two women or two men are certainly not allowed to. Even at three, Sam is quite capable of expressing feelings on these topics!

My observation of Sam has reinforced my beliefs that cultural norms, such as heterosexuality and marriage, are the result of conditioning, rather than being universal or 'natural' behaviour. Our society encourages more than just a given set of expectations, it also encourages a distorted and paralysing thinking. For example, we're not honest with children about the fact that the vast majority of farm animals do not lead the happy cosy lives depicted in children's literature, and that, in fact, we eat them every day. We adults can also find ourselves telling children that violence towards and victimizing other children is wrong, yet they see us directing just this sort of behaviour towards them, other adults, and ourselves. Given the way this sort of flawed thinking is encouraged, it is not surprising that the homo/biphobia which is alien to young children becomes more acceptable as they grow older.

I've always enjoyed living with friends. As Sam will probably be an only child for quite a while, ideally I'd like to live with friends who have children (something I experienced for six months when Sam was much smaller). For me this is an improvement on the nuclear family set-up supposedly characteristic of much of present day white British society. This sort of family still seems the goal of many, even though in its traditional form it hardly exists anymore. Many family units are characterised by isolation, either geographical or social. In these units, a lot of damage and unhappiness can go unacknowledged and undetected, with little possibility of support for children and parents.

(This is not to say that nuclear families are inherently unhealthy, or that extended families do not have problems of their own).

I have met many bi people who are interested in the idea of alternative living arrangements and/or being part of an extended family, based on choice rather than biology. This, if carefully done, can be particularly beneficial for children, who then have the opportunity to relate to others outside their immediate family. Shared childcare, leisure time, and domestic work can lessen stress for the adults and lead to more satisfaction, fun and stability all round. I'd also like Sam to be exposed to a variety of role models, of all sexualities and genders. Living communally undoubtedly requires work and commitment, and my view of it has benefited from occasionally choosing to live more conventionally!

I've become increasingly concerned, as Sam gets older, about education. Amongst many other worries I have about mainstream education, is its inadequacy when it comes to addressing issues of sexuality. Although the legislation against the 'promotion' of homosexuality in local authorities (Clause 28) has been shown to be unworkable in practice, schools still seem to see this as an excuse to be homophobic and not to address issues of homophobia (let alone biphobia).

Difference and dissent in conventional education is rarely encouraged, let alone celebrated, even in enlightened schools committed to equal opportunities. Continually instilling in children the need to submit to authority encourages them to submit to norms such as heterosexuality – and to police such norms in themselves and others.

I mentioned earlier how rarely parallels are drawn between different oppressions. It's so frustrating to see that, despite heterosexism training for staff in Sam's nursery, homophobia (and sexism) in the children's lives doesn't seem to be tackled in the way that racism is, thankfully, starting to be addressed. The more I look at it, the more the 'redeeming' features of conventional schooling (like exposure to a wider social circle) seem less important ... At present, I'm exploring the possibility of an alternative education for Sam; the sort I'm interested in seems to require other like-minded parents and a lot of parental energy. Both are in short supply. I sincerely hope I will be able to offer Sam a real choice between an education within the conventional system and one outside it.

For a bi parent with the concerns I've discussed in this piece, getting support of all kinds is crucial. I need to network with other bi parents, in order to share experiences and information – hard when so few parents can make it to bi events/groups. This I think is due to all sorts of difficulties, not just those at home. Many bi events are organised by youngish people without children. I'm thankful they've got the time, energy and commitment, but they are not always aware of children's and parents' issues. This results in events not being very child-friendly, especially for older children who don't always want to go to creches. So how about sessions/workshops for young people (where they could meet, have fun, talk)? Most importantly, what about asking kids what *they* want? I believe it *is* possible for the needs of adults, young people and children to be met without too much conflict in the bi community – as well as in society at large.

One of the other ways I get support is by reading, and books about lesbian parenting have been incredibly helpful (I have found them far more interesting on parenting than books about general parenting). But there is, not surprisingly, no mention of bisexuality in the books I have read. We need more information about bi parents and their children. We need some research into the subject. We need to know what difficulties are specific to bi parents.

Below I have listed some of the issues and questions which affect bi parents, in the hope that these will be explored further by others (with acknowledgement to those who have examined these issues already as part of other writing on bisexuality). I hope others will add to the list.

- The decision on whether or not to have a child (for those of us who have the option).
- The decision whether to bring up a child on your own. (If not, with whom?)
- Methods of becoming a parent/co-parent, or conceiving a child (by donor insemination? with a lover? a friend?).
- Co-parenting – rights, role, responsibilities, visibility (what happens if co-parent/s and biological parent/s part?).[13]
- Differences and similarities between bi parents in female-female/male-male relationships or arrangements, and those in female-male relationships.[14]
- Differences and similarities between bi parents and lesbian and gay parents.
- Pressures of a homo/biphobic society – on and from us all.
- Nuclear family living versus more communal living (possibly in extended families based more on choice than biology).
- HIV/AIDS consideration, eg, do you test before conception?
- Fostering and adoption by bisexual parents.

- The creation of social environments for our children where their parents' sexuality is sanctioned, and doesn't have to be a secret.
- Custody issues – the courts still don't like queers, whatever our sexuality.
- Families with more than two parents.
- Possible lack of acceptance, by lesbian mothers/gay parents, of bi parents.
- Gender role stereotyping, in parents and children.
- The effects of possible changes in partners/lovers on a child's future?
- Dealing with heterosexist institutions like legal, medical and education systems.
- Children and parents' non-monogamy.
- Sexism towards women in female-male relationships when children are involved; the influence of patriarchy on us all.
- Talking to your children about your sexuality.
- Pressure from children for parents to be 'heterosexual', especially when parents appear to have a choice about the gender of lovers.
- Possible conflicts with non-bi people you may be parenting with.
- Over-emphasising and over-investng in children's sexual preference (eg, do you embarrass children by frequent reference to their supposed sexuality? Do you want your children to be straight to prove that you didn't influence them?)
- The changing issues as children grow older?

I'd like to finish by emphasising how vital it is that we as bi parents get more support (in the widest sense) from our community and our movement. Our needs include the development of relevant policies, more general awareness of the issues, the collating of useful information for ourselves and others, more practical help and emotional support.[15] I think that only parents (biological or not) know the tremendous amounts of energy and commitment required for 'good enough' parenting (that sanity-saving phrase).[16] Society often presents a glamorised image of parenting, especially now that children have become something of a (largely male) fashion accessory. It feels like there's a conspiracy not to tell those without children what it's *really* like in case they don't have any! For me, one of the things that is difficult about being a parent is always having to weigh up my priorities. Sam is one of my highest priorities, and at the moment I just can't afford to have many others – I'm not into being superwoman. At times I have to consciously limit myself, which can be intensely frustrating. In writing this piece, for instance, I've had to make sacrifices, and so have Sam and my partner – although I've also gained much from it. But it's reminded me why I don't take on unplanned extra work like this very often!

Children belong to no-one but themselves, *and* they belong to all of us. Whether adults enjoy spending time with them or not, adults can still help to improve the quality of children's lives. We can all work towards a society where children and young people are able to make more liberating choices, and do so earlier than many of us adults did. Perhaps we can reconnect with the child in all of us, the child we've been encouraged to abandon and betray. Our children are the next generation, whose attitudes to bisexuality, to the value of themselves and others will be crucial – crucial in the continuation of the struggle for bi liberation and the liberation of all on the planet.

With thanks to all those who gave encouragement, feedback and support, including Sue George, Kelly Drake, Simon Scott, and especially Jo.

Notes

[1] See S. Pollack, 'Lesbian Mothers', in Sandra Pollack and Jeanne Vaughan (eds), *Politics of the Heart, A Lesbian Parenting Anthology*, Firebrand Books USA, 1987.

[2] Thanks to Sue George for this point. 'Breeder' is a derogatory term used in the lesbian and gay community for a heterosexual person.

[3] Sam is a fictitious name. It seems distasteful to use 'Sam's' real name without informed consent. Using another name also removes the necessity of constantly using the phrase 'my child', which has connotations of possessiveness that I believe our society needs to move away from.

[4] Even role reversals in a female-male relationship after a child appears (eg, woman going out to work full-time, man taking on the childcare full-time) do not eradicate some of the underlying problems of lack of support for parents. There is a lack of support both for those whose employment interferes with their relationship with their child, and especially for those who spend long periods with their children all day.

[5] I am not implying that relationships which end after undergoing these sorts of stresses are necessarily inferior to similar relationships which continue. Obviously the quality of relationship in both these situations can vary enormously.

[6] Thanks to Simon Scott for reminding me of the need to make this point. As he says, 'Choices of lifestyle tend to be an option only for the (liberal) middle classes, and not just because they can afford it, but because they have the

leisure to read outside the main propaganda institutions (school, media, government).'

[7] Introduction, *Politics of the Heart, op.cit.*

[8] Tom Kalin, in *Homophobia in Hollywood*, a programme in the series *Out*, Channel 4, 1 July 1992.

[9] Introduction, *Politics of the Heart, op.cit.*

[10] Lucia Valeska, 'If All Else Fails I'm Still Your Mother', from *Politics of the Heart*.

[11] Louise Rifkin (ed), *Different Mothers*, Cleis Press USA, 1990.

[12] Cited by S. Pollack in *Politics of the Heart*.

[13] In this piece I do not assume that relationships contain only two people, nor that families contain no more than one or two adults.

[14] I take 'female' and 'male' to denote gender rather than 'biological' sex, thus including transsexuals living in their desired gender.

[15] I am not denying that there are many other groups within the bi community that require all these things too, but they are not the focus of this piece.

[16] From Bruno Bettelheim's, *A Good Enough Parent*, Pan 1987.

Bisexuals and the Left

Zaidie Parr and Jon Johnson

It is not possible to isolate any one particular attitude or ideology which could be said to inform the political position of the mainstream left in Britain towards bisexuals and bisexuality today. The contradictory ideas and attitudes about bisexuality amongst the trade union movement, the Labour Party and the left in general include all the changing paradigms of the last thirty years – acceptance and explanation, rejection and denial, self-justification, or identity politics. All the themes that have been the common currency of the debate on sexuality, and the origins and parameters of sexual orientation, are present in the left.

It is not surprising, then, that many on the left do not even know that an organised bisexual movement exists, nor understand the importance of a body of ideas about sexuality which challenges the notion of 'sexual stasis' or of a fixed sexuality. It is for those reasons, if for no other, that the bisexual movement has to understand, educate and, if necessary, confront the left.

By and large, the left takes its ideas and cues for activity from the lesbian and gay movement, a movement which is largely dominated by identity politics and genetic determinism – both of which strands of thought are unfavourable to a social constructionist view of the world. There has also been a tradition of action for law reform, framed totally within the context of laws to decriminalise male homosexual sex.

In addition, the relative newness of the bisexual movement has meant that acceptance of the 'bisexual voice' has been slow, some of the blame for which can be laid at the left's door, a left which has historically been slow to discuss or debate new theory or ideas, although this is gradually starting to change. What then, can bisexuals do to start changing this state of affairs? What would we demand from a Labour government, from the lesbian and gay movement, from trade union activists, and from ourselves?

In *Sexuality and the State*, a report published in July 1994 by

Liberty (the former National Council for Civil Liberties), compiled with help from Outrage and Stonewall, the British government is condemned for having one of the worst records on lesbian and gay rights in Europe. Containing comprehensive, detailed and damning evidence of neglect of lesbian and gay law reform, the report highlights three areas of law where the UK is liable to be found guilty of human rights abuses: criminal justice, partnership and employment. All of these human rights abuses also affect bisexuals, and we would push any Labour government to put matters right. Launching the report, Liberty general secretary Andrew Puddephatt said:

> 25 years since the dramatic events in New York, lesbians, gays, bisexuals and transgendered people are today still faced with blatant prejudice. We need an all-encompassing bill of rights to ensure everyone's equal rights, so that the particular discrimination individuals face in their private and public lives can be tackled.

Of course, opinion in the bisexual movement would be divided about whether a civil rights bill would be the answer to all our problems, but we welcome a prominent organisation such as Liberty including bisexuals in their public statements.

One of the most momentous events for the lesbian, gay, bisexual and transgender community in the UK in 1994 was the attempt by Stonewall, a national lobbying organisation working for legal equality and social justice for lesbians and gay men, to persuade Parliament to vote for an equal age of consent at 16 (as enjoyed by heterosexuals and lesbians) for gay men. Such a vote would obviously have also benefited young bisexual men. Bisexuality has never been discussed in the Labour Party and they therefore have no policy on it. However, prior to the vote by Parliament in February 1994, the Labour Party conference had voted four times since 1985 in favour of lesbian and gay equality, and indeed they reaffirmed that commitment yet again at their national conference in October 1994. Nonetheless, David Blunkett MP, then Shadow Health Secretary, went against this policy – which was clearly for equality at 16, with conference emphasising that the only requirement for sexual relationships should be that they are based on mutual consent. When David Blunkett and 38 other Labour MPs voted against 16, they were openly defying the party conference's wishes. (75 per cent of Tory MPs also opposed equality – indeed 40 per cent of them opposed any reduction in the age of consent at all.) Outside the House of Commons, 5000 gay men, lesbians, bisexual and transgendered people waited hopefully in the bitterly cold night for what turned out to be a travesty of justice – an age of consent of 18 for gay and bisexual men, leaving younger gay and bisexual men between the ages of 16 and 18 still vulnerable to prosecution.

It is nevertheless important to note that, compared with the situation ten to fifteen years ago, where a vote in Parliament would not even have garnered a majority of Labour MPs for an equal age of consent, progress has been made – albeit too slowly.

David Blunkett's action has significance for the bisexual community because it appears that bisexuals' attempts to lobby alongside lesbian and gay activists for an equal age of consent for young gay *and* bisexual men – an aspect of equality which was hardly touched upon during the Stonewall campaign – were wilfully misconstrued by him, in as much as he attempted to put the blame for his defection on to bisexuality itself. David Blunkett claimed in an interview with Andrew Saxton in the *Pink Paper* (18.3.1994) that he had voted against 16 on 21 February because 'young people are forced into sexuality far too early'. He claimed that he would support an age of consent of 18 for everyone 'if that was a practical proposition'. However, he then went on to say: 'I don't find any difficulty accepting homosexuality or heterosexuality, but I have great problems with bisexuality and the transmission of AIDS to women worries me greatly. I'm struggling with it.' Was this the same David Blunkett who addressed the Terrence Higgins Trust fringe meeting at the Labour Party conference in October 1993, telling a packed meeting that he would lead the Labour Party from the front bench into the 16 lobby? The same David Blunkett who, when he launched Labour's HIV/AIDS strategy, wrote: 'Discrimination is not only morally abhorrent, it fuels the spread of a deadly disease. The detrimental impact of the age of consent upon health promotion work for gay men must be tackled'?

The scapegoating of bisexuality in the AIDS pandemic has been one area where the left has shown its lack of ideological cohesion. It has opened up the debate on homosexuality, with those who by and large cannot be openly homophobic, such as David Blunkett, using 'the bisexuality scare' as a prop to shield them from openly voicing anti-gay statements. A similar lack of political courage was demonstrated by failing to impose the whip on the age of consent vote in February 1994.

Recently Tony Blair made it clear that, notwithstanding the overwhelming majority (97.6 per cent to 2.4 per cent) in favour of backing an equal age of consent at the Labour Party conference in October 1994, any future parliamentary vote on the age of consent will be a 'conscience' vote, ie, no whip will be imposed. One wonders what

Labour Party members actually have to do to change party policy sufficiently for the change to be reflected in its manifesto? As leader of the Labour Party, Tony Blair actually writes the party manifesto, and thus he has the final say on what the Labour Party publicly commits itself to once in office, and on whether a whip is imposed.

On 2 July 1994 Ann Taylor, then Shadow Education Secretary, told the Labour Party women's conference in Southport that Section 28 of the 1988 Local Government Act (which forbids 'the promotion of homosexuality by local authorities') would be repealed in the first term of a Labour government. Understandably, some delegates were surprised to hear her unequivocal statement that those – like Ann Taylor herself – who had voted against an equal age of consent at 16, were united in their desire to repeal Section 28. How much faith can we put in these remarks?

Stonewall is now seeking to introduce a Sexual Orientation Discrimination bill (the 'SOD' bill), following their survey of 2000 lesbians, gay men and bisexuals in 1993, which found that 8 per cent had been sacked, 48 per cent had been harassed, and 68 per cent were not fully out at work, because of their sexuality. This would extend the Sex Discrimination Act to cover discrimination in employment on the grounds of sexuality. (It would include discrimination in recruitment, advertising, training, promotion, terms and conditions of pay, pensions and other workplace benefits, as well as harassment and unfair dismissal.) The 'SOD' bill is specifically intended to include bisexuals as well as lesbians and gay men. Such a bill is long overdue and deserves the full support of the bisexual movement. And members of the Shadow Cabinet, including Tony Blair, have appeared to express support for this piece of legislation. But unless equal treatment under the law becomes formal Labour Party policy, by being written into the manifesto, the whip will not be imposed, and the chances of the bill becoming law without a massive groundswell of public support will be much reduced.

The Trade Unions

One element of the labour movement, the trade unions, provides some useful insights into the processes which are taking place on the left today. In December 1994 we wrote to thirteen trade unions where we knew that lesbians and gays were organised, to try and discover their current attitudes to bisexuality. At the outset it is important to make a distinction between a union's not having a specific policy on lesbian, gay and bisexual issues, and their not representing and defending a member of the trade union who is being discriminated against because of their sexuality. There are cases of unions without any formal non-discrimination policy defending individual members who have been the subject of discrimination (such as the UCW, which has no policy on lesbian, gay or bisexual discrimination, but has vigorously defended lesbian members against discrimination). There are also numerous cases where a trade union has policy but nothing has been done to defend a member.

The vast majority of unions have at least some nominal recognition that discrimination against someone on the grounds of their sexual orientation must be opposed. Yet trade union members facing discrimination often find it difficult to know how to go about getting support from their trade union. If the union's policy is not being upheld at a local level, there are often few mechanisms to ensure that the union defends their members, other than by going to the next level of the union. This is often a difficult thing to do, and failure to make progress compounds people's feelings of isolation.

It is for this reason that many trade unions have lesbian and gay groups, most of which sprung up within the unions independently of their National Executives, as a response to homophobia. Recently the National Executive of at least one union has been researching its membership to test the feasibility of setting up a lesbian and gay forum (which is either good news or bad news for bisexuals depending on whether they are to be included in the forum, which varies between unions – for bad practice, see pp154–5). Such initiatives will, hopefully, diminish problems of isolation within unions.

As the articles by Frances Murphy and Kitty Rees in this book describe, bisexuality is still a political hot-potato to many trade union lesbian and gay groups. This is unsurprising, since it reflects what is going on in the wider lesbian and gay movement. Nonetheless, as it is the job of unions to defend their members' interests, where discrimination against a bisexual person occurs, in all but a few cases the lesbian and gay group representatives would pursue the case vigorously. It is this practical experience, together with the growth of the bisexual voice, which is helping to bring about a more positive attitude within the lesbian and gay trade union groups towards bisexuality.

We asked the trade unions the following questions in our letter: What is your union's policy on bisexuality? Are bisexuals included in the gay and lesbian policy? Are there any other provisions for bisexuals? Replies fell into three categories – those which had a positive policy, those in which it was implicit, and those which were actively against. Most, however, provided mainly very positive answers. The NUS said,

> The Lesbian Gay Bisexual National Campaign formally included bisexuals into our campaign in 1991. Bisexual involvement and the campaign as a whole have gone from strength to strength since. This year (1994-1995) both the National Convenors are bisexual, and we have many bisexuals at our National Conferences. We hold bisexual caucuses at national events and also hope to hold both bisexual and bisexual women's events this year. At a local level most student union societies do now formally include bisexuals, although actual involvement is less developed at this level than nationally. We are encouraging groups to set up bisexual-only spaces, to ensure high visibility for bisexuals in their campaigns and to hold discussion sessions on bisexuality to improve this.

The Transport and General Workers Union said that '... policy on bisexuality is included within our overall policy of lesbians and gays, in that we will fight discrimination on the basis of sexuality'. The First Division Association of Civil Servants was, at the time of writing, actively considering changing the name of the union's lesbian and gay network to reflect the inclusion of bisexuals. Discussion of bisexuality is 'not a priority' within UNISON, the union formed from the merger of NALGO, COHSE and NUPE. As the latter two were less biphobic in their outlook before merger, the blatant biphobia demonstrated by the organising committee of the NALGAY conference in 1986, who decided that bisexuals should be 'banned', will be increasingly a thing of the past. On that occasion, the organising committee rejected a request from NALGO members of the London Bisexual Women's group to hold a workshop at their next conference. Subsequently, the name of the annual national conference was changed by the group from the inclusive 'NALGAY' to the pointedly exclusive 'NALGO conference for lesbians and gay men'. This decision may have been connected with other political struggles that were going on in the lesbian and gay movement at the time, such as the banning of bisexuals from being members of the London Lesbian and Gay Centre, a ban that was eventually overthrown by its membership in late 1985.

A crucial area of debate for bisexuals within the unions is the wording of policies that unions urge employers to adopt. Most unions advocate a wording along the lines that 'discrimination on grounds of sexual orientation is a disciplinary offence'. Others, however, such as UNISON, advocate 'that discrimination against lesbians or gay men is a disciplinary offence'. The crucial difference here is that the former wording is inclusive, taking within its remit lesbians, gay men, bisexuals and transgendered people, whilst the latter wording is exclusive – and excludes bisexuals. These are the sort of issues which we urgently need to address if we are even to approach the more favourable situation in the USA, where an umbrella group for all trade union groups named itself from the very outset National Gay, Lesbian, Bisexual and Transsexual Labor.

Why Bisexuals
Need Trade Unions

Kitty Rees

Why bother trying to get justice through the trade unions? Surely they're too slow moving? Too homophobic? The main reason is that, through trade unions, you can reach a lot of people, who, because they're organised, have a lot of weight. Most of us don't own newspapers or control big business, so sticking together is the only way we have of protecting our interests. Unions are about collective self-defence, the notion that an injury to one is an injury to all. Their strength, whatever their leaders and 'new realists' might say, lies entirely in mass action, and ultimately in the threat that we might all stop working and stop making profits.

For obvious reasons, unions tend to concentrate on what happens in the workplace, where most of us spend much of our lives. Apart from the extreme example of being sacked, there are a lot of other ways in which discrimination can affect you at work. For example, because conditions of service tend to assume we all live in heterosexual nuclear families, it can be difficult to get leave to look after sick partners, or non-biological children. Coping with the stress of secrecy and/or hostility from workmates can affect your health; and, obviously, discrimination can damage your job prospects.

It doesn't make much difference whether you are bisexual or exclusively gay when it comes to discrimination at work. Homophobic bigots are not interested in the finer points of self-definition, and nor, usually, are supportive trade unionists. (Talking exclusively about an other-sex partner could theoretically, make you more acceptable to some people, but being 'in the closet' is possible for lesbians and gay men, too – and equally painful.)

The lack of data makes it hard to say whether or not discrimination has increased in recent years. A 1992 Labour Research survey found that a quarter of its respondents had experienced or knew personally of

265

cases of anti-gay victimisation or harassment. Since most of their replies came from the public sector, where many workplaces are covered by an equal opportunities policy, this is probably an underestimate in overall terms. Privatisation and the 'contracting out' of services have produced a number of cases of discrimination. Section 28, while rarely used in a legal sense, has led to self-censorship by local authorities and a vague acceptance that homo- and bisexuality are a Bad Thing. The British Social Attitudes survey showed an initial increase in popular homophobia associated with AIDS/HIV which has now reversed.

My own experience (which is limited to the UK trade union movement) has been as a member of and shop steward for three unions: NUPE, NATFHE and NALGO (see note). Several years' hard work by activists has meant that these three are among twenty-one unions – no longer limited to 'white-collar' occupations – which now have national policies supporting lesbian/gay rights. This usually means 'opposing discrimination on the grounds of sexual orientation', which applies equally well to bisexuals and to exclusively gay people. A good national policy is certainly helpful, but it is usually the local branch which must defend you if you are victimised. So if national policy is to mean anything the debate must also be won on the ground.

The biggest problem is often one of getting the issue raised in the first place. Censorship is often a bigger problem than expressed homophobia. Our NUPE branch secretary would reassure gay activists: 'Don't worry, you don't have to bring this issue up; it's National Policy already.' It was. Several boxes of this same national policy languished in a basement in Divisional Office, where not even the shop stewards knew about it. So, in spite of the official policy, they were obviously ill-equipped to deal with discrimination as it occurred.

Sending in items of correspondence asking for action, whether on individual instances of discrimination or on issues such as Gay Pride and AIDS/HIV is invaluable in getting the question on to the agenda. At least then you have an opportunity to argue the case. The point above all must be to get *everyone* to see discrimination as an issue that affects them personally. Sometimes people don't immediately see what lesbian and gay rights have to do with them. 'It's not a trade union issue', they say. And with no direct knowledge of lesbians, gay men or bisexuals, some people will have gone along with the anti-gay rubbish put out by the press. But views are rarely fixed, and it should never be *assumed* that heterosexual workers will be hostile.

The sort of arguments that always make sense in a trade union context includes the following: (1) No worker should be bullied or picked on because of their personal relationships. Everyone should have the right to decide for themselves without fear of violence or discrimination. (2) Our bosses have an interest in dividing the workforce, but the workforce has an interest in standing together. Blaming immigrants, blacks, gays or whatever, sets people against one another and distracts attention from those who are *really* trying to exploit us. (3) Attacks on lesbians, gay men and bisexuals are part of an offensive by the right which includes attacks on abortion rights and on single parents. By forcing a stereotyped, unreal view of the family on everybody, and using women as unpaid carers, they can justify their cuts in welfare.

It is worth trying to get bisexuals mentioned alongside lesbians and gay men in policies and resolutions, if only to demonstrate that we exist and may need support against harassment and discrimination. Occasionally (as happens sometimes in NALGO) objections may be raised by someone influenced by separatist ideas, who feels that it will 'weaken' the resolution. It is important not to allow hurt at such prejudice to jeopardise the motion or policy itself. After all, a policy supporting lesbians and gay men is a lot better than none at all. If it is impossible to get the consent of those moving the resolution, and you decide to try to amend it, the amendment should emphasise the common theme that links us – that we should all have a right to decide our own sexuality without fear.

During the 1980s, a number of unions set up lesbian and gay groups. NUT, NALGO, NCU and MSF (see note) all have a formal committee or group at national level, and fourteen other unions have informal groups or networks. Perhaps the most positive effect is the boost they give to the morale of lesbian and gay members. Bisexuals can also feel enormously encouraged to know that such a group exists. Whether or not such groups actually accept bisexuals into membership is often unclear. In NALGO, at least, some groups have what amounts to a ban, and there have been reports of women being unceremoniously ejected from even national meetings and conferences after coming out as bisexual. Bisexuals and their supporters are, of course, working to change this!

Self-organisation is valuable for the sense of confidence it creates, and it can help to get things on the agenda. Sometimes, though, recognising people's *right* to form separate, autonomous groups has been confused with the separatist assumption that only those who personally experience a specific form of oppression will ever seriously fight it. This is a great pity. Not only is it in the interest of heterosexual workers to challenge homophobia, but there is actually no reason why someone's sexual orientation should automatically cause them to have a better strategy for fighting back. And realising that you have allies can make you feel better and increase your confidence. Self-organisation is a means to an end, not an end in itself. It is through solidarity and building outwards that we start to get real results.

There is an ambiguity about being bisexual which can give you a particular angle on the question. It is interesting that our own bisexual groups are so often open to all supportive people of whatever orientation. Perhaps this is because our own experience of identity-dominated politics has so often been a negative one. Perhaps it's because we are constantly reminded how flexible sexual identity can be, and how little it need determine your views. I couldn't count the number of times that resolutely heterosexual workmates and union colleagues have ensured that harassing bigots in pubs have caused me no violence. Above all, the work of lesbian and gay support groups in the 1984-85 Miners' Strike, and in support of the Wapping printworkers not long afterwards, shows what can be done. It can be hard to remember, only a few years later, how unheard of it was for a union like the NUM to take a position on lesbian and gay rights. Our joint achievement was summed up in the NUM's motion to the 1985 Labour Party Conference. 'Support civil liberties and the struggle of lesbian and gay people. Our struggle is yours. Victory to the miners.'

Note: Over the last few years, there have been a large number of amalgamations and name changes among unions. The abbreviations in this article were those current at the time.

Thoughts of a Bisexual Anarchist

Liz A. Highleyman

My identity as a bisexual is intimately connected with my politics, especially my identity as an anarchist. Many people think of politics as voting and lobbying, but to me politics means one's ideas and philosophy, the beliefs one has about the world and how to make it better.

Anarchism is a political philosophy based on the elimination of hierarchies that limit our lives, such as the state and church over individuals, the wealthy over the poor, men over women, and heterosexuals over non-heterosexuals. Anarchists believe that hierarchical authority is not only unnecessary but harmful, and that a just and well-functioning society can be achieved in a non-authoritarian way based on co-operative, decentralised, voluntary communities. Dualistic thinking is one of the roots of hierarchy, and the existence of bisexuality presents a challenge to dualism. How can it be true that people are fundamentally different, based on whether they are attracted to the same sex or the opposite sex, when some people are attracted to both? If sexuality and gender were not regarded as a fundamental, polarising way to categorise people, sexism and heterosexism would not be possible. Thus there is an affinity between anarchist politics and bisexuality.

In recent decades, progressive political organising has evolved in the direction of identity politics, which is based on what group(s) one belongs to rather than what beliefs one holds. Within the realm of identity politics, ideological differences such as liberal/conservative, socialist/capitalist and anarchist/authoritarian are minimised in favour of an emphasis on shared characteristics such as gender, race or sexual orientation. It is often assumed that people who share identity characteristics must share a political ideology. But it is a fallacy that identifying as bisexual, gay or lesbian automatically makes one politically progressive or that being heterosexual automatically makes one politically conservative. Often gay, lesbian and bisexual activists try to gloss over political differences because these can create controversy and impede unity. Yet, given our vast ideological diversity, is it wise to try to consolidate all people who are attracted to the same sex into a common political movement?

Because of our differences, there is much tension over what the focus of the gay (or, increasingly, sexual minority) movement should be. Some want to limit the focus to expanding civil rights for people with same-sex partners. Others feel that the oppression of gay, lesbian and bisexual people is embedded in patriarchal and capitalist society and cannot be eradicated without fundamental social change. A current example is the issue of sexual minorities in the military. Should the movement support gay participation because discrimination is wrong, or should it oppose gay participation because the military is historically an oppressive institution that plays a role in maintaining the patriarchal, statist and imperialist status quo? Clearly, an anarchist position would differ from that held by political conservatives.

There are many bisexual people within the anarchist milieu in the US (more, it seems, than gay men or lesbians, and sometimes more than heterosexuals). Several anarchist publications regularly discuss issues relating to sexuality, and anarchist gatherings often include bisexual or gay/lesbian/bisexual workshops and caucuses.

In my political organising and social interactions, I associate more with anti-authoritarian groups than with bisexual (or gay/lesbian/bisexual) ones, because I find coming together with people who share my political philosophy more valuable and affirming than coming together with those who only share a common sexual orientation. Of course, I do not want to associate with anarchists who are homophobic, but I have found more bisexuals to be hostile towards anarchists (or political radicals in general) than anarchists towards queers. However, an acquaintance in the UK has had the opposite experience. He works with bisexual (or gay/lesbian/bisexual) groups rather than anarchist groups because there is support for anarchist methods and goals within the bisexual groups, while there is considerable homophobia within the anarchist groups. These examples only serve to underline some of the problems of identity-based politics.

Anarchists have often been criticised by leftists for focusing too much on the issues of sex and sexuality, which are seen as 'bourgeois' matters that will take care of themselves after the revolution. While many leftists consider sex and sexuality to be 'personal' or 'private' and divorced from politics (or at least of much less consequence than, say, economic concerns) these matters have been historically important components of anarchist theory and praxis. Many anarchists share the belief (exemplified by Wilhelm Reich) that the repression of sexuality is, along with capitalist exploitation, one of the major ways authoritarian control is maintained. Emma Goldman, and the Free Love advocates of the early 1900s, criticised misogynist sexual morality and the commodity nature of marriage and compulsory monogamy; today many anarchists continue to see the struggle against enforced gender roles and the quest for new relationship options as an integral part of the struggle for radical social change. Marx and Engels developed critiques of traditional gender roles and the property-based origins of marriage and the nuclear family, but modern socialists have often failed to expand their critique to encompass the related phenomenon of heterosexism. Some Marxist/Leninist (and Maoist) organisations and governments view homosexuality as decadent or even counterrevolutionary; in some cases this has led to active oppression of gay men and lesbians.

As identity politics has taken hold in the US, many liberal, progressive and leftist groups have begun to regard gay, lesbian and bisexual people as an oppressed minority and have sought to build coalitions with queer activists. Yet there is still often a hesitancy, even a squeamishness, about delving into sexual politics. It's often hard for people to think objectively about sex and sexuality because it hits too close to home. Anarchists have generally done a better job in both welcoming queers within their ranks and in dealing forthrightly with the politics of sexuality.

Some people become radicalised politically because of their oppression as gays, lesbians and bisexuals. Others question their heterosexuality as a result of their radical politics. I began to think of myself as an anarchist well before I thought of myself as bisexual. It was within radical political circles, in fact, that I first got to know bisexual, gay and lesbian people. I began to wonder why so many people who shared my political ideals rejected traditional notions of gender and sexuality, and I started to question many of the assumptions I had grown up with. When I thought about it, it made little sense to rule out the romantic and sexual potential of half of humanity. I had never taken gender very seriously, anyway, since I was uncomfortable with the traditional female role and generally thought of myself as 'one of the guys'. The more I learned about anarchism, the more I wanted to challenge accepted ways of thinking and living, including moving beyond dualistic conceptions of gender and sexuality.

Rejection of the patriarchal power structure, traditional sex roles, and dualistic notions of gender and sexuality has spurred many people to adopt sexual identities that they feel are more consistent with their beliefs. Often, embracing feminism shapes sexuality. Many radical women have decided that while they are attracted to both men and women, they can achieve egalitarian relationships in this society only with women. Many radical men have rejected the traditional macho male heterosexual role. Traditional gender roles limit people of both sexes and homophobia is used to keep people of all sexualities in line. Much of the privilege accorded to men and heterosexuals is based on economic privilege within the capitalist system and social privilege within marriage and the nuclear family. In seeking to change the economic system and traditional social institutions, anarchists reject this privilege and the price that society demands for it.

The most well known example of the adoption of a sexual identity on the basis of political beliefs is the 'political lesbian'. While some women have been sexually attracted to women as long as they can remember, others developed their attraction and commitment to women as an outgrowth of feminist politics. Today we have the phenomenon within radical and progressive groups of the 'political bisexual'.

There is often a temptation among non-heterosexuals to justify their orientation by claiming 'I can't help it ... I was born that way'. There is a well-grounded fear that if homophobes believe we can choose our sexuality, they will try to make us choose heterosexuality. However, being 'born that way' is no protection against hatred and discrimination, as racial minorities can attest. Some gay, lesbian and bisexual people may very well be born that way, while others probably became that way early in life, and still others consciously chose to be that way for personal or political reasons. However, some 'political bisexuals' tend to adopt an attitude of bisexual superiority, because they see bisexuality as a way to move beyond rigid notions of gender and sexuality, and see bisexuality as more equitable or more 'highly evolved' than other orientations.

The world would be a better place if everyone thought about *why* they have the preferences they do; sexual and relationship choices should be no more exempt from critical examination than choices about employment, etc. Yet no sexual orientation is inherently superior, and all people have the right to love who they choose and to be true to their own identities. There is nothing inherently better or worse about bisexuals who feel they were born with their sexuality, as compared to those who consciously chose it. If the bisexual movement wants to welcome all bisexuals, it would do well to acknowledge and value the diverse ways in which people come to identify as bisexual.

Feminist Bisexuals in the UK – caught between a rock and a hard place?

Zaidie Parr

The year of the last National Women's Liberation Conference in the UK (the scene of a decisive split between the Socialist Feminist and Revolutionary Feminist tendencies in the movement), was 1978.[1] It also happened to be the year of the first national gathering of bisexual feminists.

On a peaceful day in late summer about fifty women from around the country met up in the house and garden of a small mansion – recently liberated from the London Borough of Camden by feminists who'd squatted it for a Women's Centre. The friendly atmosphere and surroundings made me feel optimistic. And yet, despite its importance to me, the day seemed to go by in a dream. I can only remember one conversation, with a friend (obviously in the know) who declared that many, and probably the majority, of women in the Women's Liberation Movement (WLM) – including several well-known activists – were bisexual or at least had bisexual histories. This seemed such a comforting thought that despite my worries about bisexual women's poor press in the movement, I don't remember feeling that we should be (or indeed, could be) more organised. As far as I know, no significant networking took place that day.

The next national meeting of bisexual feminists was not to take place for another fourteen years, when, on 20 June 1992, the first bisexual women's day school was held in Sheffield. We had not anticipated in 1978 that the national communication network and organisational strength of the WLM would falter as it afterwards did – thus removing what opportunity we might then have had to alter the climate of repressive opinion against bisexual women which had been

274

characteristic of the WLM since the early 1970s.

In the 1970s, I saw myself first and foremost as a (radical) feminist. I did not have a primary awareness of myself then as a member of an oppressed sexual minority, which I suppose I have now. I believed that it was important to fight for the rights of all women, of whatever sexual preference, and I believed that the WLM would eventually realise this. I thought that feminists would work together to change the world. Even then, however, the writing was on the wall about the unacceptability of bisexuality. Even respected feminists believed bisexuality to be an exercise in moral and political futility.[2] We were perceived as women who were afflicted with a form of 'false consciousness'. This meant that our experience was not 'real', not experience which other women, other feminists, could or should identify with, or develop theory or practice from (the theory and practice of consciousness-raising should have suggested otherwise). We were the exceptions to the feminist rule. One day, it was opined, we would either 'see the light' and come out (self-identity) as lesbians – or we'd go back to relationships with men and stop oppressing lesbians by trying to have relationships with them in our unreconstructed state. (Opinion leaned to the view that the latter option was by far the most likely outcome, and maybe because of this, bisexual women were shunned as partners by most lesbians, thus making the theory a self-fulfilling prophecy.[3]) Bisexual women, it was felt, could safely be disregarded. Bisexual women (if they existed at all) just needed to be re-educated – and there was no shortage of volunteers.

Peer group pressure, social isolation, unavailability of lesbian partners and loss of friends and lovers usually achieved the desired result – conformity to prevailing heterosexual or lesbian norms. Nonetheless, some bisexual feminists managed to struggle on, usually opting for a lifestyle of serial monogamy, and often involving alternating het and lesbian relationships. (Triads were unheard of, of course, as they could not have been so easily disguised.) Politically active in the WLM, I felt that I was always working for the liberation of others, but somehow was not being empowered by this myself. Bisexual women were the 'Other' – prisoners of silence, of the unspoken, spoken of but never spoken to. We began to organise.

It is likely that other friendship groups of bisexual women were also meeting, unbeknownst to each other or to ourselves, when the London Bisexual Women's Group (LBWG), held its first meeting in the Cromer Street Women's Centre in London in 1985. Actually this was not the first explicitly feminist bisexual group to meet in London –

another group had started meeting some months previously. We even met up with them once or twice, but then heard that the group had disbanded as nearly all of them had decided that they were really lesbians. I remember cynically wondering if they had just succumbed to the constant pressure on bisexual women to identify as 'Political Lesbians'. This was a newish theory, which was a bit like a scientific experiment: the way forward to a better society was for all women, whatever their sexual orientation, to become Political Lesbians and stop servicing men sexually or emotionally. Bisexual feminists were clearly being given a last chance to redeem themselves with the advent of this ideology. It appears to have been a variation on an old theme.

In her acclaimed 1979 study, *The Lesbian Community*, Deborah Goleman Wolf commented that there were some women who felt that they were not 'real' lesbians, especially if they were relating to both men and women; rather they were bisexuals.[4] She noted that political ideology had played a role: 'In Europe ... bisexuality is 'chic', and it is assumed that people in certain upper class or bohemian circles are bisexual. However, in America, among many political lesbians, bisexuality is regarded as a betrayal, since it is as a *lesbian* that one is persecuted ... the politically correct thing is to define oneself as a lesbian, not as a bisexual, and to choose not to relate to men, since men are seen as oppressors of women.' Wolf goes on to note that this seemed to have led to the formation of support groups for bisexual women who were unable to adapt their affectional orientation so easily. Despite minor differences in these ideologies as they crisscrossed the Atlantic at the end of the 1970s, the message was fundamentally the same. Bisexual women were, apparently, on their own.

In 1981 the Leeds Revolutionary Feminist Group stated that, 'We do think that all feminists can and should be political lesbians. Our definition of a political lesbian is a woman-identified woman who does not fuck with men. It does not mean compulsory sexual activity with women.'[5] I thought that possibly the most difficult thing about the Leeds paper was the built-in assumption that some women have such a superior grasp of women's oppression that they have the right to tell other women how they should live their lives.

One bisexual woman, Debbie Gregory, wrote in to *WIRES* to explain what was wrong with this particular approach.[6] She began by outlining what the WLM had originally meant by the term political lesbianism; that it had been a call for all women, regardless of their specific sexual orientation, to publicly identify themselves with lesbians, as lesbians. The idea had been that if all women took a public stand as lesbians, much of the specific oppression of lesbians would then be subverted. This public identification had led to deeper changes:

> The important thing for me about political lesbianism, as it was first conceived, was that it was a call for unity among women, based on our common experience of learning to know and care for each other. I found it a profoundly creative experience, opening me to parts of myself I had never before acknowledged, opening me to other women in ways I had never dreamed possible. It allowed me to feel connected to all women, women I didn't know, women I didn't like, women I admired, women I desired.

But, according to Debbie Gregory, Revolutionary Feminists had missed the point:

> They just go on and on making statements about what every heterosexual woman's life is like, what she should think about it, what she should do about it. Rather than demanding that all women question their experience and make decisions based on their new understandings, they just tell us what that experience is and what it means. Furthermore, they tell us that if we do not accept their truth and act on it in the way they tell us to – in effect, if we do not accept party discipline – then we are collaborators with the enemy.'

Unfortunately, in spite of such critiques, the Revolutionary Feminists' analysis took hold in the WLM.

As the London Bisexual Women's Group was a consciously feminist group when it was first formed, I hoped that we might be able to challenge the ideology of Political Lesbianism, as defined by Revolutionary Feminists, and I also hoped that the recognition of bisexuality would return the WLM to the truthful accuracy of consciousness-raising and the acceptance of the need for a united struggle on many fronts. I prioritised the recognition of bisexuality as a way to heal the wounds of the fractured WLM. I did not believe that a movement which continued to accept the denial and suppression of so many women's sexuality could ever develop the valid theory and effective practice that was needed. But I failed to anticipate the difficulties which would lie ahead.

After the LBWG had been running for a few months we learned of a mixed group, the London Bisexual Group (LBG), whose origins were in the Anti-Sexist Men's Movement, and had been meeting since 1981. However, despite or perhaps because of their origins, many in the

LBG did not welcome the creation of a women-only group. We were suspected of being separatists because we identified as feminists. It was not recognised that we were organising as feminist bisexuals because there was nowhere else for us to go – exactly like our sisters on the East Coast of the United States and elsewhere were doing at that time. We were seeking sanctuary and reassurance from each other to counteract the hostility and ostracism we had experienced in the movement, and to look for a way forward for us as feminists.

The resentment toward the LBWG from the LBG had a disruptive effect. Some women decided that they ought to join the mixed group, to show solidarity, but this led to the Bisexual Women's Group being used as a recruiting ground for the LBG. Many women were also recruited whilst at LBG meetings to Re-evaluation Co-counselling – a sort of international growth movement/political party/therapeutic organisation. No doubt this seemed more enticing than mere feminism. In short, where we had expected support we were seen as a threat, or a potential recruiting ground, and this may have contributed to our failure to develop a feminist politics of bisexuality at that time. Although I am no longer a member of the LBWG, it seems unlikely to be able to challenge the direction feminism has taken all by itself.

In 1990, feminist bisexuality in the UK was given another opportunity to integrate with and receive support from the wider bisexual movement. At the National Bisexual Conference in Edinburgh that year, there was a mixed Bisexuality and Feminism workshop. This was easily the largest, and one of the most enjoyable, workshops at that Conference. There were sad moments too, when bisexual women actually shed tears of fear and despair at the treatment that had been meted out to them by lesbian groups and individuals. Although the attendance at the workshop was predominantly female, it included a minority of supportive and encouraging men. After listening to a panel of women speakers and the wide-ranging audience discussion which followed, we all overwhelmingly agreed that we were committed to building a feminist bisexual movement. However, despite this accord, no mention of this was made at the conference plenary report back, and, since there was at that time no national bisexual newsletter or magazine, the bi movement at large never got to hear of the workshop's decision, nor was there any chance to debate it.

This lack of communication meant that feminism was not adequately represented in the organisation of the next National Bisexual Conference held in London in 1991. By this time the feeling of confidence engendered at Edinburgh had somewhat dissipated, and

278

sexist behaviour by some of the men attending the conference meant that distressed women insisted upon attending a woman-only workshop, to which the four-women panel of speakers agreed. Workshop discussion centred on how the bi movement could be made safer for bisexual women. We felt that for this to happen, it was important to ensure that the bi movement was not dominated by white able-bodied middle-class men, as the mainstream lesbian and gay movement seemed to have been. All forms of discrimination – racism, sexism, sexual harassment, homophobia, misogyny, ableism and prejudice against People Living With AIDS or HIV – should be outlawed. We decided to hold a bisexual women's conference where we would have a chance to debate contentious issues relating to race and gender oppression more fully.

Most bisexual conferences which have taken place since 1992 have had to confront issues of feminism and equality. At a time when even the queer movement hosts a tendency which supports 'aesthetically pleasing' misogyny, for example, attempting to claim the film *Basic Instinct* as 'Queer Cinema',[7] it is very important that bisexual women and men make a stand for revolution, justice, and equal rights. At the very beginning of the Gay Liberation Movement, activists were clear that there could be no Gay Liberation without Women's Liberation, and Feminists asserted that there would be no Revolution without Women's Liberation. It would be a cruel irony if bisexuals, who have had to face so much discrimination and hatred themselves, could not identify with the struggles of other oppressed people. We should recognise that 'We cannot ourselves be free if others are not free', and hope that allies in the feminist movement and elsewhere will feel the same way about our own struggle for human rights and dignity.

Notes

[1] The theme of the Conference was our Differences as women, but this was not dealt with in a constructive way. Instead of celebrating our unity and strength in diversity, difference was used to divide women. The Conference ended amongst dreadful scenes of accusation and counter-accusation, leading to a profound and enduring disillusionment for many.

[2] See for example, 'Gayness and Liberalism', in *Hidden Agendas – Theory, Politics, and Experience in the Women's Movement*, Elizabeth Wilson with Angela Weir, Tavistock Publications 1986.

[3] Perhaps the assumption was that bisexual women would always opt for heterosexual privilege if it (or he) became available. If so, this assumption is probably linked to internalised lesbian self-oppression (i.e. what woman would choose a lesbian if she could have a man?) – and should be exposed as

the nonsense it is.

[4] *The Lesbian Community*, Deborah Goleman Wolf, University of California Press, 1979/1980.

[5] *Love Your Enemy? the debate between heterosexual feminism and political lesbianism*, Onlywomen Press Ltd, April 1981. (This debate first appeared in *WIRES* – the national newsletter of the WLM in the UK, – now defunct.)

[6] *Love Your Enemy? op. cit.*

[7] Talk by Andy Medhurst at the New Queer Cinema Conference held at the Institute of Contemporary Arts, London, September 1992.

A History of The Edinburgh Bisexual Group

Dave Berry

In November 1984, eight bisexual people met at a workshop on bisexuality at a Lesbian and Gay Socialist conference in Edinburgh. For most of them, this was the first time that they had been in a group with other bisexual people. It was certainly the first time that any of them had realised that there were other bisexuals active in the lesbian and gay movement. When they announced their sexuality to the rest of the conference, most of the other attendees were surprised, some were hostile, and many were unwilling to talk about bisexuality at all. This was why Kate Fearnley, one of the organisers of the conference had run the workshop. The isolation felt by bisexuals active in the lesbian and gay movement created a need to contact other bisexuals. Since several people at the workshop were from Edinburgh, the Edinburgh Bisexual Group was born.

At that time the London Bisexual Group was the only other bisexual group in the UK. It had been meeting regularly since 1981, and had been increasingly successful. Two weeks after the conference in Edinburgh, the London group held the first national conference on the politics of bisexuality. Sixty bisexuals from all over the country met there, including members of the new Edinburgh group. The second national conference was held five months later, also in London, and at that conference the Edinburgh group volunteered to run the third.

The group had started by meeting fortnightly, but soon attendance dwindled. But the other conferences had shown them what can happen when lots of bisexuals get together. And although organising the conference was a lot of work, it gave the group a sense of purpose.

At this time I had just moved to Edinburgh and was feeling very isolated. I wasn't part of the lesbian and gay movement, and didn't know any other bisexuals. The idea of a political conference didn't appeal to me, but I phoned the contact number and they persuaded me to come along and see what the conference was like. I was overwhelmed by how friendly it was and I joined the group immediately! I've never regretted that first tentative phone call. The conference was a great success, attracting sixty people, almost half of whom were from Edinburgh. Most of us hadn't known each other before. After the conference most of us started coming to the group. The group has never looked back.

Most group meetings, then as now, were informal discussions of aspects of bisexuality, such as coming out, or relationships with lesbians and gay men. People often brought along something to drink, and the meetings were lots of fun. We took turns to produce posters advertising the next meetings, and put them up in 20 or so places around the city each week. In 1986 we organised Britain's first explicitly bisexual disco (A Breach of the Genetic Peace, according to the poster). We maintained our links with lesbian and gay activists. In 1986, three of the five members of Edinburgh Lesbian and Gay Pride committee were members of the EBG.

Clearly the group was going well. Everyone was helping to keep things going, we were getting a lot done and were enjoying ourselves. But we were aware that we were lucky; many bisexual people were (and are) still isolated, with no bisexual friends and no support for their sexuality. The group was putting Kate's phone number in its publicity, and Kate had been getting phone calls from distraught bisexuals at all times of the day and night. So we decided to set up a phoneline to offer information and counselling. By advertising a fixed time and training more volunteers, we could give Kate back her privacy and offer a better service to our callers.

The phoneline could only happen because those of us who joined in 1985 were more confident of our own sexuality. Although it seemed an obvious thing to do, it seemed beyond the resources of our small group. We were worried that we wouldn't be able to carry it off. But people had the motivation to make it happen, and we succeeded.

We asked the local Lesbian and Gay Switchboard to train us, but they weren't interested. I think they thought that we were encroaching on their territory, though once the phoneline got started we soon developed a good relationship with Switchboard and other organisations. Anyway, we pooled what training and experience we had and trained ourselves. We took our first calls in January 1987, and have been running the line once a week ever since.

1987 also saw the National Conference return to Edinburgh. The Fifth National Conference on Bisexuality, jointly organised by the

Edinburgh University Lesbian and Gay Society, attracted 120 people, and was twice the size of earlier conferences. It was widely praised. At the conference we launched our pen-pal scheme. This provided another way for isolated bisexuals to keep in touch. Although it's a small-scale operation compared to a professional dating service (like everything else in the group, it's run on a shoestring) it has been well used and well liked. It now includes people from all over the world.

These events were the start of a shift towards providing a range of support services. This change was not the result of a single decision, but occurred gradually as we talked about plans over several months. It had a political slant as well. We thought that the increased visibility of the group as we offered these services would help the recognition of bisexuality in the wider world.

It's hard to compare our history with what might have happened if we had chosen to concentrate on explicitly political actions, but I think we made the right decision for the times. If we hadn't provided support to other people, we wouldn't have attracted enough people to build the successful movement that we have today. But we didn't abandon political activity altogether. Members of the group were a significant presence at several demonstrations against the notorious Section 28 of the local government bill (which has since been used against our attempts to gain funding), and at demonstrations organised by Edinburgh ACT-UP against the government's response to the AIDS epidemic.

We now found ourselves with a mix of people. Some were politically minded, some weren't. Some were completely out, some were barely out to themselves. We still managed to draw enough people into the organisation of the group to produce a newsletter, put up posters, facilitate meetings, and staff the phoneline. Some of the more experienced and self-confident of us found ourselves doing a lot of the work, but we had help from the other members, and we made sure that everyone was involved in making decisions.

In the next couple of years the British bisexual movement slowly grew. New groups appeared in several cities, although some proved to be short-lived. We helped a group start in Glasgow, as a lot of callers to the phoneline lived there. A group in London published the movement's first book, *Bisexual Lives*. The seventh national conference was held in Coventry, the first time it was held outside London and Edinburgh. We had articles published in several gay magazines, and two British lesbian and gay organisations, OLGA and CHE, decided to admit bisexuals. (The Scottish organisation, SHRG, and several short-lived Scottish campaigning groups, already supported us.) There was even a short piece on bisexuality in Channel 4's *Out on Tuesday*, although the producers tried to make a joke of the debate.

In 1989 the London and Edinburgh groups were consulted by the Health Education Authority over a health education campaign aimed at bisexual men. This was the first official recognition of the movement, although the initially strong plans for the campaign were delayed and cut by the government. It finally ran in May 1990, with greatly reduced exposure. The campaign included a national phoneline, the Bisexual AIDS Helpline. Four members of the Edinburgh group worked on this phoneline, as did members of the London group. The reduced level of campaign meant that the phoneline received a mere handful of calls each night however – no more than our own phoneline.

We had a similar experience recently, when we prepared a leaflet on safer sex for the Health Education Board for Scotland, which has never been released for use. But there have been more positive developments on safer-sex campaigning for bisexual people, particularly the national *Bisexuals Action on Sexual Health* group.

Like all groups, the Edinburgh group has had its ups and downs. We had times when it seemed that everything was going to fizzle out and times when it seemed that we were going to change the world for good within a few weeks. We had a fairly high turnover of members: some people moved away from Edinburgh, some people found friends and drifted off with them, and perhaps some people came to the group to sort themselves out, did so, and didn't need the group any more. This turnover meant that we had to keep training phoneline volunteers and finding new places to advertise. But in time the group reached some form of stability.

From this base we shifted course again. After concentrating on services for bisexuals for several years, we decided to look outward. In a way, this was bringing back some aspects of the first phase of the group. But this time we had a stronger base. We had the beginnings of a bisexual community and recognition of that community, and we were more confident. We were also less willing to treat the bisexual movement as a child of the lesbian and gay movement, and more interested in a genuine partnership, with both the advantages and the responsibilities that entailed.

We organised our third national conference in 1990, and through our discussions with lesbian and gay groups at this conference, made some new links. One result of this was that the Scottish Homosexual Rights Group added the word Bisexual to the name of their Edinburgh Centre. The EBG had always used the centre, was affiliated to the SHRG, shared some members with them, and got on well with them, but the issue of the name had never arisen. But since we had never raised it before, how were they to know that a name change would make bisexuals feel more welcome.

Another benefit of the discussions was that the International Lesbian and Gay Association decided to allow bisexual groups to join. Raising the issue in a friendly environment, where it would be discussed without antagonism, achieved results. We also formed a link with the Stonewall lobbying group, and commented on their draft bill for homosexual rights.

The 1990 Conference attracted 150 people. It was widely acclaimed as the best conference so far. For the first time we had British Sign Language signers so that deaf people could take an active part in the proceedings – which they did, to our benefit. At the end of the conference about twenty people staged a spontaneous kiss-in on the Lothian Road, one of the main roads in Edinburgh. This was a sign that the outwards shift that we were experiencing was shared by others in the movement.

Another effect of this shift in outlook was an attempt to get articles in the mainstream press. For some years we had the occasional article in the lesbian and gay press, and we felt that we had achieved a degree of acceptance there. But the straight world was as anti-bisexual (and anti-homosexual) as ever. We felt that we should shift our efforts to the larger group.

To do this we set up a media sub-group, which had some limited success. For example, two members of the group were interviewed in *Scotland on Sunday*, and some of us appeared on television discussion programmes. Organising the conference allowed us to get snippets into a variety of media. *The Observer* carried a story, and interviews were broadcast by Radio Scotland, Radio Forth and Radio Clyde. There were also reports in *Gay Scotland*, and *Rouge*, the lesbian and gay socialist magazine. We built links of a different kind when four of us went to the first USA national bisexual conference in San Francisco in 1990. The conference was quite different from ours, with more speakers, more entertainment, and with whooping and cheering at every opportunity. There seemed to be a higher proportion of therapists and counsellors running workshops. We've kept these international links since then; several Americans have visited British conferences in return.

There's more to the bi group than conferences. We still hold weekly meetings, either discussions of a topic or social nights. We organise a range of other social events, from picnics to parties. In recent years members of the group have organised several weekend retreats. We produce a short newsletter with details of events and other news, and are one of the most visible Lesbigay groups in Edinburgh. We are the most regular users and supporters of the Lesbigay Centre.

We have always run the group informally, making decisions by consensus in the group. This lets people help to run things as soon as they wish, and doesn't pressure people into doing more than they want to. We think that this is more appropriate for our group than a more formal system with committees and elections, which sometimes seem to cause conflicts that distract people from actually getting things done. We rely on donations for all our funding, including the phoneline. We maintain links with other bisexual groups throughout the world, via friendships, newsletters and computer networks.

We are open to anybody who supports our aims, regardless of sexuality. We don't require any political beliefs of our members. All we require is that people at each meeting should respect each other. In particular, we don't allow discrimination on the grounds of race, sex, age, disability, class, or any similar property. We have about 80 members, half women and half men, aged from 19 to 50. Some of us are out, some aren't; some of us are politically active, others are more interested in the social and support aspects of the group. We try to make everybody welcome.

We have no specific plans for the future, other than to continue with what we have started, and to change as our membership and the wider movement changes. We hope to contribute to the continued growth of the national and international bisexual movement. And we hope that one day people's sexuality will be no more relevant than the colour of their eyes. When that day comes, perhaps we'll disband the group. After a farewell party, of course!

Postscript: Since I wrote this article I have had to leave Edinburgh. The bisexual group still thrives. In 1994 the Bisexual Resource Centre opened in the Scottish Centre for Lesbians, Gays and Bisexuals. This office houses *Bifrost* magazine, the Edinburgh phoneline, and a bisexual archive. Also in 1994, the group combined their tenth birthday party with another Edinburgh conference. To mark this occasion, the Sisters of Perpetual Indulgence canonised Kate Fearnley for her work over those ten years, and as a representative of the bisexual movement as a whole.

Bisexuality in Brussels

A euroqueer

Let me start by introducing myself: I'm one of the many Eurocrats in Brussels, working here in a European Community institution in the capital of Europe. I'm a bisexual believer in terms of who I fancy and my sexual politics. I'll be 25 tomorrow and I've already received one birthday present – a dildo from a gay boy with whom I simulate penis envy. I've just used it – for the first time in my life I've played with a dildo – and it has inspired me to write. So here goes. These are my impressions of bisexuality in Brussels.

The bi-scene here features a few mixed sex (girl/boy) couples who hang out in the lesbian bars. The boy sits at the bar and watches his girlfriend pick up another woman, get her drunk, and take her home for what turns out to be a threesome with him. There's also the bi-woman body builder who is so butch she can pass as a man. She's been in places where no other woman has set foot, such as the backrooms of exclusively male gay clubs here.

Few people here are out about their sexuality unless they are straight, so queer organisations are weak, especially for women. We do have a women's social and swimming group, which has no straight women members. However, most of the women are too apolitical to label their sexuality, which can be a drawback (people are scared to fight for queer rights), but has one positive effect: the B-word is no more threatening than the L-word, so bisexuals and lesbians have equal status in the group.

Dykey political action does happen in Brussels, not in the swimming pool but in a bookshop run by an admirable but isolated lesbian separatist. I volunteered to work there and turned up wearing my bi-pride T shirt. She suggested I start by washing the floor. I didn't care. I just wanted her to know that a bisexual was doing her cleaning. I want people to recognise our contribution. Bisexuals are cleaning floors, fighting homophobia and building the new Europe (and working to prevent the potential benefits of European integration being limited to business people).

Bisexuals are everywhere. We're a world movement, and we are the future. When homophobia lets up, more (presently) straight people will allow themselves to feel attractions for their own sex, and queers will no longer be put on the defensive, so those lesbians and gay men who do have inklings of heterosexuality will no longer need to repress them in order to have their same sex relationships taken seriously as 'more than just a phase'. Bisexuality is beautiful. I wouldn't change my sexuality for the world, but together we will change the world with our sexuality.

A History of the Bi-Movement in the Netherlands

Wouter Kaal

In this article I shall try to give a picture of the history of the bi-'movement' in Holland. It is not without reason that 'movement' is written in quotation marks; through the years there has been little continuity, and no national coordination of local activities. Often active bisexuals suddenly appeared on the scene and disappeared just as quickly.

The 'coming-out' of bisexuals was the afterbirth of the sexual revolution of the 1960s and 1970s. The *NVSH (Dutch Society for Sexual Reform)* took the lead, concerned not so much with sexually 'deviant' behaviour as with the emancipation of sexuality in general, especially that of heterosexuals. They began to promote the idea that sex doesn't necessarily have to involve procreation. In the 1970s the subject of bisexuality was first discussed in organisations such as the NVSH, Group 7152 (founded in 1971 for lesbian and bi women) and Orpheus (founded in 1972 for married homosexuals). When talking with pioneer bi-activists I also found that some of them had previously been active in the 'men's movement'. But during all these turbulent years of sexual emancipation no separate bisexual community emerged, and bisexuality – when discussed at all – was seen mainly as a problem, and not as a positive quality.

Only in the 1980s did bisexuals begin to emerge as a separate group. At schools and universities a few theses were written on bisexuality. At the beginning of 1983 the *LSAB, (National Support and Action Group for Bisexuality)* was set up. That same year this group joined the annual Gay rights march held in Leiden, for the first time as visible bisexuals with bi-banners.

SECTION IV: BISEXUAL POLITICS

In November 1983 the LSAB organised their first big national 'happening' named 'Bi is Best!'. There was a vast programme of lectures, workshops, films, poetry, live-acts, a photo exhibition and a party. There were around 300 visitors and there was a lot of publicity in the press! Unfortunately a second meeting in 1984 was called off; the new bi-newspaper was published only three times and simply answering the mail became a great effort.

But a positive result of the event was the formation of regional or local groups. Some of them – in Zwolle, Haarlem, Amsterdam, Utrecht, Nijmegen and Eindhoven – were active for many years, organising bi meetings, often in conjunction with local branches of NVSH or COC (the Dutch Gay rights movement which was formed just after 1945).

At the end of 1985 the remaining local groups formed the LNBi (National Network for Bisexuality). The aims were to make contacts possible between bi-activists, to have a postal address and to publish a periodical.

At the national level the LNBi joined the annual Gay rights marches, provided a lot of information and published the paper *Bi-Nieuws* four times a year. Also 'bi-weekends' were organised a few times a year.

It took a few years before the government responded to requests by the LNBi for financial support. Initially the Ministry of WVC (Welfare, Health and Culture) wrote that groups like Orpheus and COC already promoted bisexuals' interests. This misunderstanding was later openly admitted by WVC and from 1989 onwards the LNBi got an annual subsidy of a few thousand guilders.

As can be expected through the years, the LNBi had their ups and downs, and people flew in and out of the organisation. In the long period between 1985 and 1990 a fairly constant core of volunteers spent a lot of time in the network and kept it going. But in 1991 real problems arose. New people stopped entering the organisation and the 'old guard' didn't want to go on in this way. The situation was complicated when a rival Foundation for Bisexuality was set up with no consultation with existing bisexual groups.

In May 1991 the LNBi decided to become a legal organisation with members. This option of becoming a society, seems the best guarantee for a lively and democratic bi-movement. It attracts members and it gives us a stronger position for negotiating, for instance with potential subsidisers.

Towards the end of 1991 *Bi-Nieuws* unexpectedly got a new editorial staff of six people, due partly to a call-for-support at the First

International Bisexual Conference, held in October 1991. The international conference was a largely Dutch initiative, with some financial support from some of the Provincial governments, the Juliana Fund and the LNBi. It took place at the Free University in Amsterdam, a two-day event with lectures, workshops, food and a disco party. It was a great success, with an attendance of almost 200 men and women, of whom about 50 were from abroad, especially from America and England. The idea to organise such an event annually arose spontaneously during the conference.

One of the main aims of the conference was to make clear to the outside world that a considerable number of people are – during part or the whole of their lives – neither heterosexual nor homosexual, but both at the same time. Other aims were to let bisexuals come out in the open and be visible, to contribute to forming an international bi-network, to encourage scientific research on bisexuality and, of course, to have a good time among bisexuals.

In Autumn 1991 a campaign was started to change the Dutch Bill for Equal Treatment, implementation of which had already been delayed for many years. The Bill is meant to protect people against discrimination on such grounds as race, religion, sex and marital status. It discusses discrimination on grounds of 'hetero- or homosexuality', bypassing all other possibilities. Our campaign aimed for the recognition of bisexuality in this law. Meanwhile the law has been passed, but without mention of 'bisexuality'.

At the time of writing, it is clear that *Bi-Nieuws* will continue, as will government subsidies. The LNBi Society has more than 200 members; we handle an average of 20 incoming letters a week; people can get information almost every day through our telephone help-line; on the local level there are about 15 contact persons who can be phoned for information on activities or just for a chat. The contact persons have joined in a National Information Group, with the LNBi Society.

Recent government cuts of 25 percent on 'homo-emancipation' have resulted in a new co-operation between all organisations that receive government subsidies. Groups like COC, Kringen, Group 7152, Orpheus and the LNBi Society are now united in promoting their common interests with the government. All these groups get their financial support in the name of the 'homo-emancipation' policy. Within this cluster, however, the LNBi Society is the only specific group on bisexuality.

The Dutch bi-movement still has quite a small social basis.

Continuity is always a problem. On the brighter side, we can see that in the past five years more than ever, we have been organised. There has been more attention in the national media, such as radio interviews, feature articles and a TV show. The Amsterdam local radio station, MVS, still has a bi-weekly programme.

Because of bisexuals' weak organisation, there is almost no way of identifying with a 'group'. Bisexual group identity and individual identity is underdeveloped and cannot be compared with those of gays or lesbians.

The creation of an effective bisexual interest group is the first necessity to be able to give bisexuality its own identity – with respect for all other forms of relationships. The LNBi-Society could perform this task in the future but only on the condition that many, many more bisexuals become active in it.

Bisexual Associations in Germany

Francis Hüsers*

In view of the low numbers and the high fluctuation of activists I still hesitate to speak of a bisexual 'movement' in Germany. Worldwide the 'movement' has only a few thousand, in Germany at most two hundred people 'actively' involved, ie, more or less regularly participating in more or less continuous meetings of bisexual people. Obviously there is not much to be enthusiastic about. On the other hand, the number of people who have at least once participated in a bisexual meeting, or been individually counselled is quite high. There seems to be more under the surface than we are able to recognise. A certain degree of fluctuation may be characteristic for bisexual associations, as many people consult a bi-group only during their coming-out process. As one result of this process they often start a new partnership – be it homo- or heterosexual – which for many may render their further participation in a bi-group somewhat redundant. Their lifestyle may now become either more 'gay/lesbian' or 'heterosexual', although they can continue to see themselves as 'true bisexuals'. Thus, fluctuation and a certain organisational instability may be a special feature of bisexual associations, to which this pattern applies even more than to the lesbian and gay movement.

And yet, if it still seems worthwhile to look back on recent efforts in Germany to start a bisexual 'movement', it is because twelve years ago there was nothing at all. Bisexuality occasionally featured in the media, but did not refer to people's lives in any 'real' or socio-political way. The first attempt to start a group of bisexual women and men was made through an article published in a fringe men's magazine in 1983. By 1984 the author of this article had joined with others to organise the first national meeting of bisexual people in West Germany. This date

* Translated by Robin Cackett

293

roughly seems to correspond to the birth of bisexual movements in other countries and it would be interesting to investigate, from an international perspective, why these attempts to get a bisexual movement off the ground surfaced at the same time in several Western industrialised countries, even though they were organisationally (almost) completely independent.

As this happened in many countries even before the mainstream emergence of AIDS, I would argue that the reason lies in certain similar aspects of social change in Western societies. Today, in these societies, sexuality is seen as a central aspect of one's identity, and this opens the possibility of new forms of partnership and gender relation. This specific process of social change is typical only for Western society in its 'late modern age', when it depends on highly developed individuality, on the basis of relative stability and affluence, at least for the majority of the middle classes, and a free choice about religion, ideology and life-style.

An example of the liberalisation that is part of the process of individualisation in Western societies is the amendments of the law that discriminated against male homosexuality in Germany (paragraph 175 of the penal code). Until 1969 this law banned all homosexual acts among men regardless of age. In 1969 it was modified, and an age of consent of 21 conceded. In 1973 this was reduced to 18. The gay movement had strongly fought for this change. But not until 1994 was the law deleted completed, so that it is only recently that there has been an end to legal discrimination against male homosexuals in Germany.

These recent trends of liberalisation and individualism create the space for bisexuals. Bisexuality, on this argument is therefore a result of social change rather than its promoter.

Since 1984 a growing number of participants has attended regular national as well as regional meetings in Germany. Until 1989 these meetings were organised by a national 'Initiative of Bisexual Women and Men' in collaboration with a growing number of bi-groups which established themselves in various cities. These meetings mainly focused on three issues: (i) the communication of individual coming-out stories; coming to terms with the 'common' denial of bisexuality; coping with conflicts bisexuals have in their relationships with lesbian, gay and heterosexual partners; (ii) the formulation and discussion of a theoretical understanding of bisexuality drawing on educational theory, philosophy, sociology, psychology, and political science; (iii) increasing bisexual visibility by participating in public discussions, by advertisements and group publications, and by joining lesbian and gay demonstrations and activities. These activities centred round weekend meetings several times a year which all bisexual women and men were invited to join. Although the organisational basis has changed, such national events are still being held and have resulted in relatively close personal contacts among people from the various bi-groups.

The national 'Initiative of Bisexual Women and Men' ceased to exist in 1989. By this time several local bi-groups had established themselves in different cities. Apart from internal group activities these groups continued organising national meetings. In 1989 a group of bisexuals collaborating with the *Deutsche Aidshilfe* (the German equivalent to the Terrence Higgins Trust) started to organise regular national weekend conferences. Today we have groups of bisexual women and men operating in Berlin, Potsdam, Hamburg, Bremen, Bielefeld, Münster, Düsseldorf, the Ruhr area (Recklinghausen, Gelsenkirchen, Wuppertal, Hagen), Cologne, Frankfurt and Munich.

It was in 1990 that bisexual women and men from the former GDR participated in a national meeting for the first time. Since then several attempts to get groups in Eastern Germany off the ground were undertaken, with different success. The bi-group in Potsdam, for instance, is very active, and organised the – probably worldwide – first Bisexual Film Festival which took place in December 1994.

By and large all the existing groups are encounter groups in which bisexuals try to mutually reinforce and support one another. Liaison with local lesbian and gay organisations differs from place to place, and according to the respective bi-group's identity, as does public relations and involvement in politics (eg, participation in demonstrations and parades etc). State subsidies have been attained in very limited amounts, and only in that the *Deutsche Aidshilfe* has helped sponsor particular events. In effect, almost all German bisexual activities and events are financed by the private means of the individuals involved.

In January 1993 the newly founded legally registered, private, non-profitable society of German Bisexuals held its first general meeting. This society is called BINE, short for bisexual network (for our address see contacts list at the end of this book). The foundation of BINE was the result of a long and controversial debate about whether we really need an official organisation in order to legally sanction the existing bisexual networking in Germany, and if we did, what we would like this organisation to look like. Some were afraid that we could betray the principles which have so far been characteristic for bisexual groups by founding this society, ie, grass roots organisation, shared responsibility, and openness towards all seriously interested people regardless of their present personal relationships and station of life.

For two years now BINE has worked itself into a position as the central bisexual organisation in Germany, coping with any matter concerning bisexuals. It promotes all local bi-groups and bisexual individuals by regularly distributing information, organising national meetings and serving as a central mailbox for contacts between bisexual associations (national and international), as well as between bi-groups and the 'outer world' (eg, 'monosexual' organisations). Today BINE has 66 officially registered members and a network of individuals serving as contact-persons in cities all over the country. Most Bi-groups are not registered members but participate in BINE events. BINE also promotes the newly founded bisexual magazine, *Bix – Infoblatt für bisexuelle Kultur*.

In these two last years German bisexual organisations also have had to face a sudden wave of public interest promoted by the media, especially by the newly founded private TV stations in Germany. A number of bisexual women and men, some from bi-groups, some without any connection to the bi-movement have participated in TV-talkshows or been interviewed or portrayed in special features. Some people felt the programmes had taken unfair advantage of them, by restricting their free speech in concentrating too much on private affairs and lifestyle issues. Others felt they actually had been able to speak their mind about bisexuality in a heterosexist society. In any case, these experiences will at least help us to learn how to cope with public interest and the media in the future.

The new interest in bisexuality has also promoted the publication of several German books about bisexuality. Some of these books are written by bisexual authors who have been – or still are – working within bi-groups, some are by professional authors who obviously felt that the growing interest in bisexuality renders it a lucrative subject. Some of the latter ones seem a bit voyeuristic, while the ones by bisexual authors can tend to treat their subject in perhaps a too scientific (philosophic or sociological) way. A reader with essays about bisexual lives written by non-professional bisexuals themselves – such as have been published in the UK, the Netherlands and the USA – can not yet be realised, for no German mainstream publisher wants to take the risk of doing it.

Compared to the bisexual movements in other countries, notably the UK, the USA and the Netherlands, the history of the German 'bi-movement' seems to me to be distinctive in two main respects. By holding national meetings, workshops and seminars right from the beginning there has been a strong emphasis on personal contacts on a national level linking the existing local groups in a more informal way; and German bi-groups have – at least in their early years – shown a strong theoretical concern, trying to achieve a philosophical, sociological and/or psychological understanding of bisexuality. Although we may learn a lot from bisexuals' more pragmatic approaches in other countries, I hope we shall manage to preserve and develop both these idiosyncrasies.

BAD (Bisexuals Affirming Diversity): Bistory

Clare Bear

The first meeting for bisexuals on campus was held in 1989 in the Auckland University Student Union. I'd put up 100 posters, many of them torn down. But still, it was *action*, something that hadn't been done before. I had no idea how many people would turn up.

Michael came up with the idea of BAD (Bisexuals Affirming Diversity). What I was aiming for was an atmosphere that was open, friendly, positive, non-separatist and non-judgemental. I was well aware of the dismissive, derisory or downright snigger-laugh attitudes. There again, gays and lesbians watched, took note of the posters, and wanted to know how many turned up. After all, we were an issue for them too. We were an uncomfortable presence in their groups, of which there was little settled on the matter of policy – how to treat us? – should we be included? Welcomed? Vilified? Supported?

On the day we had seven people turn up. All but Michael were women. Of the seven, three were new faces to me – the rest were friends, or flatmates. Yet we all knew of at least one person who could (or should!) have been there. This emphasised for us, the need to encourage people by making sure our group (if it continued) was *open*. 'No labels, no heavies, just friendly' said the posters. We needed to make it so anyone could come in the door and be welcomed without having to say 'well, I'm not really bisexual ... though maybe – I'm a lesbian, but I've had a couple of affairs with men so I don't know ...' *Anyone* could come, and not be asked how bisexual they were. Or suspected they were.

We found the problem was one of peer pressure: lesbians were too scared to admit to lesbian friends they might be bisexual. We came across this, over and over. In this sense, ironically, we found heterosexuals more accepting of bisexuality than gays/lesbians. Some people, like Helena, were suspicious of a group that had an open door

298

policy. She wanted a women-only bisexual group ('BLOC' the lesbians called her – Bisexual Lesbians on Campus). I personally found the BLOC idea depressing – yet more separatism, into smaller and smaller groups ... I felt that bi women should be able to go to BAD as bi, and go to LOC (Lesbians on Campus) for a women-only support group, and bi men should similarly have access to BAD and Unigays.

At the beginning of the meeting we were nervous but excited. The feeling an hour later was of being an entity, a group of bisexuals, instead of each of us being just an individual bi. It was strengthening. We felt that as a group under this label we could no longer be ignored as individuals, our bisexuality could not be ignored. It had been felt already. LOC was already taking note.

The idea had arisen out of a long evening 'bitch' session with me, Michael and Rosemary, as friends, over the prejudices and stereotyping of bisexuals by gays and lesbians. Michael and I had each felt the various negative or dismissive attitudes towards our bisexuality from our gay/lesbian friends. We were both bisexual, and had come from same sex relationships, and now we were going out together. Openly, much to the dismay and unease of some. Labels didn't fit us any more. And it wasn't as simple as dismissing us as a heterosexual couple, because of where we'd come from, and our continuing commitment to the gay/lesbian communities.

It got us down. We felt unfairly maligned. It seemed especially outrageous when it came from our more 'political' friends. They were hypocrites, we thought bitterly – they fight against discrimination against gays/lesbians by the straight world, yet they discriminate against *us* in turn. We felt betrayed.

Some lesbians viewed us as 'really hetero', keeping both worlds open by our false stands. Gay men tended to be less 'hysterical', though they sometimes shared the same ambivalent attitude to bisexuality as an 'illusion'. It annoyed me, to be face-to-face with Richard and hear his 'we must have a room for a support group for bisexuals', and then to hear him say privately, 'I don't believe bisexuality exists. They're kidding themselves, they're just screwed up and can't make up their minds.' Gay men had more at stake: AIDS. Hence they (officially) were less hung up about bisexuals, though this new openness to bisexual men was still filtering down from national level to these smaller groups. Unigays (for gay and bisexual men) was more sociable; camp, bitchy sessions in mostly-good humour. They never discussed how they felt about bisexuals. Unigays posters read 'Gay? Bisexual? Unsure?' – influenced no doubt by Michael going out with the poster-designer.

Section IV: Bisexual Politics

No one guessed what issues that spur of the moment 'yeah, put bisexual too' would raise. We found out at the 1989 Easter Gay/Lesbian Conference, another influence leading up to the creation of BAD. At the conference, apparently, a woman stood up and 'confessed' she was bisexual. What ensued was a rowdy and very controversial discussion of the whole issue. The conference was split as to whether they should support bisexuals or not. Were they not 'letting the enemy in'? Having their own energies diverted? Rosemary (who was a lesbian) came home extremely upset, emotionally distraught, and physically ill over the affair. She was dismayed at the attitudes, and thus she readily joined Michael and me in our despair at how some gays and lesbians treated bisexuals.

Soon after, I decided I needed to make sure, in my own mind, that lesbians *did* feel this. I went to the next LOC meeting, which (coincidentally) brought up the conference and bisexual issue ... I hadn't been to LOC before, my lesbian side had been pretty apolitical. The meeting began with the bi issue, and it became obvious very quickly that one woman was dominating the discussion. Her view was that I could come to LOC, but had to leave my bi-hat at the door. I was there at LOC's invitation only, and the condition was that I support LOC. (Surely I was supporting lesbians – just by being there, and by being a woman lover myself!)

She went on to say that bisexuals couldn't relate to the lesbian experience, we were passive supporters (as if we were heterosexual), and she gave us a 'herstory of bis' in LOC, since LOC began ... a slandering affair, bis painted as traitors who went in, sucked LOC and lesbians dry of emotional support, then left. 'We have learnt our lesson' she seemed to be saying.

Partly due to her aggressive style, it became an emotional issue, mostly her speaking and me rebutting with a bisexual view. After 30 minutes, we moved on to discussion of a different matter. During the meeting others gave me sympathetic looks, and afterwards more than half the women came up to me individually, privately outside, and said they supported me. This was very warming. The feeling was that no one agreed with what had been said, but felt dominated by the 'party line'. But no one had spoken up in my defence. Frustrating. Ironically, some of these 'lesbians' from LOC turned up at the first BAD meeting, outing each other as closet bisexuals in a lesbian group. Needless to say, they fled in panic.

At the original BAD meeting, we decided we wanted our group to be casual, open, inviting, a support group – it was, just by us talking about it! Also, we wanted to have positive action, pulling down these myths, and affirming bisexuality as a positive and desirable sexual orientation. Everyone wanted to meet again, regularly. Its impact on my own life was immediate, and in the balance, positive. When we bumped into each other there was a sharing of smiles. Also, everyone came to me within the next week, excited that they'd found someone else to come to our meeting. Our bisexual 'network' was spreading already. We all exchanged our stories with a speed and detail that was unusual in the social context – but we felt an urgent need to explode, disclose. We felt closer to each other, like we were part of a conspiracy almost. It made me feel good. Just the fact that I'd done something.

For us, bisexuality was a lifestyle and philosophy that was affirming, humane, and positive, with an open-armed acceptance and love of the diversity of people. We felt bewildered at the negative labels, from gay/lesbian and straight alike, based on their bizarre dichotomy of the world that split men and women apart. Patriarchy was the enemy, not individual men. We were all victims, all capable of changing the world – so how could you leave out great chunks of the population?

As with any interest group, we felt that our way was 'better'. Mine was an inclusive embracing philosophy, not divisive. I couldn't go to a party and mentally divide it into males and females, viewing only one group as potential lovers, the other as potential friends-only. That seemed forced, unnatural. Such an embracing and positive view gave me as bisexual an inner feeling of optimism and openness, positive 'love *people*' joy. BAD was a holistic 'gaia' approach, the sexual equivalent of the 'world as one living organism' theory. We wanted no nations, political boundaries, limitations on our personal potential. How idealistic!

No one expressed it as I just have. Rather, we giggled at how we thought we should be a club bigger than LOC or Unigays or any het equivalent, because *we* catered for all. Ours was less separatist, by its very nature, than any other. Which is one of the many complex reasons it did fizzle out. We were competing with a world with very established sexuality camps, and we didn't have the resources to suddenly whip up an alternative for all those closeted bisexuals in the het/gay camps.

Bisexuals were scared and closeted in established communities which, even if they weren't supportive of bisexuality, at least were familiar, and supportive on an individual level of the people they thought were straight/gay/lesbian. Much of the distrust, derision, contempt and non-acceptance of bisexuality, (as a *concept*, let alone as a personal label of sexual identity) was internalised by many bisexuals I met. Their fear of being 'caught' by politically correct gay/lesbian friends was far stronger than any positive 'warm fuzzies' a tiny support group could offer.

Also, it was a question of energy. I found that no one was really willing to take any direct part in the organising, or even brain-storming for the kind of social occasions that would be popular. After BAD died a fizzled death, there was the amazing first National Bisexual Conference ever in NZ/Aotearoa at Easter 1990. I went on to attempt to establish a broader-based group outside university in Auckland. Bi-Social was born then died; resurrected then waned ... but after six years Bi-Social continues to exist. But that's another story ...

Postscript: In 1993 I co-founded Uni-goblet, an inclusive group for gay, bi, lesbian and trans staff/students. It continues to thrive. In 1995 a group was set up on campus for 'women loving women'; i.e. bisexual, lesbian or 'unsure/unlabelled' women.

The Bisexual Community: Viable Reality or Revolutionary Pipe Dream?

Beth Reba Weise*

What holds a movement together is an idea. What holds a community together is a common body of symbols and folklore. In other words, a culture. Right now, the bisexuality movement has an idea, bisexuality, and no culture of its own.

Sarah Murray, reporter for the San Francisco gay weekly,
The Sentinel

There exists a set of people who are bi. I call it a movement. You have to call it something. The 500 people who showed up at the 1990 National Bisexual Conference are something. But I have real questions about what these people have in common other than a set of sexual possibilities; other than the prejudice we face. You can talk about fairly unified things early queers did, but bi's haven't really experienced that one unified source. Is there something significant about being bi? Does it have revolutionary potential?

Amanda Udis-Kessler,
Bi-theorist and sociologist, Boston

As much as there is a bi community, I feel a part of it. I think that's partly just because it's so young. Right now 'community' almost only means the people who know each other. What I want it to look like is a place where we don't ask ourselves what our labels are. I think it would have to be separate from the queer community. A really safe space would be where we're not defined by our relationships, where being queer is valued, but so is not being queer.

Cianna Stewart, member of BIPOL's Bisexual People of Color
Caucus and coordinator for the North American
Multi-Cultural Bisexual Network, Berkeley

* This article was written in 1991, and is a snapshot of the movement at that time.

303

SECTION IV: BISEXUAL POLITICS

In a sense there's a nascent community. As bisexuals, we're to an extent a part of the gay and lesbian community. I see things in the bi community forming, with a really strong effort from the leadership to include people from all over, people of color, differently abled – everybody. BiPOL's Bisexual People of Color Caucus is less than a year old. We have folks from various communities, Filipino, Chinese, Japanese, African-American, Native American, Pacific Islander, everybody.

Kuwaza Imara, Bay Area Bisexual Network and
BiPOL's Bisexual People of Color Caucus, Oakland

The bi community exists within itself and is becoming a stronger entity. But it also exists within the gay and lesbian community and that's necessary, because that's a struggle we're a part of. I'm pretty gay identified, even when I'm involved with a man. I believe the bi movement has to happen simultaneously with the movement for queer rights.

Brenda Blasingame, BiPOL's Bisexual People of Color
Caucus, Oakland

I don't think there will or should be a separate bi community. My personal vision is that we need to be part of the larger queer community, which should include gay men, lesbians, bi's, transsexuals and heterosexuals who are committed to stepping outside of heterosexism. Our bi space feels like a way station or a healing place in that our existence has been denied for so long. The purpose of bi space is to remind us that we are legitimate, and that we belong. But I don't see the need for us to form a bi community of our own. Partly because so many of us are in the gay community. It could be redundant. By doing so I'd be excluding a lot of my friends and allies.

Robyn Ochs, Bi-activist, Boston

Can there exist such a thing as a Bisexual Community? Would we want one if it could? Because bisexuals are comprised of peoples with vast and diverse experiences, identities and politics, is a monolithic bisexual community possible or desirable? In talking to bisexual people across the United States, in San Francisco, Santa Cruz, Seattle, Philadelphia, Chicago, Cleveland, and Boston, it becomes clear that every city, every group, has its own identity, its own politic, its own consensus of what it means to be bisexual, and how that is important. From sex-positive/sex-radical groups to vanilla feminist groups, married bi men's support groups to Queer Nation activist groups, strongly non-gay identified to queerer than queer, bisexual people are wildly differing in their concept of what's important, what's community.

304

Some of the points of difference that came out of these interviews include: geographic location: East or West coast, and mid-America, urban and suburban: queer identification: the strength of the local lesbian and gay community: degrees of politicisation, radical, liberal or conservative: feminist, post-feminist, non-feminist; mixed groups or women's and men's groups; mostly white groups or those with actively involved people of color. Each of these alone could be an article unto itself.

And yet even people who question whether there is a bi community use the phrase 'bi community' and 'the community' easily, without thought. Perhaps, as Sarah Murray suggests, what we really have is a movement. Perhaps there is no bisexual culture (yet) because it is hidden in gay or straight culture, or because cultures rise up from distinctive communities.

In truth, we are just like lesbians and gay men. There is no one gay culture, no one women's community. There are more and less visible pockets. The lesbian 'type' is different in New York from in San Francisco, and in Amsterdam every woman on the street looks like a lesbian to someone from Seattle. As bisexuals, we merge with all possible communities and cultures, and we're in the process of creating some of our own. You can tell a dyke walking down the street, but there's no way to know she's bisexual unless she's got a Queer Nation bisexual stickers on her black leather jacket. We don't have one unifying symbol: we don't have an agreed upon 'look'; we are in many ways invisible.

Perhaps in some ways we are in a unique position to challenge yet another patriarchal ideology by being multi-cultural, multi-racial, multi-gendered, multi-experienced, multi-sexual.

Is it possible to claim one unified bi community and still acknowledge our multiplicity? How can such a community, existing in a polarised, dichotomous social structure, still support drag queens, bull dykes, closeted straight-identified swingers, transpersons, and the same-sex couples, all under one umbrella community? It can't, in two dimensions. But as we leap off the page in three and four dimensions, we're doing just fine.

Groups of bisexuals throughout the US, Canada, Australia, New Zealand, and Europe have been organising for the past fifteen years, and in ever increasing numbers since the mid-1980s. Like the feminist and gay and lesbian movements before us, we began with consciousness-raising groups, support groups, potlucks, small photocopied newsletters, open community meetings, dances, workshops and conferences. These days you can go to most major cities in the US and find a group of bisexuals to meet with, especially if you're a woman. The North American Multi-cultural Bisexual Network (NAMBN), officially formed at the 1990 National Bisexual Conference, reports that there are over 100 bisexual organisations in the United States and Canada.

In places like San Francisco, Washington DC, Boston, Philadelphia, Santa Cruz, Seattle and Los Angeles there are several groups to chose from: women-only and mixed support and social groups; discussion meetings for bisexual married men, people of color, Jewish bisexuals; 12-step recovery groups; parenting and student/youth groups; Bi Speaker's Bureaus, and jitterbug classes. There are political groups that exist 'as the need arises', such as UBIQUITOUS: Uppity Bi Queers United in Their Overtly Unconventional Sexuality, an activist within Queer Nation in the Bay Area, and the bi political action groups, BiPOL San Francisco, BiCep Boston, BiPAC New York City and BiPAC Chicago.

So who are these bi's out there, forming groups willy-nilly leading their own individual fights in the letter columns of their local gay papers, meeting each other in ever increasing numbers until more and more bi's will tell you, 'You know, these days just about everybody I know is bi ...' What's happening out there?

Boston
In sheer numbers, the Boston area is the largest bi community, especially of bi women. They are an organised and visible force to be reckoned with in the queer community. The Boston bi movement began when a group of women met at a lesbian discussion group the night the topic addressed bisexuality. In 1982, they went on to form their own bi women's support group and took the name BiVocals. Eventually those women went on to found the Boston Bisexual Women's Network (BBWN). BBWN holds monthly open women's rap groups, many of which spin off into their own closed support groups. Robyn Ochs, one of the original BiVocals, says that presently they have no idea how many support groups are happening, on their own, throughout Boston, its suburbs and off into surrounding areas of Massachusetts. Later, the Boston Bisexual Men's Network (BBMN) emerged, and the two groups together formed the East Coast Bisexual Network (ECBN), representing bi groups from Maine to Florida. The ECBN holds annual bi retreats and has sponsored five conferences on bisexuality at the time of writing. Two years ago, BBWN and BBMN

306

became part of the Boston Lesbian and Gay Community Center. Having that space has had a strong influence on the group, says Robyn Ochs. 'Men and women are working together more than ever. The office has had a tremendous effect. We're more centralised, we share a phone, we share a space. It's beginning to create a drop-in space for bi's in Boston. Nowadays, the events we organise are more bi-space rather than specifically women's events. We're learning to work together.'

Boston's other major community-building project, not just locally but also nationally, has been the newsletter of the women's group, *BiWomen*. Over the course of its nine years of publication it has been a link between the various bi folk in Boston, and often it's the first contact people from other parts of the country have had with any kind of bi movement. In fact, it's not uncommon for people to find out about bi groups in their own city from reading about them in *BiWomen*, or ECBN's *International Directory of Bisexual Groups*, which is compiled and printed biannually.

Cleveland
In Cleveland, a Bisexual Women's Group and a Married Gay and Bisexual Men's Group formed at about the same time in 1986. Barbara Nicely began the women's group by posting an announcement in a local lesbian community centre. It was formed as a support group with a vested interest in the women's community, but without engaging in activities within that community 'as bisexuals'. According to Doug Lakacs of the men's group, the two bi groups exist not in reaction to each other, but were created out of independent and simultaneous responses to the needs of different bisexuals. He points out that a large number involved in the men's group are married men, mostly because that's where his organising efforts have been. The groups share events, and recently Lakacs' wife organized a group for Wives of Bisexual Men.

Chicago
Chicago was the home of Action Bi Women since the early 1980s, but recently the group folded due to burn-out by the women running it. Sarah Listerud, who was involved in Action Bi Women, went on to help found Chicago's bi political action committee, BiPAC.

Currently, BiPAC is working to open doors to gay and lesbian social services. One example is Horizons, a gay and lesbian service organisation. 'We've had some problems with them before,' says

Listerud. 'Women would go to programmes for women and if they came out as bisexual they'd be dis-included from the group.'

'Now Horizons has agreed to include a term bisexual in their mission statement. I met with the executive director and asked them to change their entire service focus to include bisexuals, and they did. I've been on their sensitivity panel for volunteers and that's helped. Bi's are now included in the Chicago gay and lesbian community on a very official level.'

Listerud says her concepts of community are constantly changing. 'On the whole I still have this central idea that the basis of forming a bi community is not separate from the gay and lesbian community, but distinctive. There's still a tremendous need for bisexual space, a place which we can call our own and really get into the deeper issues of what being bi means, not always going over the 'BI 101' stuff, but developing a bisexual politic.'

There are five bi groups in the Chicago area, BiPac, Review, BiFriendly Chicago, a bi group at the University of Chicago, and a bi and gay married men's group in the suburbs that's been meeting for eight years. Says Listerud, 'BiPAC has gone from about five die-hard members, all of us white, middle-class and educated, to about triple that, including African-American and Hispanic activists. I think this year is going to be our year to flower.'

'My radical bi vision is that we can go beyond where lesbian and gay people have gone, we can penetrate the heterosexual hegemony and break it up. The people we have the greatest responsibility to are people in heterosexual environments. We need to start creating places where it's ok to be queer where it hasn't been before. Basically we have gone into lesbian and gay space because that's the safest for us to be out in.'

Washington DC
Washington DC currently has two bi groups, BiWays, which has existed in various forms for over ten years, and the Bi Network of DC, which is about two years old. The Bi Network of DC was formed to address the needs of bisexual people that were not being met by BiWays, according to Margaret Rood, one of the founders. 'BiWays was overly concerned with a wider spectrum of rights for sexual minorities, not just bisexuals. At the same time, BiWays was a little intimidating for someone just coming out at the time … [Creating a new group] was an issue of social space.'

Rood and Robin Margolis founded the Washington Network two

years ago based on 'conventional socialising', a key concept for the network. They're very straightforward about it. When you call the group's answering machine their message says, 'We're monogamous or duogomous, traditional in our socialising, feminist and egalitarian in our outlook. If you're into threesomes, swinging or heavy S/M, please contact other groups instead of us.'

According to Rood, bisexuals were seen as open to threesomes and swinging, which brought some obnoxious men to meetings who were looking for sex with women. Therefore the group has limited membership to those bisexuals in monogamous or 'duogamous' (dating only two people, one of each gender at most) relationships. Rood stated that this decision was made in order to establish a 'safe place for women', and because of her perception that 'the swinger community has broken down during the AIDS crisis and needed to recruit from new areas'. Robin Margolis, the founder of the network, says she is currently writing a book with Gary Young on a 'third way' for bisexual organising. She feels that it is important for bi's to organise separately, and sees this movement as distinct from the lesbian and gay movement. She rejects what she calls the 'breaking down the stereotype model of working together with other sexual minorities to explore myths', and the 'Lesbigay' model, which locates bisexuals within the lesbian and gay communities, which, according to her, 'dilutes, absorbs, marginalises and puts down an expressly bisexual subculture, since gays and lesbians are generally so hostile to bi's ... [In DC] we have a different approach. For example, the west coast is very multi-cultural. Here we want to stay focused on bisexual issues.'

BiWays, the other DC bi group, is one of the older bi groups in the country. It's a social group, open to all bisexual and bi-friendly people. Their activities have included support groups and social events. BiWays is the home group of Loraine Hutchins, one of the co-editors of *Bi Any Other Name*.

'There's been a bi group in DC for at least fifteen years, under different names and through many metamorphoses,' said Hutchins. 'It was usually mostly men. Three years ago Robin Margolis and I happened upon the current group at the same time. At the time there was no political connection with the gay and lesbian community; it was mostly a social group and there were lots of conservative republicans who couldn't understand why anyone would march for anything.'

'Robin and I started working together and we consciously imitated the Boston model by starting a women-only group for the first time ever in DC. We met before the mixed group. Then women who wanted to meet with the men could stay and the others left. It was really active for a year in that form. There were sometimes 30 to 40 women at those meetings, which is amazing for DC.'

According to Hutchins, 'both groups are mostly white', in a majority non-white city. 'DC is a very racist place. The DC women's and gay and lesbian communities have always been white-dominated. Only in the last five or ten years have there begun to be separate black lesbian and gay organisations which have started to have some power. In some ways DC is behind other cities on dealing with racism. That's not to excuse the racism. The DC groups aren't developmentally organised for a multi-cultural bi movement right now. There are bi Black and Latin people all over town having relationships and meeting and kissing and hugging and loving each other, but it's not politicised.'

Philadelphia
The Philadelphia group, Biunity, is three years old and formed out of the March on Washington in 1987. Jill Nagle, who is involved in Biunity and a member of a collective that produces a newsletter of the Philadelphia bi community, *BiFocus*, attributes rising interest in the group to the emergence of community organisers and increased bi visibility. Nagle sees feminism, as well as a multi-cultural, sex-positive stance, as central to Biunity.

'A movement which doesn't look at itself is not worth being in,' says Nagle. She rejects the idea that multi-culturalism will dilute bisexual interests: 'I hope Philadelphia can rise to the challenge and reap the rewards of a multi-cultural bisexual community.'

Seattle
A mixed bisexual support group existed through the Seattle Counseling Service for Sexual Minorities from the early to the late 1980s. In 1986, a woman who had been attending that group put an ad in the *Seattle Weekly* for a bisexual women's group, as she felt uncomfortable with what she perceived as the sexually predatory atmosphere of the mixed group. In two weeks she received 200 phone calls. The next week, twelve women met in her living room and founded the Seattle Bisexual Women's Network (SBWN).

SBWN defined itself as explicitly feminist in its second year. An on-going discussion with some local men who felt that there need to be women in mixed groups to help educate men about feminism resulted in the line 'We remain a women's group to ensure that women's issues always remain in the forefront of our work', in SBWN's statement of purpose. SBWN has always maintained that it is not the responsibility of women to educate men about women's issues.

The group has grown to include a twice-monthly general meeting, with alternating support/check-in meetings and topic nights. Recent topics have included racism, incest survival, goddess worship and transsexualism. With so many new women attending meetings, a Newcomers' Group was begun a year ago. It is smaller and open only to women new to SBWN. It functions as a coming out group, especially for those women coming from mainly heterosexual backgrounds. For some it is a transition to the larger, more political and queer-identified Sunday group.

The Seattle Bisexual Men's Union was formed as explicitly feminist and queer-identified, and in the last two years the groups have done more work together. Recently they founded a joint speakers' bureau called Bi-Out! and are currently preparing to host the North American Multi-Cultural Bisexual Network Planning Meeting in Seattle this July. The Seattle groups also sponsor a yearly Northwest Bi Fest during Pride week in June, bringing together bi folk from the Portland, Oregon and Vancouver, British Columbia groups for a weekend of potlucks, discussion and parties.

ben e factory helped found the SBMU. 'Part of what we're doing as a men's group is addressing the experiences we have in common as men facing heterosexism. Our primary difficulty in a heterosexist culture is the oppression we face in our male-male intimate relations. Not all the men understand the desirability of having separate women's and men's groups. We're realizing that the sexism we face is linked to the sexist oppression of women. For many men that's a second step and not the first.'

San Francisco

In San Francisco, bi organising has a long and varied history. 'Bistorically' speaking, it has the oldest bi community – there has almost always been some kind of bi group active since the Stonewall era. These groups are routinely feminist and queer identified, with a strong participation by people of color and other sexual minorities.

Currently there are well over 30 bi groups in the greater San Francisco Bay Area, from Napa to Santa Cruz. They include overtly political groups such as BiPOL, the bisexual, lesbian and gay political action group, formed in 1983 and which sponsored the 1990 National Bisexual Conference; WRAMBA (Women's Radical Activist Multi-cultural

SECTION IV: BISEXUAL POLITICS

Bisexual Alliance); Queer Nation's LABIA (Lesbians and Bi-Women in Action) and UBIQUITOUS; as well as educational groups such as the Bay Area Bisexual Network (BABN) and its Bisexual Speaker's Bureau (with over 50 speakers to date); support and discussion groups like BiPOL's Bisexual People of Color Caucus (BPOCC) and Jewish Bisexual Caucus, student campus groups and Berkeley's Pacific Center. In addition, there is the purely social Bi-Friendly, founded in San Francisco three years ago, now with franchises all over the Bay Area. Bi-Friendlies meet in cafes, bars or members' homes every week to socialise in a bi-positive, bi-friendly and non-sexually focused atmosphere.

Bay Area bisexual organising is characterised by its mixed gender groups, visibility within the gay and lesbian communities, and its sex-positive approach. Bay Area bi groups have also been active in AIDS organising, local and national politics, and coalition-building agendas.

Maggi Rubenstein, a staunch advocate of civil rights for over thirty years, has been an out bisexual while active in politically progressive movements and the lesbian/gay community. She is likely the foremother of today's bisexual movement. As a mental health worker, Maggi was invited to participate in the formation of several Bay Area programs in the early 1970s, including the founding of San Francisco Sex Information (SFSI), and agreed to do so with the stipulation that bisexuality be an equal component of all the programmes. Through the visibility that came from the bi inclusion, bisexuals began to emerge and find one another, and the signs of the first organised, politically active US bi community were seen. From this networking came the founding of the Bi Center, in 1976, by Maggi and Harriet Levy.

The Bi Center, which served as a social, educational and support space brought together a slew of bi activists and educators who played major roles in the formation of many of the Bay Area bigroups of today. Most of the inclusive language and vision of the Bi Center's statement of purpose, rooted in SFSI's radical, feminist, sex-positive approach, can be found in BABN's statement of purpose and is representative of the current Bay Area bi movement and community.

The 1990 National Bisexual Conference was a major milestone for the bisexual community in terms of organising, networking and visibility; not only in the Bay Area, but also on a national level. The conference steering committee brought an inclusive feminist agenda to the organising of the event, with a strong emphasis on outreach to traditionally excluded groups. Lani Kaahumanu was a major force behind this vision, and the BPOCC, which she co-founded, played a visible role in organising the conference. The event, which brought

312

nearly 500 bisexuals together, produced not only a number of new bi groups in the Bay Area, but significantly brought the bi movement to the attention of the lesbian/gay community. The conference created the sense of a stronger, more viable bi movement and community that is clearly multi-cultural.

'Making a community is a challenge,' explains Kuwaza Imara. 'We're trying to create and build it. The focus for bi groups has been either gender or sexual identity. Focusing strictly on being bisexual can be exclusionary. Issues of sexuality are viewed differently in different groups. Also, bisexual people of color are invisible. The visible bi's are white. If the perception is that the bi community is primarily white and middle-class, how have we made it that way and what can we do to change it? Doing outreach can be a problem. Other issues come up for people of color – survival, race, or class issues.'

In terms of class, adds Kuwaza, 'we really need to take a look at our groups. We tend to be middle-class. There hasn't been much discussion of how homogeneous we are that way, and we're not doing much to change it. Working-class people may not be able to get to meetings because they're working.'

Pata Suyemoto concludes, 'One of the things that makes this area feel like a community is that there are lots of bi people who have done things, bi activists of note. We have leaders. Like any community we have many organisations; we're not cohesive. But I mean, the lesbian/gay community as a cohesive group? Ha! The Asian community? You've got to be kidding!'

As Amanda Udis-Kessler noted at the beginning of this article, the only thing all bisexual people share is a set of sexual possibilities. How we deal with those possibilities, our ethical, political and emotional choices, are creating the seeds for a bisexual identity. With the formation of NAMBN and with the increased visibility and emergence of bisexuals, bi organisers and activists are looking at the possible ways in which the bisexual identity can be represented by a cohesive and unifying framework that supports divergent cultural, sexual, political, and spiritual experiences and ideals. How can we build a community that supports individual choice and freedom and at the same time, honours the differences, dissent and non-conformity inherent in that agenda? The issue may not be whether or not there is a bisexual community, but rather, can the bisexual community adequately fill the needs of all bisexuals?

Thanks to Paul Smith, Lani Kaahumanu, and Karla Rossi.

Resources and Bibliography

Books for Bisexuals

Compiled by David Berry

The books listed below are about bisexuality or feature major bisexual characters. The listing for each book includes the UK publisher, or the US publisher for a couple of books that are of major importance or popularity but that aren't published in the UK. A few of the novels are out of print, but you may find them in second-hand bookshops.

Most of the in-print books may be purchased by mail order from West And Wilde Bookshop, 25a Dundas St, Edinburgh EH3 6QQ, Tel 0131 556 0079.

For North American readers, the East Coast Bisexual Network has leaflets available reviewing bi books of 1991, 1992, 1993 and 1994. Write to ECBN, PO Box 639, Cambridge MA 02140, USA.

Non-fiction

This list consists mainly of books published since 1990. For people who wish to study the subject of bisexuality in greater depth, four books in the list contain extensive bibliographies of books, articles, films and plays, including historical material: Geller (1990); George (1993); Klein and Wolf (1985); Off Pink Collective (1988).

Dennis Altman, *Homosexual Oppression and Liberation*, Serpent's Tail.

Deborah Anopol, *Love Without Limits*, IntiNet Resource Centre.

ANSLIM, *Beyond Sexuality*, Phoenix Press.

Warren J. Blumenfield, *Homophobia: How We All Pay The Price*, Beacon.

Susie Bright, *Susie Bright's Sexual Reality: A Virtual Sex World Reader*, Cleis Press.

Joseph Bristow and Anglia R. Wilson (eds), *Activating Theory: Lesbian, Gay, Bisexual Politics*, Lawrence & Wishart.

Marc E. Burke, *Coming Out of the Blue: British Police Officers talk about their lives in 'The Job' as lesbians, gays and bisexuals*, Cassell.

Eva Canteralla, *Bisexuality in the Ancient World*, Yale UP.

Manuel Carbello, Aart Hendricks and Rob Tielman, *Bisexuality and HIV/AIDS: A Global Perspective*, Prometheus.

Sue Cartledge and Joanna Ryan (eds), *Sex and Love: New Thoughts On Old Contradictions*, Women's Press.

John P. de Cecco and John P Elia (eds), *If You Seduce a Straight Person Can You Make Them Gay?*, Harrington Park.

John P. Decco, *Bisexual and Homosexual Identities: Critical Theoretical Issues*, Haworth Press.

Anja Feldhorst, *AIDS-FORUM D.A.H.: Band XI – Eine Dokumentation zu bisexuelle Lebensstilen und Lebenswelten*, Deutsche AIDS-Hilfe e.V. (in German).

Thomas Geller (ed), *Bisexuality: A Reader And Sourcebook*, Times Change.

Sue George, *Women And Bisexuality*, Scarlet Press.

Hannie Hansson (ed), *Biseksuele levens in Nederland*, Uitgeverij Orlando (in Dutch).

Victoria Harwood, David Oswell, Kay Parkinson and Anna Ward, *Pleasure Principles*, Lawrence and Wishart.

Health Education Authority, *Bisexuality and HIV Prevention*, Health Education Authority.

Loraine Hutchins and Lani Kaahamanu (eds), *Bi Any Other Name: Bisexual People Speak Out*, Alyson (dist. GMP).

Fritz Klein, *The Bisexual Option* (2nd ed), Harrington Park.

Fritz Klein and Timothy J. Wolf (eds): *Two Lives to Lead*, Harrington Park.

Kevin Lano and Claire Parry (eds), *Breaking the Barriers to Desire: New Approaches to Multiple Relationships*, Five Leaves Publications.

Colin MacInnes, *Loving Them Both: A Study of Bisexuality and Bisexuals*, Martin, Brian and O'Keeffe.

Pearlie McNeill *et al*, *Women Talk Sex*, Scarlet Press.

Off Pink Publishing, *Bisexual Lives*, Off Pink.

Paula C. Rust, *Sex, Loyalty and Revolution: Bisexuality and the Challenge to Lesbian Politics*, New York University Press.

Naomi Tucker (ed), *Bisexual Politics: Theories, Queries and Visions*, Howarth Press.

Martin S. Weinberg, Colin J. Williams, and Douglas W. Pryor, *Dual Attraction: Understanding Bisexuality*, Oxford UP.

Elizabeth Reba Weise, *Closer To Home: Bisexuality And Feminism*, Seal.

Biographies
James Broughton, *Coming Unbuttoned*, City Lights.

John Cheever, *John Cheever: The Journals*, Vintage.
John Cheever, *The Letters of John Cheever*, Vintage.
Kim Chernin, *Crossing the Border: An Erotic Journey*, The Women's Press.
Cyril Collard, *L'Ange Sauvage*, Flammarion (in French).
Blanche Weisen Cook, *Eleanor Roosevelt: Volume One, 1884-1933*, Bloomsbury.
Samuel R. Delany, *The Motion Of Light In Water*, Grafton.
Judith Farr, *The Passion Of Emily Dickinson*, Harvard.
Margaret Forster, *Daphne du Maurier*, Chatto/Arrow.
Barney Hoskins, *Jimmy Dean, Jimmy Dean*, Bloomsbury.
Florence King, *Confessions Of A Failed Southern Lady*, Black Swan.
Anja Meulenbelt, *The Shame is Over*, The Women's Press.
Nigel Nicolson, *Portrait Of A Marriage: Vita Sackville-West And Harold Nicolson*, Phoenix.
Tamara Nijinsky, *Nijinsky and Romola*, Bachman & Turner.
Anais Nin, *Henry and June*, Penguin.
Philip Norman, *Elton John*, Arrow.
Donna Perlmutter, *Shadowplay: Anthony Tudor's Life in Dance*, Viking.
Corin Redgrave, *Michael Redgrave, My Father*, Richard Cohen Books.
Andrew Rose, *Scandal at the Savoy: The Infamous 1920s Murder Case*; Bloomsbury.
Colin Spencer, *Which Of Us Two?*, Viking.

Fiction

The criterion for inclusion in this list is that the book must include at least one reasonably prominent bisexual character, and be reasonably positive about bisexuality. The characters need not call themselves bisexual, it is sufficient for their behaviour or thoughts to show their bisexuality. Nor does their sexuality have to be the central issue of the book; bisexuals are as entitled to escapism as anyone else. I have annotated most of the entries in this section by genre as follows: science fiction (SF), fantasy (F), mainstream fiction (M), historical fiction (H) and crime fiction (C).

Gilbert Adair, *Holy Innocents*, Minerva.
Lisa Alther, *Kinflicks*, Penguin (M).
Lisa Alther, *Other Women*, Penguin (M).
Carol Anshaw, *Aquamarine*, Virago (M).

James Baldwin, *Giovanni's Room*, Penguin (M).

Pat Parker, *The Eye In The Door*, Viking (M).

Gael Baudino, *Gossamer Axe*, Penguin (F).

Blanche M. Boyd, *The Revolution of Little Girls*, Cape (M).

Marion Zimmer Bradley, *Thendara House*, Arrow [OOP], DAW [US] (SF).

Marion Zimmer Bradley, *The Heritage of Hastur*, Arrow [OOP], DAW [US] (SF).

Christopher Bram, *Almost History*, GMP (M).

Rita Mae Brown, *Six of One* [OOP] (M).

Jackie Calhoun, *Second Chance*, Naiad (M).

Leonard Cohen, *Beautiful Losers*, Black Spring (M).

Cyril Collard, *Savage Nights*, Quartet (M).

Storm Constantine, *The Wraeththu*, Orbit (SF).

Storm Constantine, *The Monstrous Regiment*, Orbit (SF).

Samuel R. Delany, *Dhalgren*, Grafton (SF/M).

Samuel R. Delany, *Triton*, Grafton (SF).

Samuel R. Delany, *Flight From Neveryon*, Grafton (F).

Emma Donaghue, *Stir Fry*, Hamish Hamilton (M).

Diane Duane, *The Door Into Fire*, Corgi (F).

Diane Duane, *The Door Into Shadow*, Corgi (F).

Diane Duane, *The Door Into Sunset*, Corgi (F).

Larry Duplechan, *Eight Days a Week*, Alyson (dist. GMP).

Andrea Dworkin, *Mercy*, Arrow (M).

Bret Easton Ellis, *The Rules Of Attraction*, Penguin (M).

Rupert Everett, *Hello Darling, Are You Working?*, Mandarin (M).

E.M. Forster, *Maurice*, Penguin (M).

Penelope Gilliat, *Sunday Bloody Sunday*, Dodd Mead & Co OOP] (M).

Diana Hammond, *The Impersonator*, Orion (M).

Joseph Hansen, *A Smile In His Lifetime*, Peter Owen (M).

Joseph Hansen, *A Country of Old Men: The Last Dave Brandstetter Mystery*, No Exit (C).

Robert Heinlein, *Friday*, NEL (SF).

Robert Heinlein, *Time Enough For Love*, NEL (SF).

Robert Heinlein, *Number of the Beast*, NEL (SF).

Ernest Hemingway, *The Garden of Eden*, Grafton (M).

Tracy Hickman, see Margaret Weis.

Chris Hunt, *Gaveston*, GMP (H).

John Irving, *The Hotel New Hampshire*, Simon and Schuster (M).

Gary Jennings, *Raptor*, Hutchinson (H).

Dan Kavanagh (pseudonym of Julian Barnes), *The Duffy Omnibus*,

Penguin (C).

James Kirkwood, *P.S. Your Cat is Dead*, [OOP] (M).

Kathe Koja, *Skin*, Millenium (M).

D.H. Lawrence, *The Fox*, Penguin, New Windmill (M).

D.H. Lawrence, *Women in Love*, Penguin, Wordsworth, Everyman (M).

Hanif Kureishi, *The Buddha of Suburbia*, Faber (M).

Bill Lee, *Bi Ranchers, Bi Mates*, GLB (M).

Ursula LeGuin, *The Left Hand Of Darkness*, Orbit (SF).

Carole Spearin McCauley, *Cold Steal*, Women's Press (C).

Colin MacInnes, *The Colin MacInnes Omnibus*, Allison & Busby (M).

Daniel L. Magida, *The Rules Of Seduction*, Picador (M).

Thomas Mann, *Death in Venice*, Penguin (M).

Anita Mason, *Bethany*, Penguin (M).

Martin Millar, *Lux The Poet*, Fourth Estate (M).

Valerie Miner, *Movement*, Crossing Press (M).

Edna O'Brien, *Johnny I Hardly Knew You*, Penguin (M).

Edna O'Brien, *The High Road*, Penguin (M).

Joseph Olshan, *The Sound of Heaven*, Bloomsbury.

Marge Piercy, *Woman On The Edge Of Time*, Women's Press (SF).

Marge Piercy, *Summer People*, Penguin (M).

Marge Piercy, *Gone to Soldiers*, Penguin (M).

Marge Piercy, *Braided Lives*, Penguin (M).

Marge Piercy, *The High Cost of Living*, Women's Press (M).

Manuel Puig, *Kiss Of The Spider Woman*, Arrow (M).

Mary Renault, *The Alexander Trilogy*, Penguin (H).

Mary Renault, *The Mask of Apollo*, Sceptre (H).

Mary Renault, *The Friendly Young Ladies*, Virago (M).

Anne Rice, *The Tale Of The Body Thief*, Penguin (F).

J.F. Rivkin, *Silverglass*, Futura (F).

J.F. Rivkin, *Web of Wind*, Futura (F).

Michele Roberts, *The Wild Girl*, Minerva (M).

Françoise Sagan, *Painting in Blood*, Penguin (M).

Tom Spanbauer, *The Man Who Fell In Love With The Moon*, Secker & Warburg (M).

Alison Spedding, *A Walk in the Dark* (published in three volumes; *The Road and the Hills*, *A Cloud Over Water*, and *The Streets of the City*), Unwin [OOP] (F).

Darcey Steinke, *Suicide Blonde*, Picador (M).

Theodore Sturgeon, *Venus Plus X*, Sphere (SF).

John Varley, *Titan*, Futura [OOP] (SF).

John Varley, *Wizard*, Futura [OOP] (SF).
John Varley, *Demon*, Futura [OOP] (SF).
Gore Vidal, *The City and the Pillar*, Deutsch (M).
Gore Vidal, *Myra Breckenridge*, Abacus (M).
Alice Walker, *The Color Purple*, Women's Press (M).
Alice Walker, *The Temple of my Familiar*, Penguin (M).
Margaret Weis and Tracy Hickman, *The Will of the Wanderer*, Bantam (F).
Margaret Weis and Tracy Hickman, *The Paladin of the Night*, Bantam (F).
Margaret Weis and Tracy Hickman, *The Prophet of Akhran*, Bantam (F).
Stevie White, *Boy Cuddle*, Penguin (M).
Walter Jon Williams, *Aristoi*, Grafton (SF).
Jeanette Winterson, *The Passion*, Penguin (H/F).
Jeanette Winterson, *Written On The Body*, Vintage (M).
Helen Wright, *A Matter of Oaths*, Methuen [OOP] (SF).
Virginia Woolf, *Orlando*, Penguin, Virago, *et al* (H).
Eda Zahl, *Fluffy Butch*, Mandarin (M).

Short stories
John Cheever, *The Collected Stories*, Vintage (M).
Rosamund Elwin (ed), *Out Rage: Lesbian and Bisexual Women Celebrate Resistance*, Women's Press [Canada].

Contacts

Compiled by Kevin Lano

This section lists national and international contacts within the bisexual movement, and some selected 'bi-friendly' organisations.

UK National Bisexual Organisations
Following the demise of *BiFrost*, the news and features magazine for bisexuals, a group has come together to produce an as yet unnamed newsletter, which it is intended to produce monthly. It will list national and local groups and facilitate new groups setting up, as well as providing other news and information for the bi community. The address is: c/o BM QUNK, London WC1N 3XX.

Phonelines
There are two bisexual phonelines in operation in the UK:

0131 557 3620, Thursdays, 7.30–9.30pm.
0181 569 7500, Tuesdays and Wednesdays, 7.30–9.30pm.

Bi-Academic Intervention
Ann Kalowski, Centre for Women's Studies, University of York, Heslington, York YO1 5DD, 01904 433675.

Biscuits (for deaf bisexuals) contact Deaf MESMAC for further information.

Bisexuals Action on Sexual Health (BASH)
BASH, PO Box LB602, London W1A 5EQ

BiProducts
23c Stoke Newington Rd, London N16 8BZ.

Bisexual Centre Collective (Biosphere)
5 Wentworth Court, Garratt Lane, London SW18 4BT.

Bisexual Resource Centre
58a Broughton St, Edinburgh, EH1 3SA.

Bisexual Therapists Forum
Contact via London phoneline.

Off Pink Publishing Collective
24 Shandon Rd, Clapham, London SW4 9HR.
Email, alib@cix.compulink.co.uk

Quaker Bisexual Group
Contact via the phonelines.

SM Bisexuals
SM Bi, c/o Central Station, 37 Wharfdale Rd, London N1 9SE.

UK Sympathetic or Allied Groups
According to an informal survey carried out by *Bifrost*, most of the local lesbian and gay phonelines outside London are quite helpful with bisexual callers. The London Lesbian and Gay Switchboard is not recommended however.

RESOURCES AND BIBLIOGRAPHY

Countdown on Spanner
c/o Central Station, 37 Wharfdale Rd, London N1 9SE.

Deaf MESMAC, FACTS Centre, 23–25 Weston Park, London N8 9SY. 0181 341 4848.

Friend
BM National Friend, London WC1N 3XX.

Parents' Friend
c/o Voluntary Action Leeds, Stringer House, 34 Lupton Street, Hunslet, Leeds, LS10 2QW.

PASTELS (Partners and Spouses Telephone Support)
0113 267 4627/0113 257 7523. Address as for Parents Friend.

UK Local Bisexual Groups
Birmingham Bi Women's Group
BBWG, Friend, PO Box 2405, Birmingham B5 4AJ. Chris 0121 440 5586.

Brighton BiChoice, Students Union, Falmer House, University of Sussex. 01273 678152.

Eastbourne SAE c/o BiChoice, Brighton.

Edinburgh Bisexual Group
58a Broughton St, Edinburgh, EH1 3SA.

Hull Bisexual Women's Group
c/o Hull Women's Centre, Queens Dock Chambers, Queen's Dock Avenue, Hull HU1 3DR, tel 01482 226806, or Humberside University Lesbian, Gay and Bisexual Officer 01482 440550.

Leeds Bisexual Group
LBG, 5 Broughton Ave, Harehills, Leeds LS9.

Freedom of Sexuality (Liverpool)
c/o Friend Merseyside, 36 Bolton St, Liverpool.

London Bisexual Group
PO Box 3325, London, N1 9EQ.

321

London Black Bisexuals
c/o LBG.

London Bisexual Women's Group
BM-LBWG, London WC1N 3XX.

Manchester Men's Bisexual Group
MBG, PO Box 153, Manchester M60 1LP.

Newcastle ComBIne
PO Box 1JR, Newcastle-upon-Tyne, NE99 1JR.

Nottingham
Box B, Hiziki, 15 Goose Gate, Hockley, Nottingham NG1 1FE.

Bisexuals in Oxford
Oxford Lesbian and Gay Centre, North Gate Hall, St Michael's St,
    Oxford OX1 2DU.

Preston Bi Group
PO Box 375, Preston, PR2 2UP.

Sheffield Bi Women's Group
c/o General Office, Voluntary Action, 69 Division St, Sheffield, S1
    4GE.

Southampton
PinkSoc/Lesbian, Gay and Bisexual Society, Southampton University
    Student Union, Southampton University, Highfield, Southampton
    SO9 5NH.

Staffordshire
PO Box 362, Stafford, ST17 9GH.

International
This section gives the main points of contact for countries where the
bisexual movement is organised. Comprehensive details of groups in
these countries can be found in *The Bisexual Resource Guide*, edited
by Robyn Ochs, available for US $8.00 from the Bisexual Resource
Center, PO Box 639. Cambridge MA 02140, USA (E-mail:
brc@panix.com), which provides up to date worldwide information

about bisexual activity. Recent editions of the directory have listed bisexual groups in Costa Rica, El Salvador, Japan, Russia, Zimbabwe and Switzerland.

USA
Anything that Moves
The world's only glossy bisexual magazine, costs $35 for 4 issues from BABN, 2404 California Street £24, San Francisco, California, CA 94115, U.S.A. Packed with diverse and radical viewpoints.

BiNET
584 Castro St, #441, San Francisco, CA 94114.

East Coast Bisexual Network
Bisexual Resource Center, PO Box 639, Cambridge MA 02140, USA (Email, brc@panix.com).

Australia
Australian Bisexual Network
The Brisbane Bisexual Centre, 9 Hampton Street, East Brisbane. Postal address, PO Box 490, Lutwyche 4030, Queensland, Australia. Produce *National Biways* magazine, Email, re018587@mail-box.uq.oz.au.

Canada
Bi-Focus
Box 34172, Post Office D, Vancouver BC V6J 4N1, Canada.

Bi The Way
c/o University of Concordia Women's Center, Concordia University, PO 3, 1455 de Maissonneuve W, Montreal, Quebec H3G 1M8.

Finland
Women's Bi group of Helsinki
c/o Naisasialiittoo Unioni, Bulevardi 11 A, 00120 Helsinki, Finland.

Germany
BINE e.V.,
Postfach 610214, 10923 Berlin, Bermany.

Ireland
Munster Lesbian, Gay and Bisexual Collective
c/o The Other Place, 7-8 Augustine St, Cork, Eire.

RESOURCES AND BIBLIOGRAPHY

Netherlands
Vereniging Landelijk Netwerk Biseksualiteit (LNBi),
PO Box 75087, 1070 AB Amsterdam, Email, lnbi@bi-link.tdcnet.nl.

New Zealand/Aotearoa
Wellington Bisexual Women's Group,
PO Box 5145, Wellington, New Zealand.

Sweden
Bikupan
c/o RFSL, Stockholm Box 45 090, S-104 30 Stockholm, Sweden.

Electronic Mail/Newgroups
BIFEM-L: to subscribe send a message 'SUBSCRIBE BIFEM-L' to
     LISTSERV@BROWNVM.BITNET

BISEXU-L: to subscribe send a message 'SUBSCRIBE BISEXU-L' to
     LISTSERV@BROWNVM.BITNET

soc.bi: an internet newsgroup.

alt.polyamory: Internet newsgroup for those interested in poly issues.

Transgen, for people interested in gender and transgender: to subscribe
     send a message to LISTSERV@BROWNVM.BROWN.EDU with
     the words: SUBSCRIBE TRANSGEN Your name as the body of
     message.